Ethics, Ethnography and Education

Studies in Educational Ethnography

Series Editor: Professor Rodney Hopson, University of Illinois-Urbana Champaign, USA

Studies in Educational Ethnography presents original research monographs and edited volumes based on ethnographic perspectives, theories and methodologies. Such research will advance the development of theory, practice, policy and praxis for improving schooling and education in neighbourhood, community and global contexts.

In complex neighbourhood, community and global contexts, educational ethnographies should situate themselves beyond isolated classrooms or single sites and concern themselves with more than narrow methodological pursuits. Rather, the ethnographic research, perspectives and methodologies featured in this series extend our understandings of sociocultural educational phenomena and their global and local meanings.

Ethics, Ethnography and Education

EDITED BY

LISA RUSSELL
University of Huddersfield, UK

RUTH BARLEY
Sheffield Hallam University, UK

And

JONATHAN TUMMONS
Durham University, UK

United Kingdom – North America – Japan – India – Malaysia – China

Emerald Publishing Limited
Howard House, Wagon Lane, Bingley BD16 1WA, UK

First edition 2022

Reprints and permissions service
Contact: permissions@emeraldinsight.com

British Library Cataloguing in Publication Data
A catalogue record for this book is available from the British Library

ISBN: 978-1-83982-247-6 (Print)
ISBN: 978-1-80071-008-5 (Online)
ISBN: 978-1-80071-010-8 (Epub)

Printed and bound by CPI Group (UK) Ltd, Croydon, CR0 4YY

ISOQAR certified
Management System,
awarded to Emerald
for adherence to
Environmental
standard
ISO 14001:2004.

Certificate Number 1985
ISO 14001

INVESTOR IN PEOPLE

Table of Contents

About the Editors

Lisa Russell (https://orcid.org/0000-0001-7690-3060) is a Reader in Education at the University of Huddersfield. She is an active ethnographer who has chaired the Oxford Ethnography and Education Conference and sat on the Ethnography and Education Journal Editorial Board. She has over 15 years' experience of working on externally funded ethnographies that have explored young people's experiences of inclusion, exclusion, school resistance, work and unemployment.

Ruth Barley (https://orcid.org/0000-0003-0958-9619) is a Reader of Sociology in the College of Social Sciences and Arts at Sheffield Hallam University. Ruth is an ethnographer with broad research interests within the area of cultural diversity, identity and inclusion and more specifically in relation to how children conceptualise and operationalise identity and the impact that this has on their development. She has been the treasurer and co-organiser of the Oxford Ethnography and Education Conference for seven years.

Dr Jonathan Tummons (https://orcid.org/0000-0002-1372-3799) is Associate Professor in Education at Durham University, UK. He is an ethnographer with research interests in higher, professional, medical and technical education. His current research and most recent publications have centred on the ways in which people and technologies work together in a variety of formal and informal learning contexts, and on the philosophical anthropology of Bruno Latour and the evolution of actor–network theory within Latour's Modes of Existence project. He sits on the organising committee for the Oxford Ethnography and Education Conference, and on the editorial boards for Ethnography and Education.

About the Contributors

Eider Chaves-Gallastegui (https://orcid.org/0000-0002-1897-9267) graduated in Primary Education at the Faculty of Education at the University of the Basque Country (UPV/EHU). She is currently a PhD student-researcher in the program 'Psychodidactics: psychology of education and specific didactics' at the UPV/EHU. Her topics of interest include embodied learning, researcher ethics, the affective turn, teaching identity and educational innovation, among others. She is a member of the research group Elkarrikertuz, and currently participates in the R+D+i project 'Learning trajectories of young university students: conceptions, strategies, contexts and technologies'. She has also participated in several seminars and conferences.

Angeles Clemente is a Researcher and Professor at the State University of Oaxaca, México (UABJO). She received her BA from the National Autonomous University of Mexico (UNAM), and her MA and a PhD in Applied Linguistics at the University of London, where she was later a research fellow (2000-2001). Her academic publications explore the language, culture, agency and identity in Latin American contexts. She is especially interested in conducting ethnographic research on local language practices in subaltern societies, including with children and young people. She is a founding board member of RIENN, the International Network of Ethnographic Studies with Children.

José Miguel Correa Gorospe (https://reunid.portalcientifico.es/investigadores/70263/detalle) is Professor at the Faculty of Education, Philosophy and Anthropology of San Sebastian, University of the Basque Country (UPV/EHU). His research and teaching career is mainly associated with initial and continuing teacher training, pedagogical innovation, research and learning of visual culture. He is a member of the Elkarrikertuz research group (https://www.elkarrikertuz.es/), and part of the REUNI+D (http://reunid.eu) Educational Research and Innovation Network. He also is member of ARTikertuz, a network of teachers and artistic pedagogies.

Diana Milstein is a Researcher in the Center of Social Research of National Council of Scientific and Technical Research at Institute of Economic and Social Development (CIS-CONICET-IDES), Argentina. She holds a PhD in Social Anthropology from Universidade de Brasília. Her fields of interest are ethnography and education, ethnography with children, anthropology of the body and art education. Her academic publications explore social construction of bodies, childhood, politics and daily life in schools, school aesthetics, health and medical education and the ethnographic approach in collaboration with boys and girls. She is coordinator of RIENN, the International Network of Ethnographic Studies with Children.

Elizabeth Pérez-Izaguirre (https://orcid.org/0000-0003-4787-6723) is an Adjunct Professor and Vice-Dean for Mobility and Orientation in the Faculty of Education, Philosophy and Anthropology at the University of the Basque Country (UPV/EHU). She is a member of the Department of Didactics and School Organization (DOE). Her research interests are focused on education in general, including emotions, the processes of teaching and learning in formal and informal environments from a qualitative and ethnographic perspective. Some of her other areas of interest include ethnographic research in art and art learning. She is a member of the Ethics in Communities of Practice (ETICOP-IT) research group.

Fredrik Rusk is Docent of education with a focus on digital interaction at Åbo Akademi University, Finland, and Associate Professor II in pedagogy at Nord university, Norway. His research involves the employment of conversation analysis and interaction analysis with video recordings to investigate social interaction and learning in diverse settings, including screen-mediated interaction; smartphones, video conferences and video games.

Poonam Sharma has been a Teacher Educator and Ethnographer at the Tata Institute of Social Science, India, since 2018. She teaches courses in the areas of Curriculum Studies, Childhood Studies and Qualitative Research. Her doctoral research was a year-long ethnographic work focusing on the educational experiences of children in the context of low fee-paying private schools. The study focused on how disadvantaged families support their child's schooling. It brought together the new sociological perspectives on childhood and ethnographic expertise for understanding families and schooling. Her research was supported by the National Council of Educational Research and Training, India Doctoral fellowship award. She is a recipient of the DAAD Student Exchange Program Fellowship for the year 2010 (Desutscher Akadmischer Austausch Dienst, 2010). Her research interests include Pre-service teacher education programmes, Low fee-paying private schools, Childhood Studies, Ethnography and Private Supplementary Tutoring.

Regina Coeli Machado e Silva is Professor and Senior Researcher at Unioeste (State University of the Western Paraná). Researcher of Productivity at CNPq – (National Council for Scientific and Technological Development). She has a PhD in Social Anthropology from the National Museum/UFRJ (Federal University of Rio de Janeiro), with a post-doctoral fellowship in Social Anthropology at UNB (National University of Brasilia). She researches the relationship between education, school context and national borders. She is a founding board member of RIENN, the International Network of Ethnographic Studies with Children.

Matilda Ståhl is Doctor of Philosophy with education as major subject. She defended her doctoral thesis in December 2021 and is currently working as a post-doctoral researcher and university teacher at Åbo Akademi University, Finland. Her research is focused on identity (co)construction online/offline within an educational context. The ethno-case study discussed in the current chapter, co-authored with Dr Fredrik Rusk, is part of her thesis.

Yang Zhao is currently engaged in a PhD in Education in Scottish country dancing at the University of Edinburgh (funded by China Scholarship Council). She graduated with Cohort 2016 Choreomundus – International Master in Dance Knowledge, Practice, and Heritage in 2018. The Erasmus Mundus joint master was awarded by four partnership universities: Norwegian University of Science and Technology (Norway), Université Clermont Auvergne (France), Szegedi Tudományegyetem (Hungary) and Roehampton University London (UK). While enrolled in an MSc in Dance Science and Education at the University of Edinburgh in 2016, she was actively engaged in learning Scottish dancing.

Series Preface

The edited book by Lisa Russell, Ruth Barley and Jonathan Tummons, *Ethics, ethnography, and education*, presents timely and prescient contributions to topics for the novice and accomplished educational ethnographers who wrestle with questions of ethics. Within nine chapters, the ten contributors provide a landscape of challenges and complexities of shifting and responses to ethical dilemmas in the field taken from ethnographers working in the Basque Country, England, Scotland, India, Sweden and the Americas. Within the current context of the COVID-19 pandemic, the nature of fieldwork has changed for the many ethnographers and authors facing this reality. However, the book contributors also provide new ways of thinking and addressing issues related to data ownership, consent, participant representation(s), culture, dissemination of findings and working with unique country and community contexts and populations of study.

This book, volume 17 of the Studies in Educational Ethnography's book series, returns readers to the UK and Europe where the series was founded by Prof. Geoffrey Walford some 15 years earlier. From Walford's introduction to the series through this volume, the book series' primary objective is to present original research monographs or edited volumes based on ethnographic perspectives, theories and methodologies. Such research will advance the development of theory, practice, policy and praxis for improving schooling and education in neighbourhood, community and global contexts. In complex neighbourhood, community and global contexts, educational ethnographies should situate themselves beyond isolated classrooms or single sites and concern themselves with more than narrow methodological pursuits. Russell, Barley, Tummons and colleagues provide a rich and nuanced perspective an everyday ethics in a changing world, illustrating the tensions ethnographers face in managing ethics, translating ethics in multiple sites of engagement, all while paying attention to the most vulnerable, marginalised and young.

The book series is located within the College of Education, University of Illinois-Urbana Champaign. Located in the Quantitative and Qualitative Methodology, Measurement, and Evaluation (QUERIES), Department of Educational Psychology, the College of Education is home to multiple traditions of research and evaluation scholarship in humanities and social sciences for decades. On the campus, the University annually hosts the International Congress of Qualitative Inquiry (ICQI), a venue for qualitative researchers who travel from around the world to the cornfields of Illinois each May.

For more details about the series, we invite you to visit the website or communicate directly with Kim Chadwick (kchadwick@emerald.com) or me (hopson@illinois.edu).

Rodney Hopson
Series Editor

Chapter 1

Is This Ethical? Using This Question as a Starting Point

Lisa Russell

Abstract

This chapter outlines the history of ethical regulation and considers how the position of ethics has shifted. The intent of this book is to explore novice and accomplished ethnographers 'everyday, real-life' ethical challenges and considerations against a backdrop of theoretical and ethical guideline scrutiny.

Keywords: Everyday ethics; representation; tensions; voice; process; ethical dilemmas

Introduction

All ethnographers, whether regarded as novice or expert engaging with education-based research must grapple with questions of ethics. The question of what it means to behave ethically is not isolated from how we engage ourselves as 'researchers' and indeed how we operate as 'ethical beings' within the world (Dennis, 2018). It is not uncommon, in planning or in carrying out research, for the question to arise: is this ethical (Hammersley & Traianou, 2012)? Perhaps, the very first question any researcher should ask themselves before embarking upon any research journey should be this very question. At first glance such a question may seem unproblematic; however, any researcher engaging with participants in the real world knows only too well that the management of good ethical research is a very complex process that differs according to context. Particular ethical challenges related to the intimacy, complexities, and longevity of ethnography mean that many ethnographers need to negate shifting and immediate responses to ethical dilemmas as they occur, as well as consider the longer-term implications related to ownership of data, informed consent and accurate representation of participants, their culture and voices when writing about and disseminating findings in relation to their ethnographic findings.

Ethics, Ethnography and Education, 1–10
Published under exclusive licence by Emerald Publishing Limited
doi:10.1108/S1529-210X20220000019001

This is a book for all educational ethnographers who wish to learn more about the lived experiences of the ethnographer and their participants when engaging with and managing ethics in situ and beyond. The book provides a focus for discussion on how ethnographers working in the Basque Country, England, Scotland, India, Sweden and the Americas define and practise ethics in educational sites. The examples explored are taken from the ethnographers' direct experience in the field, including the ethical challenges posed by the growth of online and virtual ethnographies before and in the advent of the Covid-19 pandemic. Discussions to write this book were born from the Oxford Ethnography and Education Conference, with some chapters being presented there as 'working papers' before Covid-19 hit, whereas other chapters were written in the aftermath of the pandemic when the world and its priorities and day-to-day living changed in the blink of an eye. Some scholars have argued that the pandemic transformed the way in which academics research and thus has shaped some of the subsequent ethical dilemmas that have been experienced. Within this book, educational ethnographers from across the globe reflect on their management of ethics in situ and beyond over a longitudinal, uncertain and intimate nature.

Ethnographers delve into the everyday experiences of their participants and as such are more likely to become involved with their participants and occurrences in the field over a longitudinal, intimate period (Delamont & Atkinson, 2018). Shorter forms of ethnography are increasingly occurring however, largely due to funding and resource constraints, and with this come new ethical challenges that the ethnographer must negotiate both in situ and beyond. Ethnographers build relationships with people to understand cultures, and consequently experience a level of intimacy and unpredictability that is unique to ethnography as a methodological process and product (Russell & Barley, 2020). Based on a variety of international perspectives, this volume brings together methodological, empirical and epistemological debates regarding the current management of ethics, ethnography and education, considering too in some chapters the recent increase in Eurocentric ethical shifts.

This introduction sets the scene by outlining the premises of ethical regulation and the challenges it poses to ethnographers working on a longitudinal and intimate basis, often adopting participatory research methods with different demographic groups across varying social sites of investigation.

Everyday Ethics in Changing Times

Historically, much of the literature regarding ethics deals with the management of ethical review boards (Dennis, 2009). More recently discussions have shifted to acknowledge that while it may be relatively easy to slip into a stance of cynicism when it comes to the institutionalisation of ethical processes (Ledermann, 2007), we must as ethnographers find ways to more actively change review systems so that they develop and improve with time (Dilger, 2017; Hunter, 2018; Tolich, 2016). Most ethnographers agree that ethnography should not escape ethical scrutiny; rather, we need to re-think ethics in educational ethnography and ensure it is better subjected to more appropriate and realistic standards (Delamont & Atkinson, 2018; Dennis, 2018). This book takes a reflective view on how ethics works in situ and beyond in relation to working with a variety of groups such as professionals, children and young people, across a number of different virtual and face-to-face platforms using multiple and often participatory research methods both pre and in the advent of Covid-19 times. Ethics and their need to be managed in situ, while simultaneously recognising the participant's voice, are acknowledged. The need to challenge conventional, European/Western forms of informed consent and look at how data ownership works in practice for ethnographers is contextualised within the backlash against the increasing global shift regarding the dominance of the hegemonic approach to research, more recently epitomised by data analytics, that tends to objectify its participants as passive subjects, rather than as active participants within the research process with inherent power, rights and needs – something which is commonly critiqued within indigenous ethic paradigms (Kara, 2018).

A main purpose of this book is to contribute to the ongoing and now long-standing discussion regarding the distinction Smette (2019) makes between Silverman's (2003) notion of 'everyday ethics' and Strathern's (2000) notion of 'formalised ethics'. Everyday ethics is about building trust and field relationships that actively try and reduce power relationships between the ethnographer(s) and participant(s) while formalised ethics is concerned with institutional ethical procedures undertaken before fieldwork commences. The focus of this book is on how the ethnographer manages the 'everyday ethics'. Ethics here is regarded as connected to all dimensions of the research process and shaped by the unpredictable and messiness that ensues from the interactions between the ethnographer and participants. It is about what awkward decisions ethnographers make and how they walk fine lines of judgements within and beyond the field. In ethnography ethical research requires an ongoing and active engagement with people and the culture from which they form a part (Marcus & Lerman, 2018). This book argues that research cannot be rendered ethical by completing a one-off administrative task (Busher & Fox, 2019; Kara, 2018); rather, it requires a move towards a social justice approach to ethics that accounts for the contexts and people with which ethnographers work with and views the ethnographer as an autonomous expert. Silverman (2003) eloquently defines 'everyday ethics' and the relation this may have with the researcher and the researched positionalities, alongside the idea that ethics is about making awkward decision that may not always satisfy all related parties' interests equally:

> Everyday ethics is about crafting a persona and identity that will mutually engage both the researcher and the people, without doing damage to either. Then, it is about the continual need for choices, each day. It is about ambiguity, conflicting interests, fine lines, judgment calls and, therefore, about awkward decisions.
>
> (Silverman, 2003, pp. 127–128)

Tensions often arise regarding how the ethnographer experiences managing ethics in the field (and beyond) with participants and then how ethics is construed in more formalised arenas within academic institutions, places of social site investigation and via the implementation of policy and formal institutional, disciplinary and funding regulation guidelines, such as the implementation of the EU regulation on data protection put in place in the EU from 2018 (the General Data Protection Regulation, GDPR) or development of the British Educational Research Association Ethical Guidelines in 2018. The main gatekeepers to whether or not a study is approved to proceed are variously called research ethics committees (REC's) or institutional review boards (IRBs), seemingly defined as such dependant upon which side of the Atlantic you live (Busher & Fox, 2019). Both of these reinforce the formalisation of the management of ethics, informed consent procedures and stipulate data protection processes including use and storage of data. Such developments have particular consequences for ethnography and opinion is divided, with some arguing that ethical guidelines and regulations act to renew and improve our practice (Fluehr-Lobban, 2003; Hunter, 2018) and others stating that such stringencies have the potential to quash academic freedom and contribute to predetermined ideals about how fieldwork is conducted, and research relationships ensue in ways which sometimes presuppose opposing rather than joint interests (Banks, 2013; Lederman, 2006). It matters who we do our research with. For example, if research is conducted with the vulnerable, marginalised and young, a different set of considerations may need to ensue whereby a one-size-fits-all approach may not be deemed appropriate and may even be viewed as damaging (Albon & Barley, 2021; Pollock, 2012). The inter-related question of how we do our research also matters, with many ethnographers having to negate Covid-19 safe virtual research methods of late that change the very nature of interaction and rapport developed between the researcher and the researched. The requirement to socially distance during the pandemic in order to protect the ethnographer and participants is arguably at odds with the intimacy and need to gain rapport and spend time 'hanging around' in the field – something which lies at the heart of many ethnographers' idea of engaging with ethically sound research.

The advent of Covid-19 has illustrated the need for a flexible approach to ethics, one which shifts according to who we are working with, how and when. Ethical and equity considerations related to issues of representation and inclusion have been once again brought to the forefront, alongside the need for stable internet connection, the recognition of information technology poverty and the shifting power dynamics and positionalities between participants and the ethnographer. Our understanding of working in an ethically sound way has shifted with many questioning their own ethical practices, re-verifying necessary changes with funders and institutions to work in Covid-19 safe ways across different countries that operate different social distancing and wider ethical guideline practices. Indeed, the opportunity to work across different countries has arguably increased of late, but with this comes the need for the ethnographer to manage different countries, as well as different institutional and funding bodies ethical guidelines. Arguably power relations have been up-ended during the

Covid-19 pandemic, whereby children and young people have felt more at ease meeting in less formal spaces, have had more power to disengage by disconnecting, turning their cameras off in virtual interviews and observations and having greater power to choose when and how they partake in research. However, challenges around who is invited to take part in research and how have been noted (Lomax et al., 2021), with gatekeeper access pathways being altered by the pandemic, facilitating the re-production of adult/child power relations with researchers setting research agendas and having the control to mute participants with the press of a button, alongside the concern that lots of children and young people struggled to find 'privacy' in their own home or place of being, with parents and adults interrupting data collection and speaking for rather than with children and young people. Such ethical issues around representation and inclusion occur in situated moments. This book illustrates how some of the procedural ethical guidelines are too rigid and consequently fail to take account of the nuances experienced in practice.

Different countries operate with different yet sometimes overlapping ethical review processes, with some being carried out at the level of the individual institution and handled at national institutions (such as in the UK and Norway) whereas others start at the national level before even considering an individual social site of investigation (such as in New South Wales in Australia). So, ethics is managed differently across different regions, cultures and moments in time at a formalized, institutional level. This needs to be considered even before one delves into the messiness of 'everyday ethics' and how specific ethnographers working within particular organisations, social sites and places with different individuals, groups and cultures manage ethics in often intimate, prolonged (and as a consequence often shifting) circumstances. It is thus important to consider how ethics is implemented in educational ethnography in relation to gaining truly informed consent for those involved with participant observation on a partial and full participating collective, data ownership, power dynamics between the researched, the researcher and amongst the participants themselves and how such processes of data collection may shape the writings and dissemination of ethnography and the implications this may have for the representation of ethnography in past, present and future forms of dissemination (Russell, 2018).

About This Book

This book therefore looks in-depth at very different educational based settings and offers a reflective and truthful account of how experienced ethnographers managed their 'everyday ethics' in the field and beyond to show the nuances involved when managing ethics in situ and beyond. After reflecting upon the crucial question, 'is this ethical?' within the introduction here, the remainder of the book outline is as follows.

In chapter two, Jonathan Tummons (Durham University, UK) draws on the philosophical anthropology of Bruno Latour to construct an account of the work of research ethics. Through a consideration of the trope of the research ethics framework as text, he explores the ways in which any such text needs to be accompanied – by people, by processes, by other voices or other texts – in order to become meaningful and then impactful for the ethnographer of education and argues that the symbolic world of research ethics relies on the imaginary as much as the statutory or the political. Research ethics are thus positioned as the technological outcome of a dialogue between politics (the ethical approval process, the guidelines, ethics handbooks, committees and so forth) and imagination (the hypothesised impact of the researcher on the researched, the imagined outcomes of the research for the participant) that are prone to misunderstanding and misinterpretation, notwithstanding the strictures of the processes and policies that increasingly seek to codify the work that ethnographers do in the field.

Chapter 3 outlines how ethnographers experience managing ethics in situ when working with children and young people. Lisa Russell (The University of Huddersfield, England) and Ruth Barley (Sheffield Hallam University, England) reflect on how ethics works in situ by exploring their own education ethnographers' work with children and young people. This chapter argues that education ethnographers need to be reflexive in their consideration of ethics, especially when considering the variable fields of investigation, the closeness, proximity to children and young people over a longitudinal basis and the potential use of a plethora of research methodologies. Ethnography can be varied and unpredictable and as such have key unprecedented consequences for the use of ethics when working with children and young people.

Chapter 4 discusses research ethics in relation to child participation. Poonam Sharma (Tata Institute of Social Sciences, India) reflects on ethnographic fieldwork conducted in a town close to Delhi, India. The research focused on the schooling experiences of children from communities traditionally considered under privileged. It reflects on the ethnographer's experiences of researching with children and the ways in which child participation and research ethics emerged and shifted during the year of fieldwork. The idea of 'child participation' in the research process in the Indian context is explored. Within this context, discourse around ethics seems to be primarily concerned with ideas of consent, gatekeeping and respecting children's rights. This chapter discusses the importance of the cultural contexts of the field in shaping the research ethics and developing what 'child participation' meant for children and their parents within this specific cultural context. It does so by elaborating on contradictions that existed between the way the ethnographer positioned the child and the way children are positioned in families and schools, where children's participation, opinions and consent are often presumed by the parents much more so than in a Euro American context. Within the study, children are viewed as active agents, knowledgeable about their own positions in the research process in conflict with wider views on children and childhood emanating from the cultural context.

Chapter 5 explores ethics from an ethnographic study conducted with Higher Education students located within the Basque Country. Elizabeth Pérez-Izaguirre, Jose Miguel Correa Gorospe and Eider Chaves Gallastegui (University of the Basque Country) consider researcher and participant positionality, alongside the importance of considering the local ethical regulations for personal data protection. Nowadays most research funders require research projects to be evaluated by an ethical review board, which involves the drafting of an informed consent form that needs to be signed by research participants. Paradoxically, this raises ethical concerns related to participants' position within the field, as they are too often objectified as 'data providers' who do not own the discourse developed alongside them. This chapter argues that ethics should be practised as a collaborative approach whereby knowledge is co-constructed in a research relationship where participants are agents and co-owners of the discourse created around them.

Matilda Ståhl (Åbo Akademi University, Finland) and Fredrik Rusk (Åbo Akademi University, Finland and Nord University, Norway) explore how ethics works in online environments in Chapter 6. Doing ethnography online, partially or entirely, offers tools to better understand aspects of contemporary society in general but also how these online contexts are connected to education (see, e.g., Rusk, 2019; Ståhl & Kaihovirta, 2019). As society evolves, however, new challenges arise for ethnography to claim its position as a methodology for understanding human sociality. The definition of fieldwork is blurred when the ethnographer has constant access to the field from their computer and reaching an emic understanding is more complex when there is no or limited face-to-face interaction with the respondents (Shumar & Madison, 2013). This chapter discusses some of the challenges the authors faced during the process of an ethnographic study within the online multiplayer video game Counter Strike: Global Offensive within an educational context. The struggle to protect the participants' personal information while simultaneously conducting the analysis in a transparent manner is discussed, thus contributing to discussions around how to conduct ethnography online in an ethically sustainable manner.

Chapter 7 derives findings from an ongoing ethnography that aims to explore how people partake in Scottish country dancing in Edinburgh (Scotland) and Lyon (France). Yang Zhao (The University of Edinburgh) explores the differences between online and face-to-face ethnography in the aftermath of Covid-19 when working across different countries inclusive of native and non-native settings. Zhao argues that ethics needs to be managed in situ and issues cannot always be anticipated in advance of data collection: indeed, many projects (including this one) have needed to adapt in the advent of Covid-19. This chapter offers a reflective account of how Zhao managed these changes within the complexities of virtual and face-to-face, as well as across local and international ethnographic fields.

Chapter 8 explores ethical dilemmas and reflections in a collaborative study with children during the pandemic. Diana Milstein (Universidad Nacional del Comahue, Argentina) and Regina Coeli Machado Da Silva (Universidade Estadual do Oeste do Paraná) reflect on how a group of eight researchers from different geographical locations in the Americas understood how, in times of a pandemic, children recognise social spaces related to school, home and virtual activities; how informed consent was managed via the varying use of oral, written, recorded, drawn, photographed and audio-visual raw data among Latin American children during the pandemic whereby the children's experiences of social isolation in different locations were explored, reflected upon and problematised. These intense exchanges spurred the addition of other methodological strategies for developing virtual encounters in which there was active dialogue between the researchers and children. This strategy, consistent with the context of social isolation and with a transnational scope of the project, generated ethical concerns centred, at first, on the paradoxical coexistence that articulated the proximity of personal interactions with social and geographical distance. Important ethical implications considered within this chapter include the risks of forcing children's collaboration, conditioned by pre-established relationships (of friendship and family); contradictions regarding the 'negative' implications surrounding internet use by children and concerns regarding utilising letters and virtual encounters as ethnographic documents.

Jonathan Tummons (Durham University, UK) concludes the volume with an essay that draws together the themes outlined in the preceding chapters. In this conclusion, he focuses on those aspects of methodological debate that pertain to the ethical conduct of research that are symptomatic of the shifts in ethnography that have characterised the field during the last 20 years: the emergence of online and virtual ethnographies; the foregrounding of the voice of the researched and the decolonisation of the academy; the proliferation of codes of practice and audit cultures within educational research more widely and the subsequent impact on research governance; and the impact of notions of care within the research field. In the conclusions, Jonathan proposes a characterisation of this ethical turn as simultaneously enriching and impoverishing the lived experience of researchers, within a moment that affords new opportunities for ethnography whilst at the same time regulating the work of the ethnographer ever more closely.

References

Albon, D., & Barley, R. (2021). Ethnographic research: A significant context for engaging young children in dialogues about adults' writing. *Journal of Early Childhood Literacy, 21*(1), 82–103.

Banks, S. (2013). Negotiating personal engagement and professional accountability: Professional wisdom and ethics work. *European Journal of Social Work, 16*(5), 587–604.

Busher, H., & Fox, A. (2019). Chapter 1–introduction: Overview of the book. In H. Busher & A. Fox (Eds.), *Implementing ethics in educational ethnography: Regulation and practice* (pp. 1–16). London: Routledge.

Delamont, S., & Atkinson, P. (2018). Chapter 7–the ethics of ethnography. In R. Iphofen & M. Tolich (Eds.), *The Sage handbook of qualitative research ethics* (pp. 119–132). London: Sage.

Dennis, B. (2009). What does it mean when an ethnographer intervenes? *Ethnography and Education, 4*(2), 131–146.

Dennis, B. (2018). Tales of working without/against a compass: Rethinking ethical dilemmas in educational ethnography. In D. Beach, C. Bagley, & S. Marques da Silva (Eds.), *The Wiley handbook of ethnography of education* (pp. 51–70). Oxford: Wiley Blackwell.

Dilger, H. (2017). Ethics, epistemology and ethnography: The need for an anthropological debate on ethical review processes in Germany. *Sociologus, 67*(2), 191–208. In Duncker & Humblot (Eds.), *Spaces of belonging between Mexico and the United States.*

Fluehr-Lobban, C. (2003). An indifferent public in a world of bystanders: Unspeakable acts, ordinary people: The dynamics of torture. *Anthropology and Humanism, 28*(2), 214–215.

Hammersley, M., & Traianou, A. (2012). *Ethics in qualitative research.* London: Sage.

Hunter, D. (2018). Chapter 19–research ethics committees–what are they good for? In R. Iphofen & M. Tolich (Eds.), *The Sage handbook of qualitative research ethics* (pp. 289–300). London: Sage.

Kara, H. (2018). *Research ethics in the real world: Euro-western and indigenous perspectives.* Bristol: Policy Press.

Lederman, R. (2006). Introduction: Anxious borders between work and life in a time of bureaucratic ethics regulation. *American Ethnologist, 33*(4), 477–481.

Lederman, R. (2007). Educate your IRB: An experiment in cross-disciplinary communication. *Anthropology News.*

Lomax, H., Smith, K., McEvoy, J., Brickwood, E., Jensen, K., & Walsh, B. (2021). Creating online participatory research spaces: Insights from creative, digitally mediated research with children during the COVID-19 pandemic. *Families, Relationships and Societies, XX*(XX), 1–19. doi:10.1332/204674321X16274828934070

Marcus, O., & Lerman, S. (2018). Chapter 13-ethics working in ever-changing ethnographic environments. In R. Iphofen & M. Tolich (Eds.), *The Sage handbook of qualitative research ethics* (pp. 203–214). London: Sage.

Pollock, K. (2012). Procedure versus process: Ethical paradigms and the conduct of qualitative research. *BMC Medical Ethics, 13*(1), 25.

Rusk, F. (2019). Digitally mediated interaction as a resource for co-constructing multilingual identities in classrooms. *Learning, Culture and Social Interaction, 21*, 179–193.

Russell, L. (2018). Competing power differentials in ethnographic writing: Considerations when working with children and young people. In B. Jeffrey & L. Russell (Eds.), *Ethnographic writing.* Stroud: E&E Publishing.

Russell, L., & Barley, R. (2020). Ethnography, ethics and ownership of data. *Ethnography, 21*(1), 5–25.

Shumar, W., & Madison, N. (2013). Ethnography in a virtual world. *Ethnography and Education, 8*(2), 255–272.

Silverman, R. D. (2003). Public health law and ethics: A reader. *The Journal of Legal Medicine, 24*(2), 241–248.

Smette, I. (2019). Ethics and access when consent must come first: Consequences of formalised ethics for ethnographic research in schools. In H. Busher & A. Fox (Eds.), *Implementing ethics in educational ethnography. Regulation and practice.* London: Routledge.

Ståhl, M., & Kaihovirta, H. (2019). Exploring visual communication and competencies through interaction with images in social media. *Learning, Culture and Social Interaction, 21*, 250–266.

Strathern, M. (2000). The tyranny of transparency. *British Educational Research Journal, 26*(3), 309–321.

Tolich, M. (2016). A worrying trend, ethical considerations of using data collected without informed consent. *Fronteiras: Journal of Social, Technological and Environmental Science (Anapolos), 5*(2), 14–28.

Chapter 2

The Many Worlds of Ethics: Proposing a Latourian Investigation of the Work of Research Ethics in Ethnographies of Education

Jonathan Tummons

Abstract

In this chapter I draw on the philosophical anthropology of Bruno Latour to propose an account of the work of research ethics. Through a consideration of research ethics as text, I explore the ways in which any such text needs to be accompanied – by people, by processes, by other voices or other texts – in order to become meaningful and then impactful for the ethnographer of education. Research ethics are thus positioned as the technological outcome of a dialogue that is prone to misunderstanding and misinterpretation, notwithstanding the strictures of the processes and policies that increasingly seek to codify the work that ethnographers do in the field. Through arguing for Latour's recent philosophical anthropology as a conceptual toolkit for the exploration of research ethics, I propose that it is research ethics as object that should be the focal point for ongoing ethnographic inquiry.

Keywords: Actor-network theory; anthropology; ethics; ethnography; Latour; modes of existence

Introduction: The Less-than-Straightforward World of Ethics in Ethnography

For many of us, as ethnographers, our encounters with and enactments or embodiments of research ethics occur in several ways. The audit processes within which we are enrolled when making formal applications to institutional ethics committees or review boards exist in sharp contrast to the nuanced, rich discussions of ethical practice of actually conducting observations or interviews within

Ethics, Ethnography and Education, 11–28
Copyright © 2022 Jonathan Tummons
Published under exclusive licence by Emerald Publishing Limited
doi:10.1108/S1529-210X20220000019002

research sites or when considering the ways in which we might represent our research participants when writing journal articles or book chapters. It is not controversial to posit ethnography as a way of doing social research that, irrespective of our academic or political conceptualisations of ourselves as ethnographers, is particularly sensitive to the ramifications of conflicting discourses of research ethics – neatly summarised in the contrast between the biomedical and positivist discourse of ethics applications forms and review panels on the one hand, and the emotional, cultural, and contextual risks and dilemmas that might emerge within the field on the other.

These discussions have all been well rehearsed over a considerable period of time. Examples of such discussions include the ways that codes of ethics practice lack sensitivity to particular methods (including but not restricted to ethnography) and thereby more-or-less inadvertently constrain the conduct of empirical research (including writing), and critique the extent to which a mechanistic subscription to codes of ethics practice provides meaningful protection to research participants, in ways which might in fact increase the risk of harm (Delamont & Atkinson, 2018; Murphy & Dingwall, 2001). Feminist, post-structuralist and post-qualitative turns within social research have, alongside other ontological shifts, foregrounded questions concerning the ethics of ethnography that range from our methods when in the field – for example, the construction of power relationships between researcher and respondent – to our conduct after we have left it – for example, the maintenance (or not) of relationships and ongoing commitments to reciprocity and feedback (LeCompte & Schensul, 2015). Even well-rehearsed issues such as 'informed consent' are rendered problematic: how can an ethnographer guarantee that informed consent will be sought from all respondents, when the nature of the research being undertaken is almost by definition prone to adaption and improvisation, mindful of the emergent nature of ethnographic fieldwork? As ethnographers of education, our commitment to our research and also to well-established consequentialist ethical theory obliges us to ensure that no harm comes to our participants. But how should we respond when we observe less than ideal educational experiences due to the actions of the very same teaching staff who have given us permission to observe their lessons (Barbour, 2010)? How, as researchers, do we make sense of those experiences of our respondents that are characterised by difficulty or by trauma (Huisman, 2008)?

Both the ongoing challenges of the unexpected or underestimated as well as the epistemological and methodological fragmentations that characterise contemporary conversations about the ethics of educational ethnography all need to be accounted for, even if they cannot always be resolved (Dennis, 2018). Simply put: how might we, as ethnographers of education, make sense of what we might encounter in the field as well as what we might address in our writing? How ought the notion or phenomenon of research ethics be understood and responded to when it seems to be characterised by a fraught complexity that is black boxed by ethics forms and ethics approval panels? The world of the ethnographer in the field is quite distinct from the world of the ethics application form and the review panels that tend to privilege positivist and individualistic understandings of research (Ferdinand, Pearson, Rowe, & Worthington, 2007; Wynn, 2018). Should we therefore seek to understand them through addressing these different social experiences or phenomena rather than trying to find yet more ways to bridge, but not resolve, the distances between them?

An Inquiry into Modes of Existence: An Ontological Toolkit to Make Sense of the Social

In order to be able to say something about research ethics as they pertain to not only ethnographers of education specifically but also social researchers more generally that does not simply rehearse the kinds of well-established and well-reasoned arguments such as those that I have already cited above, I am going to draw on the conceptual as well as empirical frameworks offered by the recent work of Bruno Latour – *An Inquiry into Modes of Existence: AIME* (Latour, 2013). Latour is arguably best known for his contributions to actor-network theory (ANT), a sociological perspective that provides a framework of inquiry for an investigation of activities that take place across temporal, institutional and spatial boundaries. It is a way of thinking about how social projects are joined together in ways which can be traced through empirical research (Latour, 2005; Law, 1994). More specifically, it has been employed in a variety of education contexts including education policy, international assessment systems, professional standards and blended curricula (Fenwick & Edwards, 2010; Gorur, 2011; Mulcahy, 2011; Sarauw, 2016; Tummons & Beach, 2020). AIME, Latour's more recent project, extends the work of the earlier ANT and affords the social researcher a number of ontological lenses through which to generate their accounts.

AIME is an amalgamation of several of the strands of Latour's work in addition to ANT: anthropology, religion, law, semiotics, sociology, and philosophy (Delchambre & Marquis, 2013). Indeed, Latour himself has described AIME as a long-running project that has gradually come into being alongside all of his other work (Blok & Jensen, 2011, pp. 164–166; Latour, 2005, p. 241). It has begun to be employed in explorations of legal theory (McGee, 2014) and politics (Tsouvalis, 2016) as well as education (Decuypere & Simons, 2019; Tummons, 2020, 2021a, 2021b). AIME represents, arguably, a tacit recognition by Latour of the limitations of ANT as well as an attempt to gather the different strands of his work into one empirical investigation that does not pretend to be anything other than pragmatic, allowing the inquiry to travel where Latour wishes – to the unravelling of Modernism that has preoccupied much of his intellectual career (Delchambre & Marquis, 2013; Harman, 2016; Weber, 2016).

A *mode of existence* is a concept borrowed and expanded on by Latour from earlier works by Simondon (1958) and Souriau (1943) and is defined as an ontological feature of the world which can be brought into view through empirical inquiry: a lens through which particular aspects or elements of the world can be considered. Latour proposes that there are 15 such modes, all equally important but with distinct jobs to do: some pertain to metaphysics, some to materialities, some to epistemology. All of them are designated with a three-letter notation.

Alongside ANT, now labelled [NET], other modes that speak to Latour's broader body of work include religion – [REL], technology – [TEC], and law – [LAW]. Others are newer arrivals and include habit – [HAB], morality – [MOR] and reproduction – [REP].

Finally, it is important to foreground the empirical component of AIME, not least as it provides a meaningful alignment to the ethnography of education. Notwithstanding the ways in which Latour has long eschewed explicit methodological advice, AIME rests on and is committed to anthropology, the discipline that Latour arguably most closely attaches himself to (Berliner, LeGrain, & Van De Port, 2013; Kipnis, 2015). As a side note it is worth foregrounding the arguments that 'many non-anthropological ethnographers define ethnography more or less as anthropologists would' (Anderson-Levitt, 2011, p. 13) and that ethnography/anthropology can be seen as an analytical/empirical continuum (Hasse, 2015, p. 6). Thus, it is through empirical as well as philosophical inquiry that the specific ontologies that pertain to each mode of existence will allow us to encounter and then make sense of the distinct beings – both human and non-human (reflecting the principle of symmetry from ANT that rejects any a priori differences between humans and non-humans) – that will be encountered and must be spoken to in their own manner.

The discussion that I want to open up within this chapter rests on thinking about research ethics in a number of particular ways that are derived from AIME, from Latour's 'ontological toolkit' (Hämäläinen & Lehtonen, 2016, p. 33). Firstly, I am going to consider research ethics in terms of being objectivised knowledge; secondly, in terms of being a form of meaning and language, invariably reified within texts; thirdly, in terms of being gathered together as an assemblage of entities that can provoke agreement as well as disagreement. In order to do this, I will at first draw on the modes of reference [REF], fiction [FIC] and technology [TEC] – which will be taken together, and politics [POL]. In each case, I will briefly outline the ways in which the mode of existence in question is established and how it can inform our conceptual analysis, before then focussing specifically on the matter of research ethics as it pertains to that mode. It is important to remember that the sequence in which I discuss these modes does not imply a hierarchy: each mode is as important as all of the others. After this, I will return to the perhaps more familiar terrain of ANT in order to offer some questions and possible answers to how the social project of research ethics might be accomplished.

Ethics as Knowledge [REF]

The reference [REF] mode is the closest that Latour comes to outlining an epistemological standpoint (Reyes-Foster, 2016, p. 1181). It is the mode through which objectivised knowledge about things or people can be understood. Latour's example is geographical and topographical: Mont Aiguille, south of Grenoble in France (Latour, 2013, p. 69 ff.) I, like many other people, have never actually been to Mont Aiguille – or even to Grenoble – but I can nonetheless find out lots of things about Mont Aiguille thanks to memoirs written by mountaineers, maps drawn by cartographers, reports written by geologists, and so forth. This is not a constructivist epistemology: Mont Aiguille was always 'there', as it were, before the geologists and cartographers arrived. But it is the stuff that we can now say that we know about Mont Aiguille that is of interest to us – stuff that is the consequence of a series of processes involving careful measurements, taking photographs, analysing soil samples, and so forth. Over time, what and how much we know about Mont Aiguille has become more detailed and more robust, thanks to the fact that the tools and equipment available to us have been developed to be more sensitive, more accurate, available to a larger number of enquirers and researchers, and so forth. Or, to put it another way using the meta-language of AIME, over time, objectivised knowledge about Mont Aiguille has been established through the cumulative establishment of *chains of reference* [REF] that link (metaphorically as well as epistemologically) Mont Aiguille with what we know about Mont Aiguille. The more things that are done by geologists, or the more photographs that are taken by climbers, the stronger the chains of reference become and the more robust the body of objectivised knowledge of the [REF] mode becomes.

It is important to recognise that AIME is not proposing a positivist epistemology: things do not have one 'true condition'. Nor is it a post-modernist epistemology that accommodates multiple 'truths' that purport to be of equal veracity or merit. Knowledge can and does change over time – it is always, necessarily, mutable – but nonetheless can and does exist in objectivised forms. Knowledge is time-consuming to put together, and requires resources and effort, and we should not forget that even when objectivised, it rests on potentially fragile foundations, prone to disruption from new experiments or new enquiries. Nonetheless, 'we want to be able to say that one thing is rational and another irrational, this thing true and that other thing false' (Latour, 2013, p. 94).

If we say that we know things about research ethics, it is not at all controversial to assume that different kinds of knowing might be being enacted. AIME does not proffer a theory of knowing, but it is nonetheless not difficult to imagine that in drawing on models of cognition that are epistemologically and ontologically aligned to AIME – as well as to the earlier ANT – we might consider such knowing in both abstracted ways (knowing about research ethics by having read about them and/or studied them on a methods module) as well as more embodied ways (knowing about research ethics by having been discombobulated during a period of time in the field and being uncertain as to how to respond to the dilemma in question). Whether we are referring to the process of writing an ethics application form before beginning an empirical study or to writing to our research participants in order to outline the ways in which their practices and words have – or have not – been enfolded within our accounts, we are drawing on knowledge of research ethics in the [REF] mode. As with any other body of knowledge [REF], 'research ethics' is constituted of heterogeneous elements, variously established and inscribed, circulated and reacted to in different ways. It is a body of knowledge that has been built up over time through discussions, controversies, periods of introspection, and periods of disagreement. This body of knowledge is found within a heterogeneous array of social actors. Some of these are non-human: book chapters (such as the one that you are reading at this moment); conference papers; minutes of ethics review committees; or consent forms. Others are human: doctoral supervisors; chairs of ethics committees; students; writers. It is a body of knowledge that is simultaneously stable and mobile; stable, because it can become the focus or object of discussion, action, writing, and debate; mobile, because it can flex and change in response to new ideas, new discussions, and can also travel to new places – new social and cultural spaces – that it might not have travelled to before.

From the point of view of knowledge of the [REF] mode, therefore, we can establish that 'research ethics' is a body of objectivised knowledge that accommodates diverse standpoints and arguments, makes sense of the necessity of constant change (irrespective of the speed, impulse or source of such change), and provides us, as ethnographers, with ways of thinking about research ethics both in terms of an audit process and as an intellectual obligation. It is bound up within forms and checklists and also within unanticipated and indeterminate periods of fieldwork. The very different and long-standing enactments of research ethics that can be neatly (albeit imperfectly) summarised in reference to first, a definition of ethnography in terms of being a means of gaining knowledge about social phenomena and second, a definition of ethnography in terms of a commitment to enacting emancipatory change, can both be accommodated within research ethics as [REF], as can the audit cultures of ethics committees within higher education (Ferdinand et al., 2007; Shore & Wright, 2000; Wynn, 2018). Research ethics as [REF] shifts our focus away from considering our academic conceptualisations of ethics as necessarily increasingly fragmented as a consequence of post-structuralist or post-qualitative impulses (Dennis, 2018; Ferdinand et al., 2007), allowing us to say things about research ethics that foreground the ways in which what might be termed competing if not conflicting discourses of research ethics in fact share much more commonality than might appear to be the case.

Ethics as Fiction [FIC] and as Technology [TEC]

As ethnographers we are familiar with writing, whether this entails the writing that is so central to the work that we do both in and outside the field (Jeffrey, 2018) or the writing that we might come across during our research, the inscriptions that tell us something about the cultural locations that we are interested in (Street, 1984). Within AIME, there is no mode that directly relates to language or literacy or even to semiotics. Rather, Latour concerns himself with the figurations of language and of writing irrespective of what it is that the writing is about. That is to say, within AIME, a fictional narrative is the same as a factual narrative insofar as they are made of the same stuff – of signs, figures, words, and so forth. When Latour talks about the beings of the mode of fiction [FIC] therefore, he is talking about any 'transportable, manipulable inscriptions' (Conway, 2016, p. 9) that can translate the epistemological and ontological properties of any other being into a form – a text. These texts (of whatever modality) in turn contribute to the establishment of chains of reference [REF] of objectivised knowledge which remain mutable (as discussed above) not least because any work of [FIC] can generate divergent interpretations which in turn can be navigated and mediated through recourse to other bodies of [REF] knowledge, or through new enquires that lead to new bodies of writing [FIC] and hence generate new or more detailed chains of reference in turn. Processes of meaning making are not attached directly to beings of the [FIC] mode. Rather, there is a distinct aspect of meaning for each individual mode (Latour, 2013, p. 237): each mode has a particular way of establishing veridiction, of being able to state what is true or accurate, and what is not (Latour, 2013, pp. 53–54).

Within the earlier ANT, the role of texts as physical objects by which both meaning and intention can be carried across geographical, physical and institutional distances is well-established and in fact is central to early ANT ethnographies (Law, 1994; Nespor, 1994). Within AIME, such objects are gathered with other tools or artefacts within the technological mode – [TEC], foregrounding the importance of considering texts as reified physical or virtual forms. Reflecting once again the human/non-human principle of symmetry, it is important to remember that any being of the [TEC] mode, amongst other things, relies on being activated or manipulated. In the case of a text, such manipulation might include reading or not reading, discussing or not discussing, annotating or adapting, as well as the distribution and movement of the text either in hard copy or digital form.

Within AIME, we can combine two modes at the same time as we proceed with our inquiry, sometimes in order to extend theorisation when the phenomenon that we are interested in appears to have collapsed beings of two modes into one, at other times in order to disambiguate between two modes when what looks like a combined effect turns out, after exploration, to be nothing of the kind. Combinations such as these are referred to as *crossings* (Latour, 2013, p. 63). From this standpoint, therefore, we can think about research ethics as [FIC-TEC]: as a body of ideas made concrete – reified or instaurated into a text. As a being of the [FIC] mode, a research ethics framework (from just one institution, of course, as there will be countless other texts from other institutions, sometimes overlapping in content and intention, sometimes diverging) suffers from the same drawbacks as any other [FIC], namely that if they are put to one side or forgotten in a drawer (if referring to a paper copy) or attached to an overlooked or deliberately ignored email (if referring to a PDF) then they disappear. They must always be accompanied and interpreted (Conway, 2016). Nor is the meaning-making of our ethics guidance document a straightforward exercise: interpretations will always be divergent because the [FIC] that we are reading/ discussing by definition has had to attempt to fold up any number of problematics, subjectivities, differences, and so forth within a textual form that can be practicably distributed.

The requirement to distribute the text foregrounds the [TEC] mode, the need to think about the research ethics framework as an object or artefact. From the point of view of [TEC] it does not matter whether the text exists in a physical form made up of ink and paper, or a digital form made up of bits of information that require a laptop computer or mobile phone to read, except insofar as we would need to think about the qualitatively different ways in which the text would be circulated, by whom, at what times and across what institutional or geographic spaces, and so forth. We can think about how the ethics document as [TEC] is used, as distinct from how the ethics document as [FIC] is interpreted, whilst remembering that these two patterns of activity are often intertwined [FIC-TEC] but never conflated.

From the point of view of [FIC-TEC], therefore, we can explore the work that is done by any one of the different kinds of text-based artefact that are instaurated through/within any social practice that has the ethics of doing social research – and more specifically, ethnographic research – as one of any number of matters of concern. Any consideration of 'research ethics' needs equally to include the protocols that are agreed by an ethics committee within an academic institution and the consent forms circulated by the researcher before commencing fieldwork, mindful of the fact that the meanings that are constructed from reading them are not fixed and are only ever capable of being partial, and that the movement of the document in question – as a digital file or piece of paper – is as important to understanding how these meanings are translated from place to place as are the conversations that occur around and about them. As a *matter of concern,* (an expression familiar from Latour's earlier works (Latour, 2005)) research ethics do not 'need' to be reified into text-based forms, but without such forms it would be extremely difficult for information about research ethics (irrespective of the nature or provenance of that information) to be circulated, let alone acted upon.

Ethics as Politics [POL]

People in the social world might come together in collectives in all kinds of ways and for all kinds of reasons. Any sort of matter of concern might lead to people gathering together around and/or in response to that same concern. Once gathered, people can then begin the process of 'performing micro acts of persuasion' (Dyson, 2019, p. 217), talking in different ways in order to persuade a sufficient number of people that their interests, in relation to the matter of concern, are shared. The group or groups thus formed, setting up some sort of limit or border – an 'us' and a 'them', can be said to be acting politically, as being of the political mode – [POL]. The political mode is about more than the 'politics' that we might read about in newspapers, however, although constructions as diverse as 'constitutional politics' on the one hand and 'office politics' on the other are both accommodated within [POL]. Rather, it is the case that the political [POL] refers not only to institutions such as governments or political parties, but also to acting or speaking politically or to *not* acting or speaking politically, whether through choice (when the acts of persuasion have not been sufficiently convincing or agreeable) or whether through being disallowed from taking part in the conversation (when the acts of persuasion have not been afforded or when acts of dissuasion have been employed).

Political groupings of any kind – Latour refers to these as *circles* – are not fixed: they allow beings to come and go, all the while maintaining the delicate balance between the representation of the people and things who are enrolled within the circle on the one hand, and the requirement of obedience from those same people and beings on the other. As such, for the anthropologist or ethnographer, the interest resides not so much in what matters of concern are being addressed, but rather in how they are being addressed. And this is important because it is through this constant work of addressing that the circle persists. Tracing the circle (Latour, 2013, p. 340) allows us to see who is or has been included or excluded and at the same time exposes the twin processes of representation and obedience but does not explain how the circle endures: only by paying attention to the work being done by the people who subscribe to the matter of concern that the circle speaks to, can the ongoing renewal of the circle be explained – once again, through empirical inquiry. Once we begin to think about research ethics from the point of view of [POL], therefore, we can then make sense of the heterogeneous phenomena that characterise any appreciation of ethics in ethnographic research. We can talk about not only discourses of audit and compliance but also the everyday practice of ethics in the field. We can accommodate checklists of rights and wrongs alongside a standpoint of research ethics as being incapable of measurement.

When considering research ethics in terms of [POL], we can disambiguate processes of meaning making from processes of enactment. That is to say, instead of foregrounding our discussions in terms of a stark bifurcation between ethics committees on the one hand (beholden to audit cultures, viewing the research process in a behaviourist, predictable manner) and ethnographers on the other (committed to emergent research processes, occupying an ethics that is open for discussion), we frame them in terms of how they are made sense of and enacted in a political (in the AIME sense) manner. The dominance of the clinical/medical model of ethical governance may well be one that causes the ethnographer to chafe (Delamont & Atkinson, 2018), but the broader history of clinical/medical research on human subjects renders any attempt to gainsay such regulation as egregious if not immoral. At the same time, social research, including ethnographic research, is capable in its own way of causing harm to participants (LeCompte & Schensul, 2015). The political argument [POL] revolves not around whether or not there should be practices that render research ethics as a matter of concern, but how those practices should be enacted, to whom they ought to be reported, how they should be recorded, and so forth.

It would be a mistake to assume that one process of meaning-making or interpretation of a code of research ethics is axiomatically superior or more rigorous or more authentic than another; rather, it is simply the case that depending on context, different political circles circumscribe how they are sustained. The members of an ethics committee do not all have to subscribe to an audit culture discourse of research ethics in order to enable the committee to do its work: indeed, they may look to change the discussions within the committee from the point of view of [POL] as to how research ethics are done. Rubrics and practices have been changed before, and they can therefore be changed again.

Likewise, ethnographers and anthropologists have in the past (mindful of the fact that the ethnography of education is a relatively young academic discipline (LeCompte, 2002)) conducted research in a manner that to more modern sensibilities might be seen as unethical if not offensive, not to mention illegal. It is therefore not the case that an audit model of ethics is wrong, any more than a post-structuralist model of ethics is right. Rather, from the standpoint of [POL] we can say that there are different groups of people who have been convinced/persuaded to act/speak about research ethics in different ways. This is a process that will necessarily involve disagreement. Not every research supervisor will agree that their PhD student should have to provide an interview schedule of specific questions to be asked when they are in the field because within ethnography it might not be possible, let alone desirable, to try to predict the conduct of the research in such a manner. The logical conclusion to such a stance might be that it is impossible to obtain fully informed consent from participants in a manner akin to the consent obtained from respondents to a survey (Levinson, 2010). And one ethnographer may well disagree with another as to whether or not conventions regarding anonymity and confidentiality should always be adhered to, if not actively overturned (Walford, 2005). In just the same way that ethnographers have different political commitments [POL] in terms of the ambition or scope of their research – for example, whether or not to seek to influence practice or enact reform – ethnographers will also have different political commitments [POL] to how they should be ethical – whether in conducting fieldwork or writing approval documents, advising students or fulfilling citizenship obligations through membership of ethics panels.

Going Back to Actors and Networks: From ANT to [NET]

Up to now, I have made several references to actor-network theory (ANT) and specifically to some of the extant ethnographic research that shows ANT at work. Although ANT lacks the ubiquity of Bourdieuian or Foucauldian theories within education research, it has nonetheless become established as a meaningful, insightful and robust perspective upon which to draw (Fenwick & Edwards, 2010). Just as other strands of Latour's wider work are present within AIME (for example, his long-standing interest in technology is now located within the [TEC] mode whilst his more recent ethnography of French legal process can be seen reflected within [LAW] (Latour, 1996, 2010)), so it is the case that ANT has been absorbed into AIME. Now with the new notation of [NET], an actor-network remains the same as in the earlier ANT – a socio-technological network consisting of human and non-human actors that are enrolled within the network in order to accomplish whatever it is that the network is interested in. Within AIME, [NET] forms the starting point of any empirical inquiry: only by empirically tracing the movement of actors across their networks can we say something about what they are doing. And with the addition of a new mode, the pre-position [PRE] mode, we can now address one of the criticisms of ANT (Kale-Lostuvali, 2016) by distinguishing between the qualitative differences of any [NET]. Within AIME, the basic (although it is anything but) unit of the actor-network retains the fundamental role of providing the entry point for any inquiry: as always, we are encouraged to follow the actors (Latour, 2005). With the pre-position mode, we can sensitise ourselves to the key in which we have to interpret all of the things that we will follow: '[NET] only follows the patterns of stitching; [PRE] captures the variegation of the threads' (Conway, 2016, p. 49). To provide an analogy: if I read a doctoral thesis assuming it to be a novel, I would mistake the key in which it had been written and my subsequent interpretation would be fundamentally mistaken. Remembering the affordances of a *crossing* between modes, therefore, the [NET-PRE] crossing is our starting point: 'to understand rationally any situation whatsoever is at once to infold its network and define its proposition' (Latour, 2013, p. 66).

The Many Worlds of Research Ethics

We now have a sufficient grasp of Latour's ontological toolkit to be able to go back to research ethics and to think about what they do from the standpoint of AIME, which pushes us towards thinking about the different networks [NET] that we might find ourselves entangled within at any particular moment in time/space, and how research ethics might happen and in turn make different things happen within those networks – or, to use the meta-language of AIME: what are the beings that are instaurated across networks that have research ethics as a matter of concern? Almost by definition, any AIME-inflected account of any matter of concern does not pretend to be anything other than partial (here AIME arguably reflects the post-structuralist ancestry of ANT) whilst at the same time wanting to establish objectivised knowledge. That is to say, an AIME account of research ethics might travel in all kinds of different directions, with the scope of the inquiry not limited to a priori theoretical or empirical boundaries except for those of interest or concern to the researcher.

So, what do we know about research ethics? We know that as a socio-technical phenomenon, research ethics have become more prominent over recent years and decades in part as a necessary corrective to earlier practices that to contemporary standards would be seen unambiguously as unethical. The enrolling of an ever-greater number of institutions, processes and people within the work done by research ethics is accounted for through the proliferation of a number of heterogeneous inter-related social actors that are nonetheless familiar: ethics handbooks, review committees, conversations between researchers, methods textbooks, journal articles, definitions of terms such as 'sensitivity' and 'anonymity', participant information sheets and consent forms, and so forth. We know that the dominant discourse of research ethics is one that simultaneously is derived from and reifies a clinical rather than anthropological standpoint, and that the inherent restrictions of any text-based artefact render futile any attempts to generate a universally applicable code of ethical research practice. We know that ethical decision-making is characterised by subjectivity and partiality rather than distance and neutrality. Simply put, we know that ethnography is 'poorly served by the cultural dominance of ethical regulation derived from biomedicine' (Delamont & Atkinson, 2018, p. 121), situated within a long-established culture of audit and regulation in universities as well as elsewhere, a system 'based on visibility and coercive accountability' (Shore & Wright, 2000, p. 77) that displaces trust and autonomy.

But at the same time, we also know that ethnographers of education continue to produce rich, insightful and provocative work in ways that can be unexpected, challenging, even treated with suspicion (Dennis, 2010). And whilst ethnographers chafe at the behaviourist, reductive constraints of review boards, they/we nonetheless continue to submit our documentation to such boards and then go ahead and do research (Bosk & de Vries, 2004), to sometimes serve on such boards as an integral aspect of academic citizenship, and to 'regard the careful consideration of research ethics to be a moral imperative' (Wynn, 2011, p. 109). This might sometimes involve improvisation and workaround, an occasional willingness and/or necessity to push at the limits of the bureaucratic processes concerning ethics review that we might be enrolled in as ethnographers, but such practices are typical of many forms of activity where the work that people do (defined in the broadest sense) is required, for whatever reason, to be in some way mediated by process and/or paperwork (Belfiore, Defoe, Folinsbee, Hunter, & Jackson, 2004; Cameron, MacLeod, Tummons, Kits, & Ajjawi, 2019; Smith, 2005; Wynn, 2011).

Contrasting accounts such as these represent the many worlds of research, including those of ethnographers, that have sought to make sense of or otherwise critique aspects of the research ethics process in a number of ways. Typically, the particular phenomena that any author(s) unpack will be filtered through specific theoretical, philosophical and/or ideological lenses. That is to say, we might expect to find an aspect of research ethics as a focus for academic debate where the same element or phenomena is explained through recourse to a different conceptual framework. For example: the well-established standpoint that questions the extent to which a published set of guidelines can be more generally applied might be theorised through recourse to a post-structuralist argument that contests any modernist notion of universally applicable truths (Beach & Eriksson, 2010). Alternatively, we might draw on notions of a text as inherently open to multiple interpretations, mediated by the meaning brought to it by the reader, derived from the New Literacy Studies (Barton, 1994). A second example pertains to relations in the field. For some, the impetus for the removal of the concept of the neutral non-participant observer derives from a feminist critique of power (im)balances within the field, a political and ideological driver akin to post-colonial and post-qualitative approaches (Murphy & Dingwall, 2001; Smith, 2005). For others, the rendering as moot of any pretence to non-participation is driven by a commitment to a philosophical as well as empirical framework such as Habermasian ethical discourse, a relativist standpoint that will be negotiated within the field (Dennis, 2009; Finlayson, 2005). These are contrasting approaches but the material impact of them both includes inter alia the dismantling of the researcher-respondent hierarchy that has characterised traditional anthropological models of ethnography (Crang & Cook, 2007).

AIME takes a different approach, eschewing the importing into the discussion of overarching sociological explanations (here, as elsewhere, AIME echoes the earlier actor-network theory, this time in drawing on the post-structuralist impulse of rejecting a priori frameworks in favour of an 'insistence on painstaking ethnographic research' (Kipnis, 2015, p. 43). No one place to begin the inquiry is any better than another, except insofar as it provides a *point of entry* (Latour, 2005) into one of the networks [NET] in question. We might choose to follow a person or an object, a process or a technique: within the [NET] that we are tracing, all have equal agency: there is no hierarchy between human and non-human, or between different kinds of non-human artefact/object.

For example, an ethics document [FIC-TEC] can form the point of entry into any one of the different networks [NET] that it – and we, as social researchers – might be enrolled within, and that we can choose to follow in order to complete our inquiry. Acknowledging that at first look the ethnographer is faced with a bewildering array of possible ways forward in conducting her fieldwork, we follow the actor – the ethics form – in order to see where it travels, who writes on it, who reads/ignores it, and so forth (Latour, 2005). To choose one instance: as the ethics form travels from the committee via a virtual learning environment or email (my hunch is that few of them are completed on paper as opposed to on screen) to the PhD student, though mediated by their supervisors, we can become sensitive to the different demands made of and for it (assuming we have decided for now not to pivot on our heels and instead follow the form upstream to the point at which it was reified). The different academic disciplines or tribes (Becher & Trowler, 2001) that are required to take up the form in some way will bring their own politics [POL] to the encounter. As the form [TEC] moves from one room to another, from (for example) the supervisor's office to the student's laptop computer and then to the ethics committee meeting room, it will by definition be subject to stresses and fractures as it travels, as the imperfections of the instaurated form render the inscriptions upon it prone to multiple interpretations [FIC]. The discussions of the ethics committee constitute a nexus of practices that will necessarily involve the disciplinary politics of the committee members but at the same time also be enrolled within the dominant discourse [POL] of the auditable, accountable university: the committee members do not have to subscribe to these discourses without reservation or critique; they merely have to allow them to be enacted through their work within the committee itself, as a manifestation of pragmatism and/or strategic compliance. But if they did subscribe to the politics of audit, if they were within rather than outside the [POL] circle of accountability in the academy, their enactments would still afford the same network effect of allowing the ethics form to be able to travel to its next stopping-point within the [NET]. This might be a conversation between student and supervisor, or a conversation between student and respondent. It might be a detailed conversation that responds to a legitimate concern raised by the ethics reviewers surrounding anonymity or the suitability of a specified approach to constructing data, or it might be a cursory conversation that – tacitly or explicitly – acknowledges the structures of the process and treats it as nothing more than an administrative hurdle that needs to be cleared before a more meaningful discussion of research ethics in the field can begin.

Research Ethics – A Matter of Concern for Ethnographers

My argument, therefore, is a relatively simple one (although it has required a necessarily brief as well as partial exposition of Latour's philosophical anthropology in order to be able to set it out): research ethics deserve to be explored by ethnographers not only as causes and consequences of the treatment that our research plans receive at committee stage nor solely as the philosophical or moral lens through which we investigate aspects of our own actions within the field, but as the main object of our anthropological inquiry. If we reframe research ethics as a social actor capable of agency and intent, of being instaurated within both verbal speech and written discourse, of being able to travel in reified forms as well as through voices, then we can reframe our inquiry. Our focus shifts away from 'what are research ethics?' and 'how do we do ethical research?' (questions that we have, arguably, already answered in a satisfactory manner) to 'what do research ethics do?' Starting to build answers to this question will require us, as ethnographers, to take several steps. Although they are presented in a sequence here, they should be read as being of equal importance. Firstly, we will have to think about the different networks [NET] in which research ethics are enrolled – how they are set up and maintained, and how they then circulate in a continuous manner. Secondly, we will have to think about the pre-positions [PRE] of those networks so that we can qualify them and so that we do not mistake one kind of network for another. Thirdly, we will need to consider research ethics in their reified forms as [TEC] and as [FIC] so that we can pick them up, follow them, and read them. And fourthly, we will need to remind ourselves what it is that we already know about research ethics as knowledge of the [REF] mode, and how we might further enrich that knowledge through our inquiry.

As ethnographers we can already access a rich body of knowledge of the [REF] mode concerning research ethics as they pertain to and as they have informed ethnographies of education in a variety of contexts: further education colleges (Barbour, 2010), preschool groups (Flewitt, 2005), higher education institutions (Friberg, 2014), and adult education settings (Sabeti, 2018) – a variety of contexts rendered yet more complex once we consider the affordances of remote, online and distributed ethnographies (Forsey, 2018; Gatson, 2011; Tummons, Fournier, Kits, & Macleod, 2018). Thus, if we are to generate rich accounts of research ethics, to explore fully the connections and associations that allow research ethics to do the stuff that they do, then we need to foreground research ethics as matters of concern not because of a political commitment to a critical ethnography of research ethics as a way of overthrowing positivist biomedical assumptions and audit cultures (cf. Pels, 2000) but rather because from the point of view of AIME, we are able – required, even – to encounter the distinct beings of research ethics, to address them in their own language, and to trace their entanglements with other non-human as well as human actors in more intimate as well as larger scales (Latour, 2013).

References

Anderson-Levitt, K. (2011). World anthropologies of education. In B. Levinson & M. Pollock (Eds.), *A companion to the anthropology of education* (pp. 11–24). Oxford: Wiley-Blackwell.

Barbour, A. (2010). Exploring some ethical dilemmas and obligations of the ethnographer. *Ethnography and Education, 5*(2), 159–173.

Barton, D. (1994). *Literacy: An introduction to the ecology of written language.* Oxford: Blackwell.

Beach, D., & Eriksson, A. (2010). The relationship between ethical positions and methodological approaches: A Scandinavian perspective. *Ethnography and Education, 5*(2), 129–142.

Becher, T., & Trowler, P. (2001). *Academic tribes and territories: Intellectual enquiry and the culture of disciplines* (2nd ed.). Buckingham: SRHE/Open University Press.

Belfiore, M., Defoe, T., Folinsbee, S., Hunter, J., & Jackson, N. (2004). *Reading work: Literacies in the new workplace.* Mahwah, NJ: Lawrence Erlbaum Associates.

Berliner, D., LeGrain, L., & Van De Port, M. (2013). Bruno Latour and the anthropology of the moderns. *Social Anthropology/Anthropologie Sociale, 21*(4), 435–447.

Blok, A., & Jensen, T. (2011). *Bruno Latour: Hybrid thoughts in a hybrid world.* London: Routledge.

Bosk, C., & de Vries, R. (2004). Bureaucracies of mass deception: Institutional review boards and the ethics of ethnographic research. *The Annals of the American Academy of Political and Social Science, 595*, 249–263.

Cameron, P., MacLeod, A., Tummons, J., Kits, O., & Ajjawi, R. (2019). Unpacking practice: The challenges and possibilities afforded by sociomaterial ethnography. In J. Lynch, J. Rowlands, T. Gale, & S. Parker (Eds.), *Practice methodologies in education research* (pp. 187–205). London: Routledge.

Conway, P. (2016). Back down to earth: Reassembling Latour's anthropocenic geopolitics. *Global Discourse, 6*(1–2), 43–71.

Crang, M., & Cook, I. (2007). *Doing ethnographies.* London: Sage.

Decuypere, M., & Simons, M. (2019). Continuing attachments in academic work in neoliberal times: On the academic mode of existence. *Critical Studies in Education, 60*(2), 226–244.

Delamont, S., & Atkinson, P. (2018). The ethics of ethnography. In R. Iphofen & M. Tolich (Eds.), *The Sage handbook of qualitative research ethics* (pp. 119–132). London: Sage.

Delchambre, J.-P., & Marquis, N. (2013). Modes of existence explained to the moderns, or Bruno Latour's plural world. *Social Anthropology/Anthropologie Sociale, 21*(4), 564–575.

Dennis, B. (2009). What does it mean when an ethnographer intervenes? *Ethnography and Education, 4*(2), 131–146.

Dennis, B. (2010). Ethical dilemmas in the field: The complex nature of doing education ethnography. *Ethnography and Education, 5*(2), 123–127.

Dennis, B. (2018). Tales of working without/against a compass: Rethinking ethical dilemmas in educational ethnography. In D. Beach, C. Bagley, & S. Marques da Silva (Eds.), *The Wiley handbook of ethnography of education* (pp. 51–70). Hoboken, NJ: Wiley Blackwell.

Dyson, S. (2019). Assessing Latour: The case of the sickle cell body in history. *European Journal of Social Theory*, *22*(2), 212–230.

Fenwick, T., & Edwards, R. (2010). *Actor-network theory in education*. London: Routledge.

Ferdinand, J., Pearson, G., Rowe, M., & Worthington, F. (2007). A different kind of ethics. *Ethnography*, *8*(4), 519–543.

Finlayson, J. (2005). *Habermas*. Oxford: Oxford University Press.

Flewitt, R. (2005). Conducting research with young children: Some ethical considerations. *Early Child Development and Care*, *175*(6), 553–565.

Forsey, M. (2018). Educational ethnography in and for a mobile modernity. In D. Beach, C. Bagley, & S. Marques da Silva (Eds.), *The Wiley handbook of ethnography of education* (pp. 443–454). Hoboken, NJ: Wiley Blackwell.

Friberg, T. (2014). Towards a discovery-oriented ethnography in researching the professional context of higher education. *European Journal of Higher Education*, *4*(1), 30–41.

Gatson, S. (2011). The methods, politics, and ethics of representation in online ethnography. In N. Denzin & Y. Lincoln (Eds.), *The Sage handbook of qualitative research* (4th ed., pp. 513–527). London: Sage.

Gorur, R. (2011). ANT on the PISA trail: Following the statistical pursuit of certainty. *Educational Philosophy and Theory*, *43*(s1), 76–93.

Hämäläinen, N., & Lehtonen, T.-K. (2016). Latour's empirical metaphysics. *Distinktion: Journal of Social Theory*, *17*(1), 20–37.

Harman, G. (2016). A new occasionalism? In B. Latour & C. Leclerq (Eds.), *Reset modernity!* (pp. 129–138) Karlsruhe: ZKM.

Hasse, C. (2015). *An anthropology of learning*. Dordrecht: Springer.

Huisman, K. (2008). 'Does this mean you're not going to come visit me anymore?' An inquiry into an ethics of reciprocity and positionality in feminist ethnographic research. *Sociological Inquiry*, *78*(3), 372–396.

Jeffrey, B. (2018). Ethnographic writing. In D. Beach, C. Bagley, & S. Marques da Silva (Eds.), *The Wiley handbook of ethnography of education* (pp. 113–134). Hoboken, NJ: Wiley Blackwell.

Kale-Lostuvali, E. (2016). Two sociologies of science in search of truth: Bourdieu versus Latour. *Social Epistemology*, *30*(3), 273–296.

Kipnis, A. (2015). Agency between humanism and posthumanism: Latour and his opponents. *HAU: Journal of Ethnographic Theory*, *5*(2), 43–58.

Latour, B. (1996). *Aramis, or the love of technology*. London: Harvard University Press.

Latour, B. (2005). *Reassembling the social: An introduction to actor-network theory*. Oxford: Oxford University Press.

Latour, B. (2010). *The making of law*. Cambridge: Polity Press.

Latour, B. (2013). *An inquiry into modes of existence* [Trans. C. Porter]. London: Harvard University Press.

Law, J. (1994). *Organising modernity*. Oxford: Blackwell.

LeCompte, M. (2002). The transformation of ethnographic practice: Past and current challenges. *Qualitative Research*, 2(3), 283–299.

LeCompte, M., & Schensul, J. (2015). *Ethics in ethnography*. London: Rowman and Littlefield.

Levinson, M. (2010). Accountability to research participants: Unresolved dilemmas and unravelling ethics. *Ethnography and Education*, 5(2), 193–207.

McGee, K. (2014). *Bruno Latour: The normativity of networks*. London: Routledge.

Mulcahy, D. (2011). Assembling the 'accomplished' teacher: The performativity and politics of professional teaching standards. *Educational Philosophy and Theory*, 43(s1), 94–113.

Murphy, E., & Dingwall, R. (2001). The ethics of ethnography. In P. Atkinson, A. Coffey, S. Delamont, J. Lofland, & L. Lofland (Eds.), *Handbook of ethnography* (pp. 339–351). London: Sage.

Nespor, J. (1994). *Knowledge in motion: Space, time and curriculum in undergraduate physics and management*. London: RoutledgeFalmer.

Pels, P. (2000). The trickster's dilemma: Ethics and the technologies of the anthropological self. In M. Strathern (Ed.), *Audit cultures: Anthropological studies in accountability, ethics and the academy* (pp. 135–172). London: Routledge.

Reyes-Foster, B. (2016). Latour's AIME, indigenous critique, and ontological turns in a Mexican psychiatric hospital: Approaching registers of visibility in three conceptual turns. *Anthropological Quarterly*, 89(4), 1175–1200.

Sabeti, S. (2018). *Creativity and learning in later life: An ethnography of museum education*. London: Routledge.

Sarauw, L. (2016). Co-creating higher education reform with actor-network theory: Experiences from involving a variety of actors in the processes of knowledge creation. In J. Huisman & M. Tight (Eds.), *Theory and method in higher education research* (Vol. 2, pp. 177–198). Bingley: Emerald Publishing Limited.

Shore, C., & Wright, S. (2000). Coercive accountability – The rise of audit culture in higher education. In M. Strathern (Ed.), *Audit cultures: Anthropological studies in accountability, ethics and the academy* (pp. 57–89). London: Routledge.

Simondon, G. (1958). *On the mode of existence of technical objects* [Trans Malaspina, C. & Rogove, J.] Minneapolis, MN: Univocal.

Smith, D. (2005). *Institutional ethnography: A sociology for people*. Lanham, MD: Altamira Press.

Souriau, É. (1943/2009). *Les différents modes d'existence: Suivi de Du mode d'existence de l'œuvre à faire*. Paris: Presses Universitaires de France. doi:10.3917/puf.souri.2009.01

Street, B. (1984). *Literacy in theory and practice*. Cambridge: CUP.

Tsouvalis, J. (2016). Latour's object-orientated politics for a post-political age. *Global Discourse*, 6(1–2), 26–39.

Tummons, J. (2020). Education as a mode of existence: A Latourian inquiry into assessment validity in higher education. *Educational Philosophy and Theory*, 52(1), 45–54.

Tummons, J. (2021a). Ontological pluralism, modes of existence, and actor-network theory: Upgrading Latour with Latour. *Social Epistemology*, 35(1), 1–11.

Tummons, J. (2021b). On the educational mode of existence: Latour, meta-ethnography, and the social institution of education. *Social Anthropology/Anthropologie Sociale*, 29(3), 570–585.

Tummons, J., & Beach, D. (2020). Ethnography, materiality, and the principle of symmetry: Problematising anthropocentrism and interactionism in the ethnography of education. *Ethnography and Education, 15*(3), 286–299.

Tummons, J., Fournier, C., Kits, O., & Macleod, A. (2018). Using technology to accomplish comparability of provision in distributed medical education in Canada: An actor–network theory ethnography. *Studies in Higher Education, 43*(11), 1912–1922.

Walford, G. (2005). Research ethical guidelines and anonymity. *International Journal of Research and Method in Education, 28*(1), 83–93.

Weber, T. (2016). Metaphysics of the common world: Whitehead, Latour, and the modes of existence. *Journal of Speculative Philosophy, 30*(4), 515–533.

Wynn, L. (2011). Ethnographers' experiences of institutional ethics oversight: Results from a quantitative and qualitative survey. *Journal of Policy History, 23*(1), 94–114.

Wynn, L. (2018). When ethics review boards get ethnographic research wrong. In R. Iphofen & M. Tolich (Eds.), *The Sage handbook of qualitative research ethics* (pp. 248–262). London: Sage.

Chapter 3

Managing Ethics When Working with Young People and Children

Lisa Russell and Ruth Barley

Abstract

All research has the potential to affect people, ethnographers delve into the life of the every day of their participants, they walk their walk, talk their talk and strive for valid, in-depth contextualised data, gathered over a longitudinal and often intimate basis. Ethnography is explorative and inductive. It is messy, unpredictable and complex. Ethnography conducted with young people and children adds to the intricacy of managing ethically sound research practice within and beyond the field. In recent years, ethnographies with children, young people and families have become increasingly prominent, yet few scholars have written about conducting ethnographic research with children and young people (Albon & Barley, 2021; Levey, 2009; Mayeza, 2017). The ethnographer that works with children and young people needs to be aware that the power relationship between adults and children operates in complex and sometimes surprising ways and so needs to be ethically aware, ethically reactive and be prepared to be ethically challenged.

Keywords: Children and young people; ethical regulation; consent; ownership; representation; power

Introduction

This chapter contextualises ethics within the continual rise of ethical regulation frameworks, such as the Research Ethics Framework of the Economic and Social Research Council (ESRC), that currently dominate the research landscape. The chapter goes on to draw upon two expert ethnographers' experiences of working with children and young people. These reflexive accounts are used to reveal how

Ethics, Ethnography and Education, 29–47

Copyright © 2022 Lisa Russell and Ruth Barley

Published under exclusive licence by Emerald Publishing Limited

doi:10.1108/S1529-210X20220000019003

managing ethics in-situ is of particular pertinence to the ethnographer working with children, young people and their families since the power dynamic between the ethnographer and the participants is in a state of constant flux (Mayeza, 2017). The ethnographer requires autonomy while managing ethics soundly to work within the messiness and unpredictability of participants' lives. Educational ethnographers need to be reflexive in their consideration of ethics, especially when considering the variable fields of investigation, the closeness, proximity to children and young people over a longitudinal basis and the potential use of a plethora of research methods that may unearth data and circumstances that are sensitive and unexpected. Ethnography's unpredictable nature can have unprecedented consequences for the use of ethics when working with children and young people.

The Rise of Ethical Regulation

Ethical regulation of all social research has increased significantly in the UK; long gone are the days whereby research ethics was entirely a matter of one's own professional judgement (Dingwall, 2012; Hammersley, 2009). This increase in ethical regulation has its roots in the field of health and the trend is following that set by the USA. The Economic and Social Research Council's (ESRC) Research Ethics Framework has been imperative to the way in which ethics is managed by social scientists in universities. Ethical regulation is a requirement and failure to comply, rules out certain funding opportunities and possible practises of ethically risky pieces of research (Hammersley, 2009). This rise in ethical regulation has specific implications for the ethnographer (Delamont & Atkinson, 2018; Parker, 2007; Russell & Barley, 2020).

It is now commonplace for all research project plans to go through ethical committee clearance via formal institutional regulation boards. Such committees have an abundance of power to demand clarification and even modification of research in terms of subject choice, methods adopted, and in some instances, may prevent the research from going ahead. This increased regard held for ethical procedures has been questioned, particularly for those types of research that take place in 'natural' settings over prolonged periods (Delamont & Atkinson, 2018; Dingwall, 2012; Hunter, 2018). Such regulations have serious implications for covert ethnography, for example whereby research may struggle to gain ethical approval despite its merits in yielding valid and otherwise hard-to-access data. Furthermore, this procedure assumes that the ethics committee knows best and is in a superior position to make a better judgement about the ethics of any given research project than the actual researcher(s) involved. It also assumes that most, if not all, ethical dilemmas can be foreseen and managed in advance. Furthermore, it assumes the researcher knows from the outset what methods of data collection will be used throughout the course of the study. These requirements to foresee the possible directions a study may take make it difficult for emergent methodologies such as ethnography to reach their full potential. The field and indeed the actual purpose and means by which data is gathered is multiple and can vary and evolve within the course of any given ethnography, indeed this is deemed to be one of ethnography's strengths (Barley & Russell, 2019). While the ESRC Research Ethics Framework recognises that ethics needs to be 'continually monitored' in such forms of research, the realities of managing this in the field are somewhat problematic, especially when working with young people and children. This chapter proposes that these assumptions make dealing with ethics more problematic for the ethnographer who immerses themselves in the field for lengthy periods of time, while attempting to truly gain informed consent with children and young people (Barley, 2022; Russell & Barley, 2020). The ethnographer spends a long time 'hanging around' and familiarising themselves with the partici-pants, culture and sometimes local context, making it increasingly difficult to predict possible ethical quandaries (Delamont & Atkinson, 2018). While this emergent methodology may not easily jump through an Ethics Committee's hoops, due to a number of unknowns, it is argued that when a researcher takes time to familiarise themselves with the research context and gives their par-ticipants time to become familiar with the researcher, power dynamics can be minimised facilitating a participant's ability to actively consent, thus resulting in a deeper understanding and implementation of ethical practices (Barley & Bath, 2014).

Hammerlsey (2009) reminds us that different researchers prioritise some ethical points over others and so ethics is viewed as a variable feat, dependant on context. While Hammersley recognises the requirement for ethical consideration in *some* circumstances he reminds us of the possible dilemmas and even dangers such regulations may ensue. It is important to remember that most experienced ethnographers do hold a care of duty with regards to their participants and are acutely aware of the formal ethical guidelines that may infringe upon their practice, even if they may not be able to predict the realities of managing ethically sound practice within the field. Indeed, there is very little evidence that any recent social scientific research has actually caused harm to participants in a physical or emotional sense; in fact, many ethnographers working with young people endeavour to voice the opinion of the marginalised and empower them (Albon & Barley, 2021). Today there is an increased notion of accountability. And while there is a place for ethical regulation and review (Hunter, 2018), power placed solely in their hands could be viewed as extreme and even misplaced (Dingwall, 2012). Whereas others bring into question the idea that ethics committees should indeed prolong their role to include a consideration of ethics after a project has officially concluded in attempt to reduce harm to partici-pants and ensure the protocols of informed consent are truly upheld (Tolich, 2016). It is generally accepted that as ethnographers we do indeed need to be scrutinised and held to account (Delamont & Atkinson, 2018), but there is further work to be done here to develop and improve research ethics com-mittees so that they can be more appropriately framed and uphold realistic standards for ethnography (Hunter, 2018). Managing ethics in ethnography is inevitably messy and so there are no 'simple answers' and checklist protocols that can substitute for professional decision-making in light of unfolding events and circumstances that present themselves as the ethnography develops and quite often mutates to the needs of the field. Delamont and Atkinson (2018) argue that the ethical guidelines utilised by ethnographers would thus be better driven by positive values that ensure research is carried out humanely and sensibly, rather than by a set of predetermined procedures that will inevitably fail to anticipate all ethical quandaries.

Ethnographers are concerned with gaining valid data. Research carried out in 'natural' settings, like that of ethnography, needs a flexible procedural approach to ethics that empowers the ethnographer in their 'practical decisions which involve ethical consideration' (Hammersley, 2009, p. 215) rather than disempowers their autonomy to behave in an ethically sound manner while simultaneously gaining truly valid data. This increased regulation may increase the likelihood of ethnographers adopting a more strategic approach to their ethical considerations to satisfy ethical review committees and gain funding; consideration of ethics may affect choice of topics researched and the methods adopted to gain valid data. Researchers may shy away from taboo topics of research conducted with 'dodgy' participants via risky means of gathering data. It is also possible that there will be increased discrepancies from the official line taken to ethics and the reality of managing ethical dilemmas in the field – especially for the ethnographer working with young people. The realities of what happens in the field needs to be reflected upon to add to the novice ethnographers' knowledge and improve ethically sound practice for all. Indeed, Hammersley warns that researchers may even abstain from ethical responsibility and assign that accountability to the official ethical committees given the current regulated climate. Increased ethical regulation is thus challenged albeit something that the ethnographer cannot ignore.

Research with Children and Young People

Trust is key to any research encounter (Russell, 2005; Wilson & Hodgson, 2012) and is absolutely vital to the ethnographer who is seeking informed consent and valid data with children and young people who may be deemed 'vulnerable' (Albon & Barley, 2021). Ethics has been considered when regarding research that works with young people and children, but this is usually considered with relation to qualitative research methods in general rather than specifically looking at ethnographies (Dockett, Einarsdottir, & Perry, 2009; Sime, 2008). As ethnography is an emergent methodology that involves the ethnographer developing intimate and prolonged relationships with participants, specific ethical aspects around how one manages informed consent and deals with sensitive data need to considered to ensure ethics are managed sensitively in-situ (for more on this please refer to Russell & Barley, 2020). This chapter attempts to address this dearth in knowledge by reflecting on the work of two experienced education ethnographers who work with children and young people: Lisa Russell's work with NEET (Not in Employment Education or Training) young people and Ruth Barley's work conducted with ethnically diverse primary school age children. Doing ethnography with young people adds to the unpredictability of how ethics can be managed in the field, but also adds to the ethical sensitivity required by the ethnographer. Some scholars ask whether informed consent can be truly gained from the child or young person (in addition to the parental consent that is required by ethics committees) or if they are only able to assent to participate (Barley, 2022). Research, however, shows that a child's ability to give their consent to take part in a research study is not purely based on age but also on the child's competency, the type of research as well as the researcher's expertise in working with children. Arguably, consent needs to be thought about differently when doing ethnography with children and young people since the process of establishing relationships of trust and reciprocity are different; often participants are involved with the research as a collective as well as on an individual basis. This in turn shapes how the researcher gains access, negotiates power relations and establishes and maintains social relationships within the field (Delamont & Atkinson, 2018). So, for example, giving children and young people time to familiarise themselves with the researcher and the study before being asked to participate becomes an essential part of the consent process (Barley, 2022) as does the understanding that the nature of relationships developed in the field differ from the peripheral to the intimate and from the prolonged to the fleeting, with some participants leaving (through an intent to withdraw or unknown reasons related more broadly to attrition) and others joining and becoming more central. Ethnographic fieldwork thus follows the contours of the social setting and often include participation with a collective group of people rather than select individuals. We explore the social world, strive to understand subcultures and organisations such as schools as a whole. Considering participants as members of a collective has implications for what informed consent actually means and how it operates within ethnography. The very nature of ethnographic analysis is iterative and emergent making it all but impossible to provide fully informed consent in relation to the purposes and outcomes of the research, since they may be unintended and unknown (Delamont & Atkinson, 2018).

Another issue involves the ethnographer as a witness and questions at what point the ethnographer should intervene in potentially harmful situations (often defined as harmful by an adult) and potentially breach confidentiality, while others revolve around the need for children to be recognised as 'social actors', agents in their own right, positions that don't always sit well with national contexts and hegemonic understandings regarding age, ethnicity, gender and immigration – often these contexts act to segment children rather than work with them to generate youth-centred representations and knowledge (Garcia & Fine, 2018).

Education ethnographers need to manage ethics in the academic institutional domain as well as within the domain of their interactions with participants (Dennis, 2010). Education ethnographers place themselves in the practical domain of everyday life where the management of ethics is much messier, unpredictable and responsive to the context of particular research processes. Requirements and regulations set out by ethical review boards may not always be specific to or match those sought as important to the young people themselves. Behaving ethically in the field is complex for those ethnographers that work with children and young people. By reflecting on ethical challenges managed by education ethnographers, the formalities and the realities of ethics can be disentangled and the development of a better approach may ensue (Hunter, 2018).

Ethnographers locate ethical decisions as internal to the research process itself, linked to the everyday interactions and on-going research activities, rather than a set of principles established externally and prior to the research starting. Ethical decisions vary according to context, as well as in accordance to specific researchers' political, moral, methodological or theoretical stand-points. Doing education-based ethnography may put researchers into contact with unethical behaviour that is part of the everyday lives of the participants, and by studying them every day, the ethnographer is intrigued yet somewhat vulnerable and perhaps cautious about the ethics of researching children and young people.

The Studies

Data are drawn from two ethnographies, the first involves a three-year ethnography that explored the experiences of NEET young people as they moved from various places of employment and education sites in Northern England from 2010 to 2013 (Simmons, Thompson, & Russell, 2014). Six follow-up semi-structured interviews were also conducted in subsequent years where contact with four of the female participants remained open. The project aimed to understand the needs and behaviour of these 'hard-to-access' young people and the effectiveness of interventions aimed at moving them into sound education and employment spaces. The experiences of 24 young people identified as NEET or at risk of becoming NEET were explored with a priority being placed on gaining valid data. Fourteen females and 10 males aged 15–20 years including three self-identifying as Asian, one as Mixed Race and the rest as White participated. The level and nature of participation varied from one individual to the next and was dependent upon their personal circumstances. Levels of participation varied over the life of the project (and beyond) which has particular implications for consent (See Russell, 2013 for more on this) as does adhering to ever-changing formal ethical reviews, including changing university ethical procedures, since the start of the project in 2010.

Young people were accessed from a range of sources, including YOT (Youth Offending Team), parent groups, a housing charity, Connexions and word-of-mouth. The NEET group represents a broad range of people, and diverse sources were necessary to gain access. The main corpus of data included over 340 hours of participant observation conducted in young people's homes, schools, colleges, training providers, benefit offices, charity events, work placements, car journeys and fast-food restaurants. Fieldnotes detailed the young people's use of space and time; referral procedures and pathways, learner behaviour and relations with tutors, Connexions, benefit office staff, social workers, friends and family. Young people's activities were mapped, alongside their aspirations. Fieldwork commenced in October 2010 and comprised 79 interviews, including employers, practitioners, parents and young people. Each of the 24 young people were interviewed at least once and have been re-interviewed once or twice thereafter dependent upon their transitions or critical life moments that have arisen throughout the research. Photographs taken by the researcher and the young people, combined with official documents detailing local NEET statistics, NEET Strategy Group meeting minutes and local provision data were analysed. As is customary with ethnographic research, all data were triangulated where possible. Ethical consent was granted by the affiliated University but procedures did change after completion of the official fieldwork and commencement of additional interviews conducted. Such instances may be deemed more commonplace with ethnography given its longitudinal nature and consequent increased chances of working within and need to respond to ever-changing research contexts. This brings into question how ethics is managed after official completion of the project and what role (if any) ethics committees should hold in the aftermath of fieldwork (Marcus & Lerman, 2018).

The second study draws on two stages of a longitudinal ethnography with a multi-ethnic school in the north of England. The study included four stages of fieldwork conducted over a seven-year period:

Stage 1 (2010–2011) – Reception class (first year of compulsory education) – 4–5 years old
Stage 2 (2012–2013) – Year 2 – 6–7 years old
Stage 3 (2014–2015) – Year 4 – 8–9 years old
Stage 4 (2016–2017) – Year 6 (last year of primary education) – 10–11 years old

Two stages of fieldwork, Stage 1 and Stage 3, are referred to in this chapter.

Prior to starting fieldwork Ruth undertook a six-week familiarisation period to become familiar with the research context and start to build rapport with children, parents and school staff (Barley & Bath, 2014). A total of 31 children took part in the study: 16 girls and 15 boys. Seventeen children spoke Arabic as their first language, seven Somali, five English with the remaining child speaking a minority language that has been withheld to protect their anonymity. Eight children received free school meals.

At each stage of fieldwork, participant observations in the classroom, lunch hall and playground were the key method of data collection. Unstructured informal interviews were also undertaken with school staff. Further, based on the pedagogical principles of 'sustained shared thinking' (Siraj-Blatchford & Sylva, 2004, p. 6), children collaboratively designed research activities which were used to initiate research conversations. These data were then collaboratively analysed alongside more traditional hand-written fieldnotes. Adopting a participatory approach in relation to the design and development of the study helped to reduce some of the power differentials between an adult researcher and child participants (Cheney, 2011). This participatory framework provided a basis on which to reflect on other ethical issues throughout data collection and analysis. Formal ethical approval was gained at the start of the study from the university ethics committee and updated before each subsequent fieldwork period.

The Personal, Professional and Political

Education ethnographers have long recognised the significance of the researcher's self upon research (Burgess, 1984; Russell, 2005; Troman, 2001; Walford, 1991). The ethnographer enters the field for long periods of time and engages in close contact with participants. Due to this intimacy, the personal, professional and political standpoints in addition to the institutional and societal climate are of particular importance in ethnography and have specific implications for the management of ethics. These three related aspects influence choice of topic, where and how research is conducted, with whom, where and how findings are disseminated (Miller & Russell, 2005). These aspects are particularly salient for ethnographers who regard themselves as criticalists – a tradition that broadly refers to researchers who are concerned with issues of social justice and enter the field with an aim to change the community for the better (Carspecken, 1996; Dennis, 2009; Korth, 2005). Within this tradition injustices are confronted head on, the research undertaken is unashamedly political and purposely aims to emancipate the vulnerable and marginalised. When working within this tradition, the ethnographer might be especially willing to risk intervening or not intervening if this action is perceived to benefit the community or participants in some way (Dennis, 2009). Both Lisa and Ruth would place themselves in this camp, thus having particular consequences for modes of participation (or 'intervening' as Dennis would describe it) and reasons behind those decisions which in turn can complicate the manifestation and management of ethics.

The majority of literature on research ethics focuses on the challenges, limitations and ethics of review board requirements and practices, usually addressing issues regarding the need to gain informed consent (from parents and guardians in addition and in some cases instead of the young people themselves if under the age of 16), protect participants from any physical or emotional harm and ensure their and the related institutions anonymity if deemed necessary (Dennis, 2009). For more on this related to Lisa's research on NEET young people please see Russell (2013) and for Ruth's work within an ethnically diverse primary school classroom see Barley (2014). Modes of participation and decisions about how and when, or even if, to intervene in the life of the participants may implicate the management of ethics and indeed throw into question the issue of who owns the data and for what purpose (Russell & Barley, 2020).

Issues of Consent, Data Ownership and Intervention

Ethnographers have long debated the ethical challenges of 'intervening' with the participants they work with; however, few have stipulated the specifics involved when working with young people, when arguably the need to intervene for safeguarding and other related issues may more likely arise (Garcia & Fine, 2018). Lisa faced a decision to intervene in her work with Isla a young mum who was having incredible difficulty accessing services and gaining information needed to help her maintain custody of her baby. Isla and Lisa met on an employability course that was put in place for those who were part of the Leaving Care team. Isla had done some level one and two hairdressing training, but failed to gain the certification after completing the course. During the fieldwork she returned to her hairdresser training (a decision of her own making), repeating levels one and two after the birth of Oscar. The majority of fieldwork was conducted in Isla's various places of residence (she moved three times during the research) as she remained NEET for the majority of time over the life of the project. Becoming a mum was a significant life event for Isla. Lisa only ever observed Isla at home with Oscar; however, they did discuss photographs she had taken with Oscar's dad Lucas and other members of her family in a semi-structured interview.

Through the Eyes of Isla

09/02/12

12.00–1.00 p.m. As soon as I enter, Isla informs me that she and Lucas have separated. Oscar is asleep on a bouncer near the radiator. Isla seems pleased to see me and is eager to talk about recent life events. She walks over and uses the hob on the cooker to light a cigarette. She says a lot has happened since our last meeting. She has an injunction out against Lucas. His mum comes and picks Oscar up to see his dad, and the visits are supervised by Lucas' parents as ordered by social services. Lucas has him about three days a week.

   She describes going out to her cousin's 21st birthday party, a male friend came by and slept on the chair sofa in the living room with his baby in the room. Oscar was at the parent-in-laws overnight. Lucas suddenly got mad, broke a bowl and threw it off the table in a rage, he went to bed and she didn't go with him as she didn't want to go to bed with someone who was 'like that' – he later came down the stairs shouting saying she needed to leave the house, she refused, reasoning that all her belongings were there and he started a chainsaw up and threatened to saw her legs off if she didn't get out. She ran out of the house to her neighbours with no shoes on and called the police.

Ethics are an important consideration in any research setting, but when the research is conducted in a young person's home, specific issues can emerge that require careful consideration. One issue involves consent and the other includes ownership of data. Central to working with children and young people is the issue of gaining consent. Consent requires continual renegotiation especially when the research uses different research methods and is longitudinal and intimate in nature. Lucas the father and indeed Oscar who was too young to talk did not give their consent to take part in the ethnography, yet parts of their (intimate) lives were made available for Lisa to observe and document through the eyes of Isla. Members of Isla's family and some of her friends and professionals who worked with her made an appearance in Lisa's written fieldnotes; photographs taken by Isla and interviews. Some of these research methods are deemed more participatory than others but all were largely participant led. Participatory methodologies assume that data will be owned by the people involved with the research. All young people had first inspection of the photographs taken by them; two copies were made so they could keep one for themselves. In all instances, no photographs were censored for analytical purposes of the research. However careful consideration of some photographs was needed for publication purposes, with some depicting sensitive types of data such as young people partying and others portraying people who were not directly part of the ethnography. Content of such data is deemed sensitive and, in some cases, can only really be considered in relation to the young person themselves, since it is their viewpoint, their reality of a particular point in time that cannot be triangulated with other sources; indeed, they represent data that may otherwise have remained hidden.

Some of the data Lisa was exposed to were highly sensitive in nature. Examples of issues raised during the course of fieldwork with NEET young people included non-consensual marriage amongst school age Asian females; benefit fraud, theft, drug-marketing and domestic violence. Dealing with sensitive material may be commonplace for the ethnographer working with marginalised young people and children but questions about data ownership require further interrogation (Russell & Barley, 2020). The Data Protection Act 1998 and Freedom of Information Act 2000 (relevant policies at the time of fieldwork; with the General Data Protection Regulation coming into effect in 2018 in the UK) ensure that the participant may have access to any information at any point the researcher may have regarding them. Fieldnotes for the ethnographer have sometimes been viewed as a personal record, in their raw form kept only for the eyes of the researcher. Questions of data authenticity and validity come in to play if ethnographers allow their participants to view fieldnotes, edit interview transcripts, photograph selection and indeed any other data source, as they may edit data according to their own agendas. However, it is not uncommon for the ethnographer to allow participants to see all data as they are being recorded and after they have been documented, indeed many view this as being ethically sound practice that allows the ethnographer to gain trust and valid data (Albon & Barley, 2021; Barley, 2022; Russell, 2005). The ethnographer has to be highly reflexive and keep reflective accounts to help uphold validity of findings, but also has to be aware of how to deal with sensitive data that involve other people who are not directly part of the research. Careful deliberation is required when considering what to do when the participant asks to have access to their data. In this instance, Isla asks Lisa to provide a statement for her child custody case; Isla trusted Lisa, as did Isla's parents. Lisa supported Isla and the family to manage formalities regarding child benefit, documenting crime references and providing car transport to and from the solicitors. Lisa's response to this unpredictable sequence of events is partly shaped by her own political and philosophical standpoint; like Dennis (2009), she too felt morally obliged to help Isla.

Supporting Isla

05/07/12

10.30–11.30 a.m. We sit in the garden on the back doorstep in the rain, she says, 'I've loads to tell you'. Lucas and his parents have asked for sole residency of their son Oscar.

Her parents tell me that Lucas' parents have applied for child benefit; Isla shows me the letter from HM Revenue asking her to respond within 21 days or her money will be stopped. Her parents urge her to inform her solicitor about this. She says Lucas just wants to make her life a misery and is doing anything he can to achieve this.

She asks me to read her statement, written by her solicitor, it state's Lucas' episodes of violence. It states he controlled what she wore; called her 'slag' accused Isla of sleeping around and stopped her friends from visiting.

Isla asks if I would be willing to give a statement. Saying the more she has the better, I agree to this but worry about the ethical considerations involved. She was supposed to see her solicitor today but will now see her tomorrow with me.

She says it is sad when Oscar leaves but is convinced she will gain full custody, as the violence has been well documented. Charges against him were dropped for the chainsaw incident as the neighbour wouldn't provide a statement for fear of getting involved.

Her solicitor has said they can't stop her child benefit until court in August. She rings her solicitor as I am there to arrange me coming in tomorrow.

06/07/12

10.30–2.30 p.m. I arrive at Isla's parents wet and late after a horrendous journey in the rain. I give her mum a lift into town while we park.

Caroline, her solicitor, states that my statement will be short as I can only comment on the state of Isla's residences. She says I may be summoned to court and need to keep the 3rd August free for this reason.

Caroline states that Isla has to prepare herself for the fact that she might lose Oscar. She says Isla needs to get police incident reference numbers, any medical records and letters from her Sure Start group to confirm her attendance at the parenting groups.

Lucas' ex has given a statement saying Lucas has displayed threatening behaviour towards her; she is currently in a safe house for witness protection (OC I worry about my own safety, Isla paints Lucas to be a threatening character).[1] When I ask Caroline about this she says, 'I don't blame you' – this doesn't fill me with confidence. Caroline says I may have to give evidence if summoned in a family court in front of Lucas.

Isla says she is struggling to get people to do statements as people fear Lucas and what may happen. Others haven't got round to doing it. Caroline says Isla needs to be more pro-active.

We walk back to the car and I drive her home. I go in the house for a cup of tea, her dad asks how it went and I say Isla has a number of things she has to do, like get hold of her social worker, find her crime reference numbers, and ring her health visitor and Sure Start contact. Upon my recommendation Isla uses my phone to try to contact these people.

Lisa appeared in county family court with another member of the research team on the set date, but was never called. The above depicts the emotional cost to the researcher such dealings can have, but also made Lisa re-evaluate her political and moral stance. Concerns about who might ask for the fieldnotes and other data were called into question, what if the courts or Isla demanded to see fieldnotes that detailed her time at home with the baby, how should Lisa as an individual and as a researcher working in a university manage this ethical dilemma? The fieldnotes depicted Isla's day-to-day activities and at the time of writing them Lisa had no idea who or why other audiences might want to see the raw material. Furthermore, some of the data involved other people who were not directly involved with the research. All raw data would have to be screened to reveal data pertinent to the case in question. This episode confirms that ethics is important when working with children and young people; one does need to be aware of their political standpoint and how it might affect their position and rationale to intervene (or not). Lisa had seen Isla caring for her baby in her home and had no cause for concern She also wanted to help Isla who she deemed to be a vulnerable young lady. Lisa too felt frustrated by the lack of support Isla was able to glean. This situation reveals the need for the ethnographer to be prepared to manage the unpredictable in-situ and beyond.

Managing the Unpredictable In-Situ

The ethnographer has to expect the unpredictable when working with children and young people, manage the emergence of sensitive issues and trust his/her own judgement based on his/her ethnographic expertise about his/her own and the participants' safety (Russell, 2013). Certain procedures can of course be implemented before the ethnographer enters the field such as gaining a valid Disclosure and Barring Service check, ensuring all university, related institutions, participants and funding body ethical regulations are adhered to. The ethnographer may need to question their own moral and political viewpoint and be prepared to intervene. Managing the unpredictable in-situ is a complex ethical challenge for the ethnographer.

An example from Ruth's study reveals how this became apparent to Ruth in terms of racial discrimination. The fieldnote extract below describes a participant observation session involving three children in Ruth's study: Annakiya (a girl from Nigeria), Kareem (a boy from Libya) and Fariido (a girl from Somalia).

18/11/10: She's Black

10.30–11.35

The class moves to the outdoor play area. I walk to the steps and sit down and watch as the children play. Annakiya picks up a ball and asks me to play with her. We throw the ball back and forth to each other. After a few minutes Kareem comes up to us – also with a ball in his hands – and asks me to throw his ball to him. I throw Annakiya's ball back to her and then Kareem's ball to him and so on alternating between the two children.

Fariido comes, looks at Kareem, and asks if he will throw his ball to her so that she can also join in. He says 'No' and throws the ball directly back to me. As I throw it back to him, Fariido asks him again if he will throw the ball to her, and again Kareem replies, 'No', but this time also shakes his head resolutely to emphasise his meaning. He then turns to me and says 'She black', offering an explanation for why he won't throw his ball to her. I tell him that isn't nice and that everyone can play. Kareem, however, keeps a tight hold on his ball and starts to back away from us.

Annakiya turns to Fariido, who is upset by the encounter, and says to her 'Play with me'. The two girls then start to throw Annakiya's ball to each other.

While Ruth normally did not get directly involved in social encounters and disagreements between children so that she could observe how they resolved them on their own, in this case she felt that there was a safeguarding issue and potential for harm if she did not step in and tell Kareem that his behaviour was unacceptable and reassure Fariido (and also Annakiya) that this type of behaviour was not allowed at school. Brown's (2007) work supports this approach by saying that quick responses that promote equality and inclusion are needed in situations like this to send clear messages to children. Further, Ruth felt that she had a moral obligation to counter racial discrimination. Sending this message was more important to Ruth throughout the course of her fieldwork than collecting data. After this incident, she also immediately discussed what had happened with school staff asking them if they had observed similar incidents and helping them to plan a longer-term strategy to deal with this issue.

Around this time The United Nations Human Rights Council (2010:2) issued a statement calling for Libya 'to end its practices of racial discrimination against black Africans'. After this incident informal conversations that Ruth had with Kareem during the first phase of fieldwork revealed that the only ethnic minority individuals he had previously known while living in Libya were servants. He described an ethnically segregated environment where he was taught that he was different from 'the black helpers' who he described to Ruth (see Barley & Merchant, 2016 for a more detailed analysis).

Notably, during the third phase of fieldwork just over four years after this incident Ruth observed that some of Kareem's closest friends at school were Somali like Fariido. Ruth observed Kareem regularly playing and conversing with them as equals. Ethnography's in-depth nature allowed Ruth to reflect on Kareem's actions on other occasions and within a wider context in a way that other methodologies do not allow.

It is not possible to ascertain if Ruth's intervention on 18.11.10 helped to change Kareem's views but it is notable from both phases of fieldwork that after this incident Kareem continued to confide in Ruth both in relation to his views on ethnic diversity and in relation to other aspects of the research focus. In this case, stepping out of the researcher role and commenting on Kareem's behaviour towards Farrido did not appear to affect Ruth's research relationship with Kareem.

Dealing with Sensitive Data

Ruth's fieldwork also produced instances of sensitive data relating to children's discourses around armed militias in North and Sub-Saharan Africa which, as with the incident described above, raised safeguarding questions for Ruth. Ruth's fieldnotes from the first phase of her data highlight one example which raised ethical issues for her relating to publishing sensitive data:

3/2/11: A Data Bomb

14.00–14.40

I am sitting in the outdoor play area just under the cover watching Kareem and Lina play in the home corner. Abdul comes over and sits at the Lego tray and starts to build a model car. I watch as he pushes it around making 'brum' noises.[2] He lies on his tummy and pushes it under the bench. When he reaches where I am sitting, he asks me to move my legs so that he can continue to push the car past me. When he gets to the end of the bench he turns the car around and comes back with it.

He leaves the car next to where I am sitting and goes to get some wooden blocks. He brings some blocks back and starts to build what I think is a tour. He goes to get more bricks and adds them to the tower. He then gets a longer thinner block and leans this against the tower to make a ramp. He comes back to me smiling and picks up the car. He adds some Lego bricks to it before taking it to the top of the ramp. He pushes the car off and shouts 'bang, bang' as the car hits the floor and smashes into pieces.

He picks up the pieces and puts the car back together quietly saying to me 'It's a bomb'. 'A bomb?' I ask. 'Yes', he replies, 'a car bomb'. He pushes the car off the ramp again and shouts 'bang' as it smashes. As he is rebuilding the car he tells me, 'There are lots of car bombs in [...] to stop the English people'. 'To stop the English people?' I enquire. 'Yeah', Abdul replies, 'English people are Christians'. 'Are they all Christians?' I ask. He nods as he collects the pieces and starts to build the car again. The teacher rings the bell signalling that it is time to tidy up. I help Abdul pick up the bricks and Lego pieces and sort them into their boxes.

Due to the wider political context of the UK Government's controversial 'Prevent Strategy' (The UK's counter-terrorism strategy) and its questionable safeguarding links Ruth decided not to publish data relating to these discourses from Phase 1 of her fieldwork in her PhD thesis or subsequent book. The Prevent Strategy was first published in 2008, before being reviewed during Ruth's first stage of fieldwork in 2011 resulting in the statutory Prevent Duty being introduced during the third phase of her fieldwork in 2015 placing a number of statutory duties on schools and other organisations.

After observing this event Ruth's immediate reflections focused on whether there was a Safeguarding issue in relation to the game that Abdul created on this particular day. Her reflective notes the week after this observation give an insight into some of her thoughts at this time:

10/2/11: Reflective Notes

After talking to Abdul today I have some answers to the questions that I was unsure about after last week's observations particularly in relation to my question about where Abdul got the inspiration for creating the car bomb. We talked today about watching the news and he described to me seeing a story on the news about a car bomb. He wasn't sure where this was but said that 'it was in a Muslim country'. He also told me that he often watches the news with his older brother.

After this conversation, a week after the original observation, Ruth's initial interpretation that Abdul's game was recreating an event that he had seen or heard about was confirmed. This interpretation corresponds with Holland's (2003) findings that young children (and in particular young boys) make sense of violence and fighting through their peer games. She concludes that banning fighting tools, such as guns, can have a negative impact on young boys' development. Reflecting on this, and other similar research, informed Ruth's decision about whether or not to act on this observation. In contrast to the incident she observed in relation to Kareem (above) Ruth had no Safeguarding concerns in relation to Abdul's game.

Despite this, Ruth was concerned how these data would be received in the wider political context of the 'Prevent Strategy' and its questionable relationship with a Safeguarding Agenda. This impacted on her decision not to publish these findings at the time as she was unsure if she could protect Abdul from harm in a way that she felt ethically bound to do. Given the wider political context Ruth was concerned that publishing this and other similar narratives may cause children's families to be targeted (under what she sees as a morally dubious Prevent Strategy) and/or give fuel to right wing groups who want to further stigmatise Muslims living in the UK. If she had observed a White child engaging in similar play, she would not have hesitated in publishing these data at the time.

Conclusions

Doing ethnography with children and young people raises particular ethical challenges regarding consent, dealing with sensitive data and intervention decisions that the researcher may need to negotiate. Conducting ethically sound ethnography requires constant negotiation and vigilance. The ethnographer must respond to issues as they appear in the field and cannot always foresee how their position, the research they conduct and the data derived from that can impact upon the participants and other audience members. Current ethical guidelines and procedures are useful but somewhat problematic; especially when considering the multitude of ethical challenges, the ethnographer may need to face in and beyond situ. The ethnographer has to have a degree of experience and confidence to regulate themselves in the field and not fall into the temptation of allowing university and other ethical guidelines and procedures to debunk their sense of ethical conduct.

Notes

1. OC – Observers Comments – is a section of the field notes dedicated to the researchers reflexive account as derived from Carspecken's (1996) 5-stage critical ethnography format.
2. When editing the fieldnote above Ruth gave Abdul a second pseudonym so that this data cannot be connected to a wider narrative in previous publications. As Abdul is no longer in the country Ruth feels that it is possible to now share this data four years after the observation took place with these changes.

References

Albon, D., & Barley, R. (2021). Ethnographic research: A significant context for engaging young children in dialogues about adults' writing. *Journal of Early Childhood Literacy, 21*(1), 82–103.

Barley, R. (2014). *Identity and social interaction in a multi-ethnic classroom.* London: Tufnell Press.

Barley, R. (2022). Assent or consent? Engaging children in ethnographic study. In G. Spencer (Ed.), *Ethics and integrity in research with children and young people* (pp. 29–41). Bingley: Emerald Publishing Limited.

Barley, R., & Bath, C. (2014). The importance of familiarisation when doing research with young children. *Ethnography and Education, 9*(2), 182–195.

Barley, R., & Merchant, G. (2016). 'The naughty person': Exploring dynamic aspects of identity and children's discourses before and during the Libyan uprising. *Childhood, 23*(4), 477–491.

Barley, R., & Russell, L. (2019). Participatory visual methods: Exploring young people's identities, hopes and feelings. *Ethnography and Education, 14*(2), 223–241.

Brown, B. (2007). *Unlearning discrimination in the early years.* Stoke-on-Trent: Trentham Books Ltd.

Burgess, R. G. (1984). *The research process in educational settings: Ten case studies.* Lewes: Falmer Press.

Carspecken, P. F. (1996). *Critical ethnography in educational research.* London: Routledge.

Cheney, K. E. (2011). Children as ethnographers: Reflections on the importance of participatory research in assessing orphans' needs. *Childhood, 18*(2), 166.

Delamont, S., & Atkinson, P. (2018). Chapter 7 – The ethics of ethnography. In R. Iphofen & M. Tolich (Eds.), *The SAGE handbook of qualitative research ethics* (pp. 119–132). London: SAGE.

Dennis, B. (2009). What does it mean when an ethnographer intervenes? *Ethnography and Education, 4*(2), 131–146.

Dennis, B. (2010). Ethnography and education ethical dilemmas in the field: The complex nature of doing education ethnography. *Ethnography and Education, 5*(2), 123–127.

Dingwell, R. (2012). How did we ever get into this mess? The rise of ethical regulation in the social sciences. In K. Love (Ed.), *Ethics in social research* (pp. 3–26). Bingley: Emerald Publishing Limited.

Dockett, S., Einarsdottir, J., & Perry, B. (2009). Researching with children: Ethical tensions. *Journal of Early Childhood Research: Experimental Cell Research, 7*(3), 283–298.

Garcia, A. E., & Fine, G. A. (2018). Fair warnings: The ethics of ethnography with children. In R. Iphofen & M. Martin Tolich (Eds.), *The SAGE handbook of qualitative research ethics*. London: Sage.

Hammersley, M. (2009). Against the ethicists: On the evils of ethical regulation. *International Journal of Social Research Methodology, 12*(3), 211–225.

Holland, P. (2003). *We don't play with guns here*. New York, NY: McGraw-Hill Education.

Hunter, D. (2018). Chapter 19 – Research ethics committees – What are they good for? In R. Iphofen & M. Tolich (Eds.), *The SAGE handbook of qualitative research ethics* (pp. 289–300). London: SAGE.

Korth, B. (2005). Choice, necessity, or narcissism? A feminist does feminist ethnography. In G. Troman, B. Jeffrey, & G. Walford (Eds.), *Methodological issues and practices in ethnography*. London: Elsevier.

Levey, H. (2009). 'Which one is yours?': Children and ethnography. *Qualitative Sociology, 32*(3), 311–331.

Marcus, O., & Lerman, S. (2018). Chapter 13 – Ethics working in ever-changing ethnographic environments. In R. Iphofen & M. Tolich (Eds.), *The SAGE handbook of qualitative research ethics* (pp. 203–214). London: SAGE.

Mayeza, E. (2017). Doing child-centered ethnography: Unravelling the complexities of reducing the perceptions of adult male power during fieldwork. *International Journal of Qualitative Methods, 16*(1), 1–10.

Miller, H., & Russell, L. (2005). The personal, professional and political in comparative ethnographic educational research. In G. Troman, B. Jeffrey, & G. Walford (Eds.), *Methodological issues and practices in ethnography*. London: Elsevier.

Parker, M. (2007). Ethnography/ethics. *Social Science & Medicine, 65*, 2248–2259.

Russell, L. (2005). It's a question of trust: Balancing the relationship between students and teachers in ethnographic fieldwork. *Qualitative Research, 5*(2), 181–199.

Russell, L. (2013). Researching marginalised young people. *Ethnography and Education, 8*(1), 46–60.

Russell, L., & Barley, R. (2020). Ethnography, ethics and ownership of data. *Ethnography, 21*(1), 5–25.

Sime, D. (2008). Ethical and methodological issues in engaging young people living in poverty with participatory research methods. *Children's Geographies, 6*(1), 63–78.

Simmons, R., Thompson, R., & Russell, L. (2014). *Education, work and social change: Young people and marginalisation in post-industrial Britain*. Basingstoke: Palgrave Macmillan.

Siraj-Blatchford, I., & Sylva, K. (2004). Researching pedagogy in English preschools. *British Educational Research Journal, 30*(5), 713–730.

Tolich, M. (2016). A worrying trend, ethical considerations of using data collected without informed consent. *Fronteiras: Journal of Social, Technological and Environmental Science (Anapolos), 5*(2), 14–28.

Troman, G. (2001). Does gender make a difference? A male researcher's reflexive account of gendered fieldwork relations in ethnographic work on stress in teaching. In G. Walford & C. Hudson (Eds.), *Genders and sexualities in educational ethnography*. Bingley: Emerald Publishing Limited.

Walford, G. (1991). *Doing educational research*. London: Routledge.

Wilson, A., & Hodgson, P. (2012). Trust, coercion and care: Researching marginalised groups. In K. Love (Ed.), *Ethics in social research*. Bingley: Emerald Publishing Limited.

Chapter 4

Research Ethics: Reflections from Fieldwork with Children in India

Poonam Sharma

Abstract

This chapter derives from ethnographic fieldwork conducted in a town close to Delhi, India. The research focused on schooling experiences of children from communities that are traditionally considered underprivileged. It required shadowing children throughout the day. This chapter reports on the experiences of researching with children and the ways in which child participation and research ethics emerged during the year of fieldwork. The idea of 'child participation' in the research process – within the Indian context is explored. The discourse around ethics in the current literature is primarily concerned with ideas of consent, gatekeeping and respecting children's rights. This chapter discusses the significance of the cultural contexts of the field in shaping the research ethics and developing what 'child participation' meant for children and their parents within this specific cultural context. It does so by elaborating on contradictions that existed between the way the ethnographer positioned the child and the way children are positioned in families and schools, where children's participation, opinion and consent are often silently presumed by the parents much more so than in a Euro-American context. Children are viewed as active agents, knowledgeable about their own positions in the research process.

Keywords: Research ethics in practice; child participation; Indian childhood; cultural context; ethnography; reflexivity

Introduction

What does it mean to behave ethically in the field? Can official codes of practice provide an adequate or universal means of navigating the field? Can ethics be prescribed, or do they emerge on the field? Where does or should the researcher's ethical ground for researching with children emerge? None of these questions have

Ethics, Ethnography and Education, 49–65

Copyright © 2022 Poonam Sharma

Published under exclusive licence by Emerald Publishing Limited

doi:10.1108/S1529-210X20220000019004

a straightforward answer. These questions become even more complex in the context of ethnographic work with children in a country like India, where the lived realities of children are far away from the idealised notions of childhood. Western imagination of childhood occupies the way childhood is projected, theorised in the minds of policymakers and research committees. Scholars have reflected on how the notion of ideal childhood promoted by the discourse of developmental psychology (Vasanta, 2004) and 'global childhood agenda (Nieuwenhuys, 1999) of child rights fails to account for the everyday realities of Indian children (Ramam, 2000). Cultural notions of childhood shape the fieldwork and children's participation in research. Researcher's own notions of childhood may or may not sit well with the cultural notions of childhood posing difficult situation to the researcher.

In this chapter, I problematise some of these situations by reflecting on my own practice. The aim is to make the practice of ethics amiable to discussion; thus the nature of this chapter is illustrative and not prescriptive. It illustrates how ethics were constructed as I encountered situations and struggled through my fieldwork with children and families. These examples that I share may, at best, offer an insight into my thinking of those situations and do not indicate any right or wrong way of ethical behaviour. Taking an ethical position involved a reflective process; questioning, challenging and thinking through of strategies used to resolve them in the best interest of forefronting children, their cultural contexts and their lived experiences.

Ethical dilemmas arise out of moral reasoning that belongs to the individual consciousness. Ethical decisions are taken within the cultural context and do not lend themselves to objective definitions and agreements. What is right and wrong is personally established within one's personal, social, moral and professional stance (Paoletti, Thomas, & Menendez, 2013). Ethical issues are embedded in specific situations within cultural forms (Christians, 2007) and in the network of relationships (Etherington, 2007). In this chapter, I attempt to make ethics describable and an object of empirical documentation. I argue that children and families participating in research cannot be taken as homogeneous, as the field may have participants with diverse communities that include a range of interests and values, notions and lived experiences of childhood to which the researcher must be vigilant and accommodative. I also assert the inclusion of cultural context as a central dimension in the theorisation of research ethics with children.

Ethnographic Research with Children in India

Childhood in India has primarily been understood within the discourse of 'problem' (Newhanways, 2009, p. 147) and is projected as undesirable and deviant (Ipe, 2019). Two major ideas that have shaped childhood studies in India are: (1) the colonial heritage and (2) the general Euro-American scholarship (Balagopalan, 2011). Both seem to be constructing Indian children as helpless 'victims', waiting to be rescued by the west. There has been an aggressive approach to find out what is undesirable and needs to be immediately addressed through interventions. This portrays Indian childhood as pathological and in need of intervention to be able to catch up with the west. Such anxiety has left little space for any other alternative imagination of children and their lives. The discourse of child rights (UN convention) and saving children has dominated the research and policy for children. However, ethnographers of education have attempted an alternative imagination of children and their research participation. These researchers share their ontological grounds with the New sociology of childhood (James & Prout, 1997) in viewing children as social agents and active in the construction of their reality and knowledge. These ethnographies have focused on the everyday lives of children and their participation in social interactions. It includes Sarangapani's classic work (2003) that positioned children as epistemic subjects actively taking part in the knowledge community. Other studies have focused at children's identity as a learner (Chawla-Duggan, 2007), their conception of a 'real school' Vs 'local school' (*Mohollla club*) (Balgopalan, 2005) and projected them as 'strategically opportunising actors' (Maithreyi, 2018).

These studies established the value of children's agency and took an ethical stand of bringing forward accounts and experiences of children. They highlighted the idea of children's active role in the construction of their lives and an interpretive reproduction (Corsaro, 2004) of their life circumstances. These studies have contributed to indigenous sociology of childhood and consequently, deconstructed the notion of childhood (and the meaning of researching with children), that has so far prevailed in the policy and practice space of childhood studies in India. This chapter shares its ontological position with these studies and views children as active social agents, knowledgeable about their own positions in the research process.

In terms of writings on ethical issues of researching with children, there is very little work in the space of education research in India (Ipe, 2019). Ethical aspects of researching with children are often subsumed in the section on fieldwork (as in the case of Sarangapani, 2003) and rarely get highlighted as research writing. There are fewer accounts of researchers that discuss their rapport building with children and their position in relation to children's positioning on the field. Sarangapani (2003) in her note on her fieldwork reflects on how children perceived her and her attempts to reduce the adult-child gap while researching with children. She writes about her efforts to 'present herself' as someone with whom children interacted in school but neither as a teacher nor as an inspector. She made efforts to convince the children that she was primarily interested in knowing them better and in her interactions with adults communicated to children that she was not there for any evaluation purpose. Gradually she noted a change in the way children approached, interacted and questioned her. Chawla-Duggan, Wikeley, and Konantambigi (2012) elaborated on her observations of the power dynamics that existed between the teacher, parents and the researchers and how these impinged upon her research work with children that intended to prioritise the voices of children. In the coming passage, I describe the cultural scenarios on the field and how that shaped child participation in my research.

Child Participation

In the social science research space, there has been a paradigm shift from doing research 'on' children to doing research 'with' children; that is children are no more seen as an object of study but as competent informants about their life experiences and issues concerning them (Christensen & James, 2008; James, 2009). The new conceptualisation of children is loaded with ideas of agency and individual autonomy and looks at children as reliable informants on their lives and that is seen as a valuable contribution to knowledge production on childhood. Participation of children is seen as having more genuine accounts of children's life experiences and stabilising the researcher and the researched power equation (Dennis & Huf, 2020; James & James, 2004).

Dennis and Huf (2020) reconstructs and problematises both the adult-child binary and a belief in the authenticity of the 'voice' of children. She discusses the possibilities where children do not wish to and resist the participation in research and argue that the notion of 'voice' is wrongly conceptualised as individual agency. She advocates for an alternative kind of participation in which ethnographers practise *their participant observation as a playful openness in engagement with the children that allowed for reconfigurations of researchers and children entangled with one another* (Dennis & Huf, 2020). Child participation is also often misunderstood and overrated. Twum-Danso Imoh and Okyere (2020) argues that participation cannot be thought of being separate from the context within which children live. The researcher's idea of child participation, that is, ways in which access to children is made while respecting their rights may stand in contradiction with the way the children are construed on the field. These situations offer unprecedented ethical dilemmas for the researcher.

Idealised Notions of Childhood and Adult-Child Continuity in India

The UN convention[1] of 1989 has been under criticism (most of all articles 28 and 32) for ignoring the realities of children of the majority world and propagating a standardised notion of 'the child' (Raman, 2000), yet they have powerfully sustained the notion of 'ideal childhood' and a 'normal child'. These notions have not only shaped the international policy, expert opinion, but also cultural practices of child-rearing (Vasanta, 2004). These ideals have spread through the expansion of compulsory schooling and have been strongly imposed on the children of the majority world (Ipe, 2019).

Scholars have paid attention to the contrast between the rights discourse and the experiences and perceptions of children from impoverished communities where cultures are in sharp contrast with the dominant rights discourse (Raman, 2000; Twum-Danso Imoh & Okyere, 2020). The rights discourse has percolated a dominant model of adult-child relationship, wherein the child is the one in need of protection from adults and adults are the caregivers. On moral grounds, this model looks so convincing that it leaves no room for imagining a different version of adult-child relationship.

The key difference between western imagination of childhood and the one lived by large numbers of Indian children is in terms of the adult-child relationship. Scholars have noted that Indian society is characterised by adult-child continuity, unlike the segregation of adulthood and childhood in the western discourses (Kumar, 1999, p. 70; Vasanta, 2004; Viruru, 2001). Murphy's[2] analysis of Indian children illustrated adult-child continuity in terms of physical proximity between the adult and the child. She observed a weak adult-child differentiation and the adult and child sharing of the physical and social spaces. In addition, she also supported her observations through religious and cultural lore. The child world and the adult world were not so separate, and the child was viewed very much as part of the larger unit of family, tribe, clan etc. (Raman, 2000, p. 4056). The transition from child-hood to adulthood was more fluid and not of a dichotomy. Nevertheless, the adult-child relations are relations of power, with children often assuming a subordinate position.

These international discourses and indigenous ways of life shape the structure of childhood and allow differentiated childhoods to coexist. Within the small geography of the town, I noticed the differences in the ways families included children in their daily lives, assigned them roles and approved of their interactions with the others. On one hand there were children living the protected childhood governed by adults that aspired to catch up with the 'ideal childhood' and on another, there is childhood that is lived within the realm of 'adult-child conti-nuity'. The adult-child relationship in both cases are in great contrast. In the two families that I discuss here, one childhood was shaped by the forces of 'ideal childhood' and in another it was construed in the indigenous and cultural ways of bringing up their children. This logic of child-rearing dictated the daily schedule of the family, expectations from children, and the roles that they play in the family.

Family one (Parsa family) had two children, created a protected and safe space for their children. Children's physical and social space was cut off from the adult world and they lived a protected childhood where the entire family's routine revolved around children's schooling and care. The other family (Kannojia family) had four children (three daughters and youngest being a son). The parents focused on earning their livelihoods and children were looking after the house and managing their time all by themselves. Parents fought in front of children and discussed the town gossip with a range of topics from black magic to divorce rates in the town. Whereas in the Parsa family, the parents carefully chose the topics they should or should not discuss in front of their children. With regard to the space of school, scholars have noted that school is characterised by highly unequal adult-child rela-tionships (Iyer, 2013; Sanangapani, 2003). Parents and teachers shared folk ideologies about disciplining children and physical punishment was a norm in school.

I was witnessing two diagonally opposite cultural contexts and family settings as my research site. And this had implications on my interactions with children, in the ways they perceived and approached me and allowed me into their lives. This contrast offered opportunities to enact and respond but also dilemmas to ponder and reflect. This also had an influence on the stance that I took as a researcher. Were children to participate in my research at all? Or were they to make attempts to escape or resist the structures of my research (Dennis & Huf, 2020). Were they to position me as an authoritative adult or have a more shared relationship with me? Were children to independently interact with me or was their consent to be coerced by powerful adults (Alderson & Morrow, 2011). Of course, a lot of this depended on how I 'presented' myself to the children (Sarangapani, 2003). But my presentation of self and my research was to be understood by them in the cultural frames within which the children otherwise operated. My interaction with children was to be played out in the cultural and historical context of the family and children's everyday experiences.

The Study

The fieldwork discussed in this chapter is part of an exploratory study that looked at the family-school relationship through children's experiences. I begin with an open-ended and wide-ranging inquiry, seeking to answer how children navigate the two spaces of family and school. I lived in the field (a village turned into town) for about a year. The research site was not very far from the place of my upbringing and I was thus familiar with the language, cultural beliefs and lifestyles and in some ways (though not completely) as an insider (Webster & John, 2010). However, I was also understood as an outsider on account of me belonging to the city and being 'too much into studies'. School was one of the entry points for the field, but since I was staying in the town itself for the coming year, I also made friends in the neighbourhood and contacted families on personal account. Within the inner part of the town (the original village), families had dense social networks, with extended families and kinship ties, staying closer to each other. This allowed me to gain multiple contacts and there came a point where there was no further distinction in my association with the family being rooted in the school or independently. Initially, I interacted with about 20 families before selecting four families for a closer ethnographic work. Four families were from traditionally marginalised social communities and have also been economically disadvantaged.[3,4] For the purpose of illustration, I have used data from two families (described above) who were in great contrast in the way they organised the childhood of their children, adult-child relations, responsibilities between adults and children. In one family, the adult-child continuity was prominent and the childhood space of the other family was shaped with the notions of western childhood.

My interactions with the families were informal and unstructured occurring in several natural settings inside homes, at the school and on the way to/back from school. It all started with very awkward situations while obtaining permission from families for interactions and observation where people often viewed me with considerable scepticism. However, by the end of my fieldwork, I had developed relationships with families and they understood the needs of my work. I was receiving invitations from families for special occasions that they thought would be relevant for me to attend. This was a long way from my starting point when I had begun with an intention to explore the family-school interphase. All my hard work and struggle of gaining access to families in the initial part of my fieldwork paid rewards later in terms of access to children's experiences that are otherwise hidden when researchers sit at school and speculate about family scenarios. Being in the site of home bestowed upon me a variety of other scenarios including internal family dynamics, the adult-child relationship, intergenerational relationship and associations with their neighbours and so on. While the families were told that I am there to understand children's schooling experiences and their relationship with the school, families gradually opened up and assumed my interest in other matters of their lives. This was, of course, very useful as these narratives gave me a holistic picture of their world view and the lives of children. It also gave me more naturalistic settings to interact with children.

Ethical Dilemmas Faced 'on the Ground'

Central to my ethical framework was the idea of reflexivity (Delamont, 2009, p. 58), i.e. to be acutely sensitive about the interrelationship between myself and the focus of my research and the other was the focus on children's views and action in their cultural context. The first implied challenges of being able to think through situations, question my own beliefs and observe things as they were on the field (Berger & Luckman, 1971). These were internal and hard challenges. These required what any dedicated ethnographer must do, that is to have reflective journaling, to observe, record and reflect on one's own behaviour and emotions as we experience the field. The second implied even harder challenges as I had to do this in scenarios where adult authority operated in enormous and intimidating ways. And there was a huge difference in the way I tried to relate to children and the way other adults on field related to children. I had to do this at the risk of being ridiculed, thought of as a 'city girl' (Sharma, 2018) and at times, my relationships with the parents.

Besides the approval of the doctoral advisory committee, I had to undergo no other ethical approval for working with children. Since a large part of the research was concerned with observing the children in the space of family, I did need to first build the rapport with the parents, gain their consent and then gradually interact with the children and grandparents. In both the families, parents were the gatekeepers of the children and their permission was required before entering into any conversation and relationship with the children.

Dilemma 1: Rapport Building with Children

Rapport building is an important aspect of ethnographic work. It needs to be carefully invested upon and is a continuous and dynamic process. In order to gather the insider perspective and develop *analytic understanding of per-spectives, activities and actions* (Hammersley, 2006), establishing a rapport with the people on the field is the key. In the Parsa family, I had begun my interactions with children through story telling. I knew from previous ethnographies where researchers choose to do paper folding (Sarangapani, 2003) activities or asked children to draw (Balagopalan, 2005; Gupta, 2015) as a means to gain access and break the ice with children. While storytelling did help in comforting the children and allowed me vantage points to open up discussion with children, I soon begin to realise that this resonated pedagogic activities at school and was reinforcing the traditional adult-child relationships. Children are submissive to these activities and assume certain power relationship as soon as these are introduced in the setting (Dennis & Huf, 2020; Gallacher & Gallagher, 2008).

Within a gap of few days, I also began to visit the Kannojia family where the father promptly introduced me to the children. Children were unbelievably quick to gel in with me. From day one, they exposed me to their internal dynamics and peer culture. The interactions with these children were comforting as I did not have to resort to any artificial methods. However, for quite some time I struggled with the thought 'should I not have a similar approach to interacting', with the children of the two families?', or should I allow myself to flow with the situation and let the children lead? What was the root of my differentiated approach to children in two families? I knew that the paper folding or storytelling activities were not worth it when it came to the Kannojia family children. These children were not docile to the school activities and had a counter-culture (Willis, 1977). They actively participated in creating a non-academic yet positive school identity (Sharma, 2018). My struggle here, however, was to reflect and think through the fact whether it was me who was imposing certain approach to rapport building with children, or was it the children who were also actively co-opting in the research process and taking up certain roles.

Given my ethnographic approach, I had the luxury of time and multiple visits, and a long-term engagement with the children. I allowed the field to take over me and let the children guide me; I subsumed myself into the leads of children. It may look rather simplistic now while I am away from the field, but at that time, it was a real question. For my entire communication with close to 20 families, with whom I interacted at the beginning of fieldwork after the first few initial interactions with the adults in the family, I approached the children. In this period, what could be called my 'familiarisation period (Barley & Bath, 2014)', my strategy was to begin with storytelling sessions with the children. This was meant to be a buffer time for me to engage with children and allow them time to think whether they wish to participate in the research or not. But apparently, not all children allowed or responded to these. This dilemma enticed me to think of the problem of homogenisation (Levinson, 2010) of children as a category when we approach the field. I could not have assumed a similar approach and a similar engagement with the children in these two families.

Dilemma 2: My Perceptions of the Field

In the initial phase of my fieldwork as I enthusiastically moved around in the town, approaching and figuring out the families who would participate in the research, I (did not realise but I) became the talk of the town. Approaching and self-inviting myself to families did not come easy to me as a researcher. I had to learn the skill of self-inviting[5] myself to the families and social meet up in the town. While I was picking up this skill, an unprecedented incident happened. This incident demotivated me enormously but turned out to be an immense opportunity as I describe here:

August 2011: Field Notes. RJ- D Family

I write this note in a very depressed state of mind, I am not very keen on this part of the research, and breaking ice with the researched can be so dangerous at times....one can get into severe identity crisis.... The researcher profile is not a known image here in the town like the other of baba (religious disciples), police inspector, journalist and teacher. I have to all the time explain and re-explain in different ways and vocabularies to people, what I was doing there...My interest in children and their ways of thinking is often misunderstood and questioned. Today on my way to the Kannojia family their neighbour caught hold of me and took me on remand.

P – why are you here?

R – I have come in this family (pointing to the Kannojia family house) to research about children, to know their views about their schools, to learn and understand about their lives at home. I am here to understand how and what children learn, what they do after coming from school. This research is part of my studies for a degree.

After this long and rather simplified version of my introduction, she said to me.

P – '*manne na samajh aai to kai bole hai*? I don't understand what you are saying.

Tu padave hai kaya yahan kai school me? Do you teach here in some school?

R – No. But I also go to school to see children and meet their teacher.

P – *tujhae pta hai na, aysi hi ate hai log jo bacche churate hain. Pichle saal ik ladki ayi thi, ye do gali chod kar, ik do din gali me aayi aur fir baccha gayab ke bhag gai.*

I am sure you are aware of the people who kidnap children. Last year a girl, just like you, used to visit in the street just adjacent to ours, she came for a day or two and then stole the child and ran away.

I was emotionally too disturbed. While she was speaking to me, Mnjali the youngest of the four siblings passed by. I was embarrassed and decided to return to my room and not visit the family. With my all other struggles to set up my room and dealing with the fears of self-inviting myself to the families, this conversation was a total fed up. My conversation with her ended in my unsuccessful attempts to convince her of my authenticity as a researcher. I was there to research with children and not to steal them away. After this, I did not feel like speaking to her. I don't plan to visit the children anytime soon.

Unexpected situations are the most difficult (Delamont, 2009). But in these situations lies the best opportunity. While I was making intense efforts to present myself as a non-threatening adult, this situation did the exact opposite; it framed me as a potentially harmful person. I thought about the situation and several thoughts occurred to me. Should I go back and have a word with the neighbour? Or should I just drop this family and look for a new one? Should I just be honest and visit the family and brief them about my discussion with the neighbour? I struggled with these questions in my mind, as I controlled myself and yet eagerly waited to visit the family. I also thought about getting some help from a school teacher to validate my authenticity. Still, then I also realised bringing in a teacher (an authority figure) would risk my otherwise organic relationship with the children in the family. Another way was just to ignore and act as if nothing happened. But based on my interactions with the children, I had an intuition that children would have spoken about the episode at least amongst themselves if not with their parents. Having read the previous literature, I was conscious of the significance of children's perception of me. With fears of having my earlier efforts of rapport building with this family being destroyed, I decided to just be honest and persist with my research interest. I decided to meet the family. As soon as I entered the house Mnjali (the 8 year old) said to her mother:

> A – 'see mummi wasn't I telling you, didi must have felt bad about how anuty spoke to her. Didi, You don't worry about them, they don't like us as such and they are always fighting with us. Don't stop coming to our house. Let them be.

I was delightfully surprised firstly, to experience that she still held a positive view about me, and secondly about the fact that the mother had nothing to interfere with what she spoke. Her silence and later conversation with me highlighted an independent child capable of intervening and meaningfully contributing to the construction of adult world around her. Post this event, children explained to me that perhaps the reason for such behaviour by the neighbour was the fact that she was jealous of me not visiting them as part of my research. Children acquainted me with the dispute with their neighbours and many more stories that would otherwise be part of the adult world. This was the turning point in my relationship with the children, also an evidence of the adult-child continuity. And it is in the realm of this adult-child continuity my relationship with the children was organic. They shared their social spaces with me and related to me as they related to other adults around them. They actively took part in the conversations of the parents' town gossip and did work at the shop their parents owned.

Having gone through this, I became vigilant to the child-led discussions and activities. It was a right decision not to introduce any other adult to legitimise my involvement with the children and also not to ignore a situation in which children had stakes. I allowed the children to lead the conversations and never hesitated in showing my complete lack of knowledge about the town and town gossip. Within the cultural context of the complex power relationships, children became my most relied informers. Children '*co-opted and co-laboured*' the research (Dennis & Huf, 2020) and allowed for co-production of knowledge. I felt no need to 'reduce' the adult-child gap.

I had a unique advantage of meeting children at sites other than school. Often, it was their homes. Gradually, weekly markets, tuition centres, en route to schools, places students visited (and I shadowed them there as well), became my research sites. I write this chapter with the awareness that these were the advantages of an ethnographic study. Within the first week of the field, I also realised that I was hugely advantaged by selecting the site of the family. This allowed both children and me to get the space away from school authorities and also at times away from parents.

Dilemma 3: Contradiction in the Positioning of Children

I was researching the space where adult authority was paramount. Like other researchers (Sarangapani, 2003), I too faced problems in confronting children. Adults in the Parsa family often appropriated children's responses and prompted them towards specific answers. The 'concerted cultivation' (Lareau, 2003) is characterised by correction of children's behaviour to align their behaviour to what is expected and appreciated in school. Parents in this family were very conscious of the way the teacher perceived their children. This was extended to children's interactions with me. Parents ensured that I see children in specific ways and corrected their language quite often. In such situations, I begin to seek opportunities when children could be away from the adult gaze.

After every comment by the adult, I had to always add a tag line for my interest in children's views and experiences. On occasion, my persistence on children's views led to offending the adults; at times, they viewed me in exclamation and several times just asserted their own opinions, paraphrasing it as children's sentences. In each of the scenarios, three parallel forces were operating (Fig. 1). One is the way adults positioned the children, another is the way children positioned themselves and me, and the third was the way I positioned children. In many episodes, these positioning sat uneasily with each other. This was counter-intuitive to many adults with whom I otherwise shared a good rapport. The adults' positioning of children had implications on what was expected out of me, while interacting with children. It took a lot of persistence on my part to assert that I was genuinely interested in children's ways of being and doing.

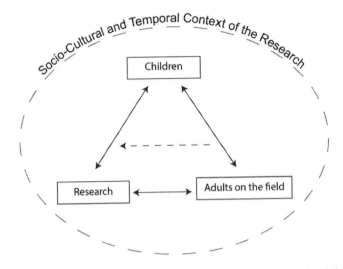

Fig. 1.   Diagrammatic Representation of the Research Field.

Dilemma 4: Should I Intervene?

Ethnographers have grappled with the difficult situations of observing from a distance and intervening. Barley and Bath (2014) described that she took a 'non-teacher' role and avoided getting involved with the children's peer argument and their resolutions as she was interested in observing ways in which they negotiated with their peer culture. But she also argued that negotiating this non-teacher role was an on-going process and recollected instances where she had to step back in and take up the role of the mediator. Besides this, there has been far less writing of 'confessionals' (Dennis, 2009) in which the researchers take the opportunity to revisit the multiple dimensions within which a decision was made. One such rare collection of work is in the book collated by Lareau and Shultz (1996) that is the realistic accounts of ethnographic fieldwork. The book collates the aspects of the research that did not proceed as anticipated and pushed the researcher into complicated decision-making; it is argued that these are the processes through which individuals learn to deal with difficult situation on the field while carrying out qualitative research.

On the field, I experienced several situations where I felt a pressing need to intervene. In these situations, I did not want to lose my established rapport with the participants and influence their behaviour and thus had to be very mindful in dealing with them.

One such situation occurred in the private school. An excerpt from my field notebook is here to illustrate the point.

March 2012: Field Notes

It was a rather busy morning assembly at the school. The principal (school head is referred as principal) seemed disturbed about something and aggressively moved in the assembly lines, as if he was searching for someone. As soon as the assembly was over, the students and teachers returned to their respective classes. The principal asked a child to stop until the assembly area was vacant.

...

After a few questions to the child, he started aggressively beating the child. I was stunned at the way he handled the child and the child's complete surrender to him. None of the teachers came in for support or to cover for the child's mistake. It was unbearable for me. Despite knowing about the national level ban on corporal punishment, I was witnessing the child being beaten by the principal. I could not control and went upon to indirectly intervene and ask about the matter with the school principal, implying that he stops beating the child and engages with me. He gave me his narrative about 'these children' (children of poor and low caste parents) who need to be disciplined.

...

I also discovered later from the teachers that the child had spoken a lie about something which in my perception was not a big deal. I also understood from the teachers that the principal had parents' permission to beat the child. So I was dealing with an adult world that subjected children to their authority.

In such scenarios, I wondered should and why did I not intervene and help the child? To my understanding, it was wrong and objectionable. Was it possible to be culturally sensitive at this point? I wondered when I totally disapproved of it, why did I not stop the principal right in the beginning. Did some kind of gender dynamics operated in this situation? Had this been a case of sexual harassment wouldn't I have been more prompt? Later in the process of reflective writing, I was able to discover that my lazy reaction to the episode was rooted in the normalisation of physical punishment of children as part of the culture in which I was researching and partly belonged to. It was sort of a disadvantage of being an insider. Also, in those moments, I failed to bracket (Berger & Luckman, 1971) my own beliefs and 'make strange' (Barley & Bath, 2014) the social context that is needed to beware from 'over familiarisation'.

There were other situations wherein parents sought my advice in helping them choose the right school or the right private tuition centre for their child on account of me being an educated person and belonging to the city. However, these situations were not that intense as the one described earlier. I could deal with them through tactics of probing and paraphrasing their own interest. However, I also suffered from tensions of misleading the participants through the impressions I gave them and obtaining original data in terms of their beliefs and value systems.

Discussion

Behaving ethically in the field is a multifaceted, multi-layered and vigorous venture for education ethnographers. This chapter has focused on ethical issues that shaped the relationship between the ethnographer and the child participants in an Indian cultural context. The episodes laid out here highlight the specific difficulties with regard to the access, prioritisation of children's voices and the context of the research with the disadvantaged.

There are no easy solutions to the situations that arise in the field. In India, there is a fortunate or unfortunate lack of ethical guidelines for researching with children (Ipe, 2019). University departments for ethical clearance are interested in the formal consent, maintaining the privacy of data, any potential harm caused to participants (if any), the rewards of participating in the research and the direct benefits of the research. While these are indispensable and insufficient parameters on which ethical concerns regarding research work with children are to be understood and theorised, any attempt of developing a comprehensive set of principles that govern the ethnographer's relationship with the child participants will always be superficial. In my view, ethics emerge organically through the culturally sensitive conduct of the researcher. This chapter brings out the nuances of the ethical dilemmas and the complexities the field offered for the work of the ethnographer.

I feel the ethical stance of privileging what children say and do allowed me to notice the heterogeneity within the structure of childhood. It allowed me to critically examine and include the multiple discourses of power and contexts that permeated children's lives. There is a need to engage with ways in which children respond to these power equations. Children need to be viewed as cultural agents (Qvortrup, 2009), who resist but also submit to systemic injustice. There is thus a need to not only focus on agency, but to notice the entire material and social context within which children behave with agency. As an ethnographer of education and childhood, we are not only interested in priming the child, but also in illustrating the processes and interactions in which children's agency emerged or subsumed. Such a research will allow for an ethically sound theorisation of childhoods. Therefore, I argue that cultural context must be invoked as a non-negotiable category while theorising ethics.

Just like the way childhood cannot be understood without its time and socio-cultural space, research ethics/child participation (Boyden, 1997; Twum-Danso Imoh & Okyere, 2020)[6] can also not be just 'applied' or flow out of researcher's behaviour without the context. Ethics get generated on the field, with ethnographer's presence on the field and her mindfulness to the various power equations, her role as an observer, and her commitment to the wellness of the research participants. These are the sensibilities that develop on the field through a rigorous experience of being in unexpected situations and through constant retrospection and note-taking of one's own behaviour on the field. What is needed and will be more useful is to have more accounts of researcher's writing about the ethical dilemmas they encountered on the field and ways in which they deal with them. This will allow new researchers to know the length and breadth of the issues that can potentially emerge. And this will enable a more informed approach towards ethical conduct on the field. Such efforts make 'ethics in practice' an object of documentation and description rather than ignoring them or taking them for granted.

Based on my own fieldwork, I advocate ethnography as a powerful method to gain insights about children's lives, opinions and actions. Having an ethnographic approach allowed for a broader, dynamic and collaborative engagement with children and their cultural context. While I acknowledge that ethnography and participant observations are time-consuming and have colonising roots, I assert that the core component of participation possibilities offers methodological and ethical vantage points for initiating child participation in a dynamic, collaborative and interrelated way. This allows for ethically sound co-production of knowledge.

Notes

1. In the UN Convention on the Rights of the Child, a majority of the world's governments agreed on what children have a right to, and what the obligations are of the state and of care givers. The agreement is written in such a way that all aspects of a child's life, including survival and development, protection and participation, have been articulated as 'ideal' (Bissell, 2003, p. 51).
2. Lois Barclay Murphy, in 1953, visited India as part of a UNESCO project and studied Indian children and youth post-independence (Kumar, 1999).
3. Caste groups that are considered socially low, for more details see Maan (1979) and Sarangapani (2003).
4. However, one of the family benefited from employment in public services and their changing economic situation due to its bureaucratic association.
5. My own subjectivity of being born and brought up as a middle class Hindu family girl, conditioned to not visit places to which I had not been invited interfered with my attempts to pick up a new role as an ethnographer that required self-invitation and intrusion into peoples' affairs.
6. Twum-Danso Imoh and Okyere (2020) argues that the one-dimensional approach to child participation has led to the ignorance of views, experiences and perceptions of children growing up in impoverished communities within cultures that contrast sharply with dominant children's rights discourses.

References

Alderson, P., & Morrow, V. (2011). *The ethics of research with children and young people: A practical handbook*. London: Sage.

Balagopalan, S. (2005). An ideal school and the schooled ideal: Some reflections on educational experiences at the margins. In P. e. Jeffery (Ed.), *Educational regimes in contemporary Indian*. New Delhi: Sage.

Balagopalan, S. (2011). Introduction: Children's lives and the Indian context. *Childhood, 18*(3), 291–297.

Barley, R., & Bath, C. (2014). The importance of familiarisation when doing research with young children. *Ethnography and Education, 9*(2), 182–195.

Berger, P. L., & Luckman, T. (1971). *The social construction of reality*. Harmondsworth: Penguin Books.

Bissell, S. (2003). The social construction of childhood: A perspective from Bangladesh. In N. Kabeer, G. B. Nambissan, & R. Subrahmanian (Eds.), *Child labour and the right to education in South Asia: Needs versus rights*. New Delhi: Sage Publications.

Boyden, J. (1997). Childhood and the policy makers: A comparative perspective on the globalisation of childhood. In A. James & A. Prout (Eds.), *Constructing and reconstructing childhood: Contemporary issues in the sociological study of childhood* (2nd ed.). London and New York, NY: Routledge Falmer.

Chawla-Duggan, R. (2007). *Children's learners as identity as key to Quality Primary Education, Eight case studies of schoolong in India Today*. Lewiston, NY: The Edwin Mellen Press.

Chawla-Duggan, R., Wikeley, F., & Konantambigi, R. (2012). Researcher–child relations in Indian educational settings. *Ethnography and Education, 7*(3), 345–362.

Christensen, P., & James, A. (2008). *Research with children. Perspectives and practices* (2nd ed.). London: Routledge.

Christians, C. G. (2007). Cultural continuity as an ethical imperative. *Qualitative Inquiry, 13*(3), 437–444.

Corsaro, W. (2004). *The sociology of childhood* (2nd ed.). Thousand Oaks, CA: Pine Forge Press.

Delamont, S. (2009). The only honest thing: Autoethnography, reflexivity and small crises in fieldwork. *Ethnography and Education, 4*(1), 51–63.

Dennis, B. (2009). What does it mean when an ethnographer intervenes? *Ethnography and Education, 4*(2), 131–146.

Dennis, B., & Huf, C. (2020). Ethnographic research in childhood institutions: Participations and entanglements. *Ethnography and Education, 15*(4), 445–461.

Etherington, K. (2007). Ethical research in reflexive relationships. *Qualitative Inquiry, 13*(5), 599–616.

Gallacher, L., & Gallagher, M. (2008). Methodological immaturity in childhood research? Thinking through 'participatory methods'. *Childhood, 15*(4), 499–516.

Gupta. (2015). *Education, poverty and gender: Schooling Muslim girls in India*. New Delhi: Routledge.

Ipe, R. (2019). Ethical tensions in designing ethnographic research with schoolchildren in rural Karnataka. *Global Studies of Childhood, 9*(2), 120–131.

Iyer, S. (2013). An ethnographic study of disciplinary and pedagogic practices in a primary class. *Contemporary Education Dialogue, 10*(2), 163–195.

James, A. (2009). Agency. In J. Qvortrup (Ed.), *The Palgrave handbook of childhood studies*. Singapore: Palgrave.

James, A., & James, A. (2004). *Constructing childhood. Theory, policy and social practice*. Basingstoke: Palgrave.

James, A., & Prout, A. (1997). *Constructing and reconstructing childhood: Contemporary issues in the sociological study of childhood* (2nd ed.). London: Routledge.

Kumar, K. (1999). Children and adults. In T. S. Saraswati (Ed.), *Culture, socialisation and human development: Theory, research and applications in India*. New Delhi: Sage.

Lareau, A. (2003). *Unequal childhoods : Class, race, and family life*. London: University of California Press Ltd.

Lareau, A., & Shultz, J. (1996). *Journeys through ethnography: Realistic accounts of field work.* New York, NY: Routledge.

Levinson, M. (2010). Accountability to research participants: Unresolved dilemmas and unravelling ethics. *Ethnography and Education, 5*(2), 193–207.

Maan, R. (1979). *Social structures social change and future trends.* Jaipur: Rawat Publications.

Maithreyi, R. (2018). *Children's reconstruction of psychological knowledge: An ethnographic study of life skills education programmes in India.* New Delhi: Sage.

Nieuwenhuys, O. (1999). The paradox of the competent child and the global childhood agenda. In R. Fardon, W. van Binsbergen, & R. van Dijk (Eds.), *Modernity on a shoestring: Dimensions of globalization, consumption and developments in Africa and beyond.* Leiden and London: EIDOS.

Nieuwenhuys, O. (2009). Editorial: Is there an India childhood? *Childhood, 16,* 146–153.

Paoletti, I., Thomas, M. S., & Menendez, F. (2013). *Practice of ethics and empirical approach to ethics in social science research.* Newcastle: Cambridge Scholars Publishing.

Qvortrup, J. (2009). The development of childhood. In J. Qvortrup, K. Brown Rosier, & D. A. Kinney (Eds.). *Structural, historical, and comparative perspectives (sociological studies of children and youth* (Vol. 12). Bingley: Emerald Publishing Limited.

Raman, V. (2000). Politics of childhood: Perspectives from the South. *Economic and Political Weekly, 35*(46), 4055–4064.

Sarangapani, S. (2003). *Constructing school knowledge: An ethnography of learning in an Indian village.* New Delhi: Sage.

Sharma, P. (2018). Management of home-school relationship: Role of schools principals in low fee paying private schools in Manisha Jain. In A. Mehendale, R. Mukopadhayay, P. Sarangapani, & C. Winch (Eds.), *School education in India: Market, state and quality.* New Delhi: Routledge.

Twum-Danso Imoh, A., & Okyere, S. (2020). Towards a more holistic understanding of child participation: Foregrounding the experiences of children in Ghana and Nigeria. *Children and Youth Services Review, 112.* 104927. doi:10.1016/j.childyouth.2020.104927

Vasanta, D. (2004). Childhood, work and schooling: Some reflections. *Contemporary Education Dialogue, 2*(1), 5–29.

Viruru, R. (2001). *Early childhood education: Postcolonial perspectives from India.* New Delhi: Sage.

Webster, J. P., & John, T. A. (2010). Preserving a space for cross-cultural collaborations: An account of insider/outsider issues. *Ethnography and Education, 5*(2), 175–191. doi:10.1080/17457823.2010.493404

Willis, P. (1977). *Learning to labour: How working-class kids gets working class jobs.* London: Routledge.

Chapter 5

Revisiting the Ethics of Basque Educational Ethnographic Research Based on a Post-Qualitative Inquiry: A Proposal for Inclusive Ethics

Elizabeth Pérez-Izaguirre, José Miguel Correa Gorospe and Eider Chaves-Gallastegui

Abstract

This chapter reflects on how ethics was managed in Basque educational ethnographic research. Specifically, it addresses researcher positionality when relating to research collaborators in an attempt to manage inclusive ethics in situ. Nowadays, most research is evaluated by an ethical review board that ensures adequate research practice. However, unexpected field-work events need to be managed in the field, and this chapter addresses the impact of these events on the relationship between researchers and collaborators. Influenced by a post-qualitative stance we posit that research collaborators should be included in the research process. It reflects on the data collected during an ongoing ethnographic study with higher education students. The method used includes several interview meetings between researchers and collaborators, multimodal representations of collaborators' learning, and participants' self-observations. In the interviews, participants' discourses, representations, and self-observations were collaboratively analysed. The ethnographic data from these meetings show how researchers use a collaborative approach to practise ethics. Through such meetings, the knowledge derived from the ethnographic data is co-constructed in a research relationship where participants engage in dialogue and negotiation about the discourse created around them. Based on this relationship, we propose the concept of inclusive ethics as a process requiring an honest, inclusive, and collaborative relationship with the research subject.

Ethics, Ethnography and Education, 67–86
Published under exclusive licence by Emerald Publishing Limited
doi:10.1108/S1529-210X20220000019005

Keywords: Inclusive ethics; Basque educational ethnography; post-qualitative inquiry; researcher positionality; collaborative research; higher education

Ethics in Educational Ethnography

Ethics in educational ethnography has been a topic of constant debate for many reasons, including ethics review boards' scepticism when evaluating an ethnographic research proposal (Busher & Fox, 2019), the need for informed consent, and data protection during ethnographic research (Smette, 2019; Walford, 2009). Russell and Barley (2020) problematised the process of obtaining informed consent and personal data in educational ethnography, considering these to be the central elements in research ethics that need to be managed in the field. Drawing on this, we focus on the ethical dimension of relations during fieldwork. More precisely, we address the relationship between the researcher and the collaborator during ethnographic data collection and analysis. Our focus differs from previous studies, as it does not refer to the regulatory framework that usually governs research ethics.

The research project itself was conducted in collaboration with the University of the Basque Country and the University of Barcelona that investigated the learning trajectories of third- and fourth-year university students. Learning trajectories refer to the interweave of connected ideas, people, relations and contexts that shape how, who, what, where, when, and how much individuals learn. Learning trajectories need to be considered from a holistic, relational and biographical perspective (Jornet & Erstad, 2018). Furthermore, the project is structured according to four axes: contexts, technologies, conceptions and strategies of learning. In this project, researchers compromise with various collaborators in order to reveal and analyse their learning trajectories in a collaborative way.

Ethnography production is less prolific in higher education than at other educational stages (Lucas, 2012). This is unsurprising, as university students share a working and learning space with professors and researchers. The challenge for ethnographers in this case is precisely to speak with, interview, and observe students in relation to their peers, which might add difficulties to their usual task of observing others. Furthermore, doing research with young people could pose 'specific methodological challenges', as often contacting and maintaining research relationships with youngsters becomes complex (Russell, 2013, p. 47). To avoid these difficulties, new modes of ethnographic research are required.

Ethnography implies compromise with collaborators and investment in the field on the part of the researcher (Pérez-Izaguirre, 2021). Such investment not only refers to the time the ethnographer invests in the field, but also includes emotional aspects related to field devotion. Guided by questions from a post-qualitative perspective, this work questions the 'who' and the 'how' of such immersion. Post-qualitative inquiry enables the traditional modes of research (in this case, of ethnography) to be questioned (Koro-Ljungberg, 2016). Fieldwork is essential for ethnography, but who is in the field can be debated. In this study, we consider that collaborators can be observers of their own history; hence, they are the ones in the field.

We use the term 'collaborator' in a conscious way. We argue that students who participated in this research were our collaborators, as without them our research would not exist. Collaboration implies an interaction fundamental for ethnography (Shagrir, 2017). In this case, however, collaboration was more than simple interaction directed to collecting data. From our perspective, collaborators' voices were heard and the meanings in their narratives were analysed with them.

Following Nind (2014), we embraced an inclusive research perspective, as collaborators are part of our research. Our aim in this paper is to relate the concept of inclusive research to that of ethics, proposing the concept of inclusive ethics. The concept of inclusive ethics was developed by Persson (2017) in moral philosophy to explain the problems associated with common morality. Our perspective differs from Persson's (2017) proposal and refers to a relational concept of ethics in ethnographic research. Inclusive ethics enables questioning traditional modes of research and makes the whole process more honest. In fact, honesty becomes central to our research, as it allows the relationships between collaborators and researchers to be more reliable and authentic. In this chapter, we reflect on the cases of three university students and showing the interactions and analysis made between researchers and collaborators, we outline a concept of inclusive ethics in ethnographic research.

Doubts Cast by Post-Qualitative Inquiry

Post-qualitative research has been particularly influenced by new materialisms and new empiricisms, which offer alternative ontological, epistemological, and methodological approaches to research on education (St. Pierre, Jackson, & Mazzei, 2016). The new materialist inflexion enables not only matter to be reimagined as an active and vibrating force but also the analysis of growing intersections between materialities and broader geopolitical, biological, and social problems associated with the Anthropocene (Coole & Frost, 2010). These new materialistic concerns have made ontological work in the social sciences more urgent, as researchers strive to respond to new ethical problems provoked by rapidly accelerating material change (St. Pierre et al., 2016).

Thanks to the development of critical perspectives on traditional paradigms, our relationship with knowledge has been transformed, leading to questions about the status of knowledge production. The transformation of knowledge moves us away from consolidated strategies for studying a certain and stable world. It also demands new creative perspectives for addressing research within a constantly changing education.

Despite increasing discussion about the effects of permanent change and transformation on living conditions and education, much work remains to be done on their influence on ethnographic research and knowledge production. Due to permanent and unpredictable global mutability, society changes so rapidly that truth and the relevance of knowledge itself are constantly defied, taking by surprise even the most informed subjects (Bauman, 2007). These changes transform the notion, production, relation, and representation of knowledge, and they question the research methodologies and strategies that have been conducted to date.

This ontological turn has involved distancing from epistemological debates about knowledge, verification, and evidence. Instead, it raises speculative questions about the nature of being and the metaphysical conditions in which life, experience and research are possible (Lather & St. Pierre, 2013). As the ontological turn in the social sciences accelerates, some researchers have regarded post-qualitative research as an alternative to conventional modes of qualitative research. For example, St. Pierre (2011, 2013; St. Pierre et al., 2016) proposed post-qualitative inquiry as a mode of research that refuses all qualitative methodology and even the concept of methodology itself. Other authors have advocated a methodology that overcomes linearity and static knowledge categories produced by experts. For example, Lather (2015) suggested developing different routes to knowledge that highlight a variety of experiences. Such shift would enable a diffractive position in how we relate to data, resisting normativity and implying different starting points and investment with research participants.

What is usually understood by 'post-qualitative' is the compromise with the ontological, Deleuzian and new materialist changes in a wide range of disciplines, including education. We understand the post-qualitative perspective as a diverse movement of alternative forms of fluid and porous research in the social sciences, which can also be designated as new materialism, new feminist materialism, new empiricism, post-humanism, post-qualitative inquiry, or the ontological turn (Correa Gorospe, Aberasturi Apraiz, & Gutiérrez-Cabello, 2020). We maintain that a post-qualitative perspective refers to the constant change and transformation that provide conceptual and practical tools for analysing ethnographic research processes. These are always open and unfinished, and they enable us to establish other forms of relations among and representation of emergent and creative knowledge.

Post-qualitative inquiry also emphasises the importance of new research perspectives that analyse social difference and inequality to overcome dualistic human categories and knowledge sustaining humanist thinking, such as objective/subjective, reason/emotion, culture/nature, mind/body, human/non-human and self/other. Furthermore, post-qualitative inquiry exceeds theory/method and fundamentally defies the ontological assumptions in traditional qualitative humanistic tradition that have focused on the meanings of individual and social human experience. Some of these ontological assumptions have masterfully represented participants' humanistic realities.

To summarise, post-qualitative inquiry offers new relational, collective, fluid, and porous methodologies (Koro-Ljungberg, 2016) as possible forms and examples of uncertain research processes that enable us to overcome stable, objective and fixed methodological thinking. We embrace the ethnographic apparatus as a research method, but we consider that the post-qualitative turn has blurred its limits.

Ethics in a Volatile Research Context

As researchers, we have navigated through qualitative research, especially ethnography, narrative research, and life stories. We are aware of the flow of movements and uncertainty that blur the limits of the researcher's position in a volatile, uncertain, complex, ambiguous, and constantly changing world. This questions our previous ethnographic research methods and practice. We are drawn to the post-qualitative focus, motivated by the desire to do critical research that generates different forms of knowing to respond to the challenges of knowledge in this changing world (Jackson & Mazzei, 2012).

Researchers experience academic pressure to conduct a certain type of research that receives funding and is published in specific journals. Such processes are often opaque and exclude certain topics and research perspectives. However, this kind of research also depends on specific socio-political values and follows hegemonic discourses that enable telling the 'truth'. We are aware that these forces often work against new ways of generating knowledge and devalue some research positions, which in the social sciences and humanities pose ethical-epistemological questions about knowledge practices and knowledge itself.

More precisely, the doubts generated by post-qualitative inquiry enable us to permanently revise older paradigms and conditions – hegemonic discourses, power or oppression – that sustain knowledge generation. It also enables an evolving narrative, open to the unknown, in a process of fluid ethnographic research in a constantly changing scenario. According to Romm (2020), research that is intentionally performative and necessarily oriented to transformation needs post-qualitative ethics.

Post-qualitative ethics add value to scientific knowledge production and are common in research as a whole, since ethics go beyond academic ethical review boards. We do not reject the need for ethical review boards, as they are funda-mental for research institutions, but they cannot help when researchers face unexpected and difficult situations in the field, need to make immediate decisions in ethically sensitive situations, or when information reveals researchers or par-ticipants to be at risk (Guillemin & Guillam, 2004). According to Riera-Retamero, Estalayo-Bielsa, Hernández-Hernández, de Riba-Mayoral, and Lozano-Mulet (2021, p. 173):

> …it is necessary to develop ethical devices that respond to specific necessities of what happens in the field, not as systematic formulas of caption, as a process of performative reflexivity of the encounter itself, of how researcher interact with their counterparts.

In critical educational ethnography, this involves the researcher's active participation and firm commitment to research participants, requiring interaction and involvement in the field (Stith & Roth, 2006). Research processes, such as this one, involve questioning the researcher's authority and reviewing how the research affects participants in it (Parrilla-Latas, 2010; see also Haraway, 1988; Rosiek, Snyder, & Pratt, 2020). It also relates to the idea of inclusive research, or the critical view on the relationship between researchers and researched (Nind, 2014; Nind, Chapman, Seale, & Tilley, 2016; Seale, Nind, & Parsons, 2014). It requires collaborative sense-making in the research process, which helps raise awareness of inclusion in research (Nind & Vinha, 2014).

Ethics and politics in research imply considering the consequences of tangles established in a research project, as well as those not established (Romm, 2020). These actions alter the ontology of the topic by constituting the ethnographer not as a critical spectator or observer, but as a participant in an ethical relationship with other agents. In this case, the ethnographer contextualises academic discourse, analyses power relations with science and knowledge, considers the conditions of subalternity in academic production, and advocates a more inclusive and democratic relationship with participants that focuses on the conditions of inequality and reproduction of power. Hence, ethics in ethnographic research influenced by a post-qualitative perspective are not limited to providing faithful and precise descriptions of objects, since they also question the traditional positionality of researchers.

Method

The method employed was a variety of traditional ethnography influenced by the hybridity and porosity of the post-qualitative perspective. According to Mills and Morton (2013), ethnography in education constitutes a mode of seeing, being, thinking, and writing. In this sense, ethnography is not an instrument for data collection, but a set of methods with a shared disposition. Disposition refers to the ethnographer needing to understand the subjective experiences of others, which implies being exposed to others and their complexities in education. For this, a high degree of conceptual and methodological openness and empathy is needed.

Walford (2009) specified that ethnography (1) needs to study a specific culture or group that shares certain values, practices, relationships, and identifications; (2) uses diverse methods, including interviews, other recorded conversations, and field notes; (3) implies a compromise with the obtained material, for which an investment of time and a trusting relationship with participants in the field is needed; and (4) considers the researchers' subjectivity. At the same time, (5) participants' voices remain central. This means that ethnographers need to find a middle ground between their undeniable power and the actions and narratives of participants. Finally, (6) ethnographic research needs to have an emergent nature that modifies hypotheses and theories as data are collected.

Our ethnographic approach consisted of two main phases that happened simultaneously:

> Ethnography with research collaborators. In this phase, a set of encounters with the collaborators is proposed to collect multimodal material based on interviews, graphic representations of the learning trajectories of each collaborator, and self-observations. All the data generated are analysed collaboratively.

Collaborative Autoethnography (CAE) between researchers. According to Chang, Ngunjiri, and Hernández (2013), CAE is the study of the self in collaboration with others, including in the 'self' the life experiences in work, family, academic and social environments. In our research, meetings/seminars were held fortnightly. In these, we discussed reading material, the evolution of each case, and researchers' experiences during the processes. It became a space for collaborative discussion about the data and reading material provided by each researcher and was essential for clarifying the researchers' positionality.

This chapter focuses on the first phase, which refers to the ethnography with research collaborators. Each researcher in this chapter presents the follow-up of a case involving ethnography with a collaborator. Fieldwork lasted between two weeks and five months in each case. Collaborator selection was made according to the project's aims: studying the learning trajectories of university students following completion of their undergraduate studies.

Following Walford (2009), our study focused on the culture around university students as university, school, family and social learners. It involved diverse data collection techniques: interviews, graphical representations of each student's trajectory and students' self-observations collected in a field notebook. Students' voices were listened to and their contribution collaboratively interpreted for analysis in each encounter. Accordingly, the theories and hypotheses were emergent, and they were negotiated and modified in each encounter. This implied the researcher compromising and developing a trust relationship with the students, although the researcher was not in the field. Our proposal differed precisely in that it was the collaborator in the field collecting their data as an auto-ethnographer of their own learning.

This proposal was influenced by the openness of alternative methodologies rooted in the post-qualitative perspective. It included the collaborator and their vision and experience in the field. More precisely, it began with their vision of their own learning and needs, using theoretical and methodological tools that were shared with them during the encounters. The material produced by each collaborator was revised, discussed and analysed with the researcher.

Our proposal could be compared to Ruth's (2015) ethnographic research that used the field notes generated by her colleagues in the university context, leading to a 'productive insight into myself' (p. 3). In this case, the boundaries between researchers, the researched, object and method became blurred and the material generated brought all parties knowledge about the researched. In our proposal, emic and etic perspectives were also negotiated, as the collaborators' perspective (emic) was shared and negotiated with the researcher (etic) (Bergman & Lindgren, 2018).

The methodological approach included four encounters with the collaborators in which interviews were conducted. Following Blommaert and Jie (2020), the interviews were ordered conversations in relation to a series of topics. In the first encounter, the research project was presented and each participant was shown a series of statements reflecting popular prejudices about young people. Some of these statements were constructed in a positive way (e.g., 'if young people love something they explore it deeply') and others in a negative way (e.g., 'young people have difficulty in maintaining attention'). After the initial discussion, the central concepts of the project were presented: the notion of a learning trajectory, and the conceptions, contexts, technologies and strategies of learning. Collaborators were asked about their ideas of learning in these terms and their expected contribution to the project.

At the end of the first encounter, the participants were encouraged to make a graphical representation (or mapping) of their own learning trajectory. These consisted of drawing lines, indicating a chronology, on paper, although participants were also encouraged to make multimodal (e.g., rhizomatic or digital) representations. It should be noted that the representation of learning trajectories has limitations, because maps and representations can be considered hegemonic, fixed and non-fluid modes of such representation (Sefton-Green, 2017). This limitation can be mitigated by creating a collaborative narrative about it. Indeed, the graphical representation of the trajectories was analysed with the researcher during the second encounter.

At the end of the second encounter, collaborators were introduced to the field notebook elaboration (Facer & Manchester, 2012). During each week, the collaborators self-observed and noted when they considered they were learning, according to the axes of the project and bearing in mind the notion of the learning trajectory. It was discussed and analysed during the third encounter, which became a narrative and collaborative elaboration of a field diary – that is, we designed the analysis around the 'the collaborative field diary', which included events, relationships with the axes of the projects, and the beginning of an analysis about them.

Once the interviews, graphical representations, and collaborative field diary had been finalised, the researcher more directly related them to each theoretical axis of the project. The researcher elaborated a tale about the learning trajectory of the collaborator, which was shared and discussed in a fourth encounter.

We considered the analysis as a process, rather than a product, throughout the data collection (Barley, 2014). This involved constantly applying a collaborative analysis to enable continuous revision, dialogue with, and negotiation of the project's principal ideas. This was also related to the post-qualitative perspective influencing our work and the concept of inclusive research, as in this case collaborators were the main characters in their own tale.

Finally, it is important to mention that although we followed the same methodological approach, the three cases varied in both content and form. This points to a complex ethnographic research panorama where one size cannot fit all. However, it also provides research with a rich variety of data that cannot be ignored. Being conscious of such variety and complexity has direct effects on the concept of inclusive ethics, as it embraces volatility.

Each of the researchers were involved in one case: José Miguel Correa worked with Pablo, Elizabeth Pérez-Izaguirre collaborated with Marina and Eider Chaves Gallastegui worked with Lucía (all participant names are pseudonyms). The cases of Pablo and Marina followed the methodological pattern proposed at the beginning of this section. However, the availability of each collaborator varied, which obliged us to postpone the encounters. Lucía initially compromised with the research project, but after a first virtual encounter, she decided to discontinue her involvement. Consequently, the researcher in charge of her follow-up reconsidered what to do with the generated data and whether it was valid. Indeed, all these changing, un-patterned, and unexpected elements directly impacted on the collected data; for instance, learning trajectories were lineally represented by Pablo and Marina, but not by Lucía. As related to the ethnographic diary, Marina wrote 48 diary entries, Pablo 12 and Lucía did not reach such point. This fact precisely highlights the need for the inclusive ethics, as proposed in this chapter.

Reflections. Case 1: Participant Withdrawal from the Research

When Lucía told me (Eider) before our second encounter that due to work and personal commitments she could not continue collaborating in the research, I was beset by many questions. Before understanding her motives, I admit I felt some guilt. Perhaps I had not shown enough gratitude or compromise; perhaps she had not agreed with the ethical or researcher positionality; or perhaps I had not insisted enough that she continue her involvement in the project.

I remembered the idea of Parrilla-Latas (2010) about questioning the researcher's legitimacy in adopting an ethical position, in light of whether participants feel they have been favoured or ignored during the research process. I re-read the interview with Lucía and focused on the part of the conversation about our research collaboration.

Eider: Before mentioning the ethics protocol, I would like to share with you how we reach this interview: the doubts, expectations, desires… to understand where the other person comes from. What do you think?

Lucía: I agree.

Ei: I don't know whether you thought about it, if have a clear idea about it…

L: I have a clear idea about it. Basically, when I was told about the (research) project, I was interested because I believe I can contribute quite enough. I also think that we don't study well at university and, unfortunately, this is an experience I have to carry with me. Hence, I was interested in seeing what was going to be researched and whether something could be changed with this research… And I feel encouraged [to start working] as I don't know how it is going to be. I am intrigued.

Ei: Great. I'm happy that you approach the research in this way. The truth is, I am also intrigued, because even though I am 'qualified', I also do not know its drift. I admit I'm a bit nervous, but I am keen on seeing where this research will take us and on exploring together… I am happy to know that you are interested and feel implicated.

Reviewing the text helped me accept and integrate the drift and uncertainty revealed in the first encounter. I now realise I was not conscious of its value. Ethics relates to the exploration of unexpected possibilities, and the fact that Lucía had to leave the research for unconnected reasons implied a non-established tangle, an unforeseen consequence that simply happened. Moreover, it made me think about the implications of researching with young people, and asking myself if this 'category' was somehow defining ethnography. At this point, I agreed with Russell (2013), as doing research with young people involves specific complexities; 'their individual circumstances and characteristics can have an impact upon how and why they participate' (2013, p. 46).

The change of drift was not exhausted, but emphasised certain insecurities and tensions in me regarding whether my youth and inexperience might have influenced her decision to leave the study. It also occurred to me that she might have felt empowered to exercise her will or show less compromise. I wondered if I was being regarded as an authority figure. A final question concerned the concept of ethics: how could inclusive ethics be understood in this tangle? Lucía's discourse provided some hints about it.

> L: I realise I will not be able to continue doing the research [...]. The truth is, I don't have time to do the activities you propose or almost even for meeting with you. I feel angry, as when I compromise with something I like doing it until the end... but my situation is becoming worse and I don't have time. I believe that while COVID-19 is still 'with us', I won't have time. I couldn't find any other way. You adapt to something, and suddenly you need to adapt to another thing.

From the perspective of inclusive ethics, I recognised Lucía as someone with knowledge, and this implied that the encounter needed to be founded in the interchange and co-construction of knowledge. However, such co-construction was paused, or was modified because of her decision. At this point, I accepted the impossibility of continuing knowledge generation without her collaboration, which led me to think about researcher vulnerability. I also assumed its consequences. Considering the collaborator an active subject and agent of the research made me reposition myself as a researcher and look for spaces and new perspectives, which involved questioning pre-established, inherited and learned roles.

Furthermore, I assumed the need to accept both the unanticipated behaviour and the point of view of the participant. As Russell (2013) mentions, the changing nature of the research sample in ethnography commits both the researcher and their methodology to be more flexible. It also requires the researcher to be prepared for the unexpected moves of participants, such as disengaging from research or not being available to collaborate as pre-arranged.

Reflections. Case 2: Considering Unexpected Characteristics of Participants during Fieldwork

As previously mentioned, post-qualitative ethics focus on the transformation of power relations between researchers and collaborators from a democratic perspective. As a researcher, I (José Miguel) was surprised when, at the beginning of the second encounter, Pablo and I were reviewing his biography and he told me he had been diagnosed with ASD. My initial surprise at this confession led me to reflect on the concept of inclusive ethics (Nind, 2014, 2017). It also made me wonder how this would affect our researcher–collaborator relationship and the value of each interview's content.

Despite having to wear masks due to Covid-19, everything happened naturally, which was possibly ignited by the surprise created by the confession. At first, I tried to understand Pablo's situation, how the ASD diagnosis had affected him, and how it might impact the research objectives. Our conversation explored the initial meaning he attributed to ASD and sought to understand the scope of his confession. This was motivated by reflecting on the validity of the encounter and the content of our conversation. The dialogue started with the following question:

José Miguel: Why did you select these experiences from your memories [...] in your school biography? [...]

Pablo: I should have mentioned this last week, but I have Asperger's. [...] This is why the social issue is so important for me. [...] I discovered my Asperger's [...] when at the end of my baccalaureate diploma studies I had to go to therapy because I did not feel emotionally well. Then, I discovered it [...]. Throughout my childhood, I had been living without being able to connect with people or not knowing how to relate to others. After this confession, I tried to identify anything in our first encounter that could have led me to realise this. In reviewing our first encounter, I found no hint of it, but neither did it seem out of place. Without much time to think about what I needed to do after his declaration, but conscious of the importance of his words for the research, I intervened:

J.M.: Had you been diagnosed before? [...]

P: When I was six [...]. It was then I was diagnosed and this was written in a report. But that did not have any follow-up [...]. During my baccalaureate diploma studies, I had to go again due to my distress and my mother was told about it. She was told that in my situation it was normal 'taking into account what I had', referring to the diagnosed I had received during primary education. Pablo's ease of speaking about his ASD made me realise how the meaning of our encounter was changing. I Experienced doubts: I Wondered how I could gain the students' trust, what I should do, if empathy could offer him a space to speak freely about his experience with ASD, and how this conditioned his school biography. Showing interest in his history in order to create a trust-based relationship, I asked him:

J.M.:   How did childhood terrors break out? [...]

P: When I watched a film [...] I didn't want to sleep because I thought if I slept my parents would be kidnapped [...]. These were my first anxiety episodes, when I couldn't sleep. During primary education my disorder was quite present [...], I was very obsessive. My parents also suffered my anxiety at night.

After Pablo's confession about his ASD, the conversation and research were transformed, as if new communication channels had opened. Following Veck and Hall (2018), the type of participation demanded an inclusive ethics perspective, as we needed to question the established order and distant relations between researched and researcher, which implied a series of breaches and transgressions in knowledge production. The decision at that moment was how to proceed: whether just to listen to what he wanted to mention or to explore more deeply how ASD affected his learning. I also wondered if he was asking for help, and whether I should help him by acting in a particular way or by questioning his discourse about ASD to mobilise him out of it.

I already knew I was involved in inclusive research, but I now realised I needed to rethink how this affected my researcher role and our research objectives, and to embrace inclusion as an essential factor potentially affecting what we were saying. I realised that our conversation was transforming the communication and relationship based on trust, which also transformed research relations and the problems that were being explored (Nind, 2016; Walmsley, Strnadová, & Johnson, 2018). Hence, this had a greater and more profound impact than our first idea of studying university students' learning trajectories, contexts, conceptions, strategies, and technologies. I also wondered whether the student's confession would change how I participated in the research. I decided to let Pablo speak by asking him:

J.M.: How does it affect you to think you have ASD? [...]

P: I am still 'in my bubble', but at least I am able to act. I have tried to learn how to integrate in society.

Time has passed since the interview and the ASD aspect has been diluted. Indeed, the attention we devoted to ASD during the second encounter has now lost power, as the analysis of the interviews and content did not focus on the research project's objectives. I obviously cannot ignore the presence of ASD and its impact on Pablo's learning trajectory, but the experiences shared with the collaborator transcend the research project itself. A contribution from inclusive ethics proposes a methodological turn that implies changing from researching subjects, collectives or communities to researching with them (Smith-Merry, 2019).

Reflections. Case 3: Dialogue and Negotiation between Researched and Researcher

The post-qualitative influence our research involved being open to theoretical and practical proposals from collaborators. In my case (Elizabeth), this implied listening carefully to Marina's theoretical ideas. This philosophy student brought a field notebook full of very specific and detailed entries about her own learning. From the outset, I was surprised by Marina's level of precision and reflection in her self-observation. In the following excerpt, I show part of the conversation in which we analysed one field note entry during our third encounter:

> Marina: We are studying some authors [in different classes and we were asked whether...] cognoscitive efficacy is related to character or content. Character is the normal and common meaning, and content is the non-expressed proposition. As I was reading a paper [...], [I realised] I couldn't answer the question. The paper used the term 'cognoscitive significant', but I didn't know that cognoscitive significant and cognoscitive efficacy were the same thing. Well, it makes sense, as it contributes to knowledge, doesn't it? But I didn't know they were the same thing, and this was important information to be able to answer to the question. [...] Kripke [...] mentions all this inside modal logic, which is necessity, possibility, and where possible worlds operate. That is, [...] it is true: in all possible worlds, and possible may be true, it is true in any of the possible worlds, but not in all [worlds]. [...] Here Kripke talks about rigid designators that, in an identity relationship, if both are designators, these are going to be true in all possible worlds. Hence, in philosophy of mind, the principal evidence is reducing mental states to physical states, and Kripke says that for this, such identity should be a rigid designator's identity.

This is the example of an explanation of the field notebook by Marina, narrated by herself during the third encounter. Marina presented a précis of the theories learned in class and the connections she made between different subjects. These connections were clearly a 'conceptual revelation' for her. However, I must admit that the connection between the concepts was not clear to me because I do not have enough training in philosophy.

Marina delivered her narrative rapidly because she was motivated by what she had learned. She probably thought I could follow her arguments, but I found her narrative too fast; only after reviewing the interview transcripts did I fully comprehend these conceptions. The unpredictability of these elements (Bauman, 2007) led me to embrace the perspective of inclusive ethics and make a specific decision during our encounter: Aware of my limitation, I decided to focus on the project objectives when trying to understand what Marina was attempting to explain to me – that is, beyond the conceptions that I was struggling to understand at the time, I needed to understand what Marina was trying to tell me. Thus, I asked her the following question:

Elizabeth: Alright, if I followed you correctly, did you already have some information about this conception? [...]
M: Well, in this subject I hadn't [already acquired the conception]. I just understood part of it. But when I studied this conception in another subject, I understood it all. I tried to rephrase what marina was saying as I wanted to be sure that what she was explaining to me was how she had learned to connect the conceptions from one subject with another. She corroborated it, making a small correction:
E: Alright, in the academic context [you acquired both conceptions...]. And the [learning] strategy was simply classroom dynamics. [...]
M: Yes, I made sense of the same paper from two different perspectives, and then I connected them, making more sense out of it. That was it. Moreover, I like these authors, so [...] it was important.
E: I notice you like them.

In this excerpt, Marina's and my perspectives were more clearly expressed and negotiated with regard to the conceptual contribution of the project. Negotiation from a post-qualitative perspective derives from the idea that collaboration in any research, hence, any ethnographic research, needs to be understood in a process of negotiation (Bengry-Howell & Griffin, 2012). Inclusive ethics necessarily implies a negotiation between researched and researcher's voice and is directly related to the collaborative perspective in this project. Such collaboration transcends the ethnographic field and meetings. That is, even though such negotiation happened during fieldwork, it had a direct impact on the process of analysis and written material produced afterwards.

Such collaboration during our conversation continued to focus more on the conceptions and learning strategies relating to interest, as something that motivates the student. Interest is an element that appeared on various occasions in relation to learning conscience:

M: Yes [I like the authors...]. In relation to this, there are two different conceptions: (1) That of direct reference by Russell and all that, and (2) Frege's indirect reference, social, descriptions, and so on. We were speaking about these in class. There I realised that I feel more identified with direct reference. [...] I realise I am more keen on philosophy of language. Well, analytic philosophy in general. I tend to like more those areas. And well, if these conceptions had not been explained, maybe I would not have realised about those [...] even if I read the article. Or maybe the ability to relate complex authors is greater when you are in class, not alone.

E: Well, all that made you reach your reflection [...] and this is related to your own [learning] conscience.

M: Yes, it is.

E: Where you stand ...

M: This is the academic context, but it is also related to you personally.

In this excerpt, Marina and I explored more deeply the learning conscience – that is, when Marina realised what she had been learning and what the consequences of such learning were for her own positioning. This was a central part of our project: it was present in her learning trajectory and we considered it within the idea of inclusive and collaborative ethnographic research.

Conclusion

Our chapter has addressed ethics in educational ethnography by focusing on the relationship between researchers and collaborators, going beyond the normative and formal aspects that are inevitable considerations of ethical review boards. More precisely, influenced by the post-qualitative perspective, we proposed overcoming traditional modes of research in order to adopt a more inclusive (Nind, 2017) and collaborative research (Bergman & Lindgren, 2018). Inclusion and collaboration are essential for this or any ethnographic research, as without collaborators there would not be any study.

Lucía's case questions some researcher roles, which is fundamental from our ethical positioning. Lucía spoke about adaptability and the unexpected element in life, but this also relates to our research. It refers to drift and considers the unexpected and unestablished tangle in a particular research (Correa, Aberasturi, & Chaves Gallastegui, 2020). It reaffirms that research is a process of mutual exploration and learning (Romm, 2020), and that ethics relates to the spaces we share. It also raises the question of when the relationship with the collaborator ends and when it can be concluded.

This reminds us that researchers lose their supremacy when they enter the game and open the possibility of affecting and being affected by the other, exposing themselves to drift. In this way, the role of the 'voyeur' who observes from a distance and does not intervene is dissolved (Stith & Roth, 2006).

The researcher as a distant witness disappears (Haraway, 1988); instead, the researcher has an ethical relationship with other agents (Correa et al., 2020; Rosiek et al., 2020). In this sense, Lucía became an active agent capable of making decisions, and of affecting, participating in, and modifying the research process.

It opens new avenues for emergent topics derived from research practice. It enables reflecting on what happens when we consider collaborators to be active subjects. It also reconsiders researchers' recognition, as researchers are affected by considering collaborators as active agents. We wonder whether researchers are prepared for this ethical and onto-epistemological turn, taking into consideration our tradition of privileges and power in research.

Pablo's confession of being diagnosed with ASD made him vulnerable but also the main character in the encounters. After the confession, the research was transformed, and ethical implications multiplied as new challenges appeared. The relationship between Pablo and the researcher was more equal, calling into question the usual power imbalance, as the relationship was democratic and collaborative. This promoted a different way of listening and integrating collaborators in our research. It also added a new factor to take into consideration, as ASD involves belonging to a group that has traditionally been excluded. This process generated numerous questions about the project and the methodological approach. We wondered whether this pattern was valid for all cases, given students have diverse communication and learning needs. Other concerns related to whether the questions or answers were all equally valid, or to whether their meaning was understood differently by the researcher and collaborator. There were conceptual differences in the project, as it might be different to investigate how university students learn than to explore how diverse university students learn.

This experience has an important added value as it increases awareness of inclusive processes of research (Nind & Vinha, 2014). By reviewing research patterns, language use, relationships, and researcher competence, it explores how inclusive research processes are addressed (Nind et al., 2016). It also helps by looking beyond research production to question the level of inclusion in relation to other projects and their quality (Seale et al., 2014).

Marina expressed clear ideas about her learning and about how she experienced and registered them in her field notebook. Following Nind (2014), Marina's conviction led to the researcher revising her position of power and authority, as Marina was certain of her ideas. This had direct consequences on the negotiation of the collaborative analysis. Indeed, Marina led the collaborative analysis, which made the researcher a mere guide in clarifying what Marina was trying to say. This questions the traditional authority of the researcher, which has been problematised by other authors (Parrilla-Latas, 2010; Walford, 2009).

In line with the cases of Lucía and Pablo, Marina's case opens new research questions relating to drift and the conceptual contribution of participants. It shows how the collaborator knows and makes sense of her own conceptions in her learning trajectory. It also suggests that knowledge is not solely the researcher's property and that an inclusive ethnography should provide the collaborator with specific tools to recognise and study their own learning. This should be made collaboratively, and the researcher should not be the only interpreter. As Marina's example shows, interpretation is shared, negotiated and discussed, becoming an open, fluid and porous element in research, which relates to the concept of fluidity and volatility as specified by Bauman (2007).

All these examples show a type of relational ethics in ethnography that we have designated as inclusive. Inclusive ethics are negotiated and discussed with collaborators during data collection in the field. In this case, the field was located beyond meetings between researchers and collaborators, and this was possible due to constantly questioning researchers' awareness of their power and authority and their inevitable need of the others. It reveals traditional oppression dynamics and power relationships that exclude, control, authorise and regulate how participants and researchers could work. An inclusive ethics perspective moves away from this view in educational ethnography and opens new alternative and promising spaces for collaborative work. Hence, we pose that inclusive ethics refers to the necessity of collaborators for doing ethnography and to the creation of a middle ground where the researcher meets the collaborator and they both do ethnography in collaboration with one another. The middle ground where the researcher and collaborator meet enables the creation of an authentic research relationship. Authenticity is created in an environment of trust where all perspectives are heard and taken into consideration.

Inclusive ethics are also necessary for making sense of the new processes of ethnographic research that extend beyond the researcher's physical and direct observations. In other words, inclusive ethics enables questioning any collaborative research and refers to the blurred lines between the researcher and collaborator, which paradoxically makes the processes of data collection and analysis more honest. This is possible due to the doubts cast by the post-qualitative perspective and the porosity of research methods. Inclusive ethics allows us to analyse our research practices with greater complexity. By questioning the conditions and relationships within which knowledge, research relationships, power relations and our own motivations as researchers are generated, inclusive ethics enables addressing the complexity of our researcher role and moving towards greater authenticity. In sum, inclusive ethics enables opening new debates about researcher positionality with research collaborators doing educational ethnography. Future research should focus on the impact of researcher positionality and relations in the field to understand the kind of ethnography they produce.

Overall, this chapter contributes to a broader debate about ethics in ethnographic research based on the relationship between researcher and collaborator, and influenced by post-qualitative inquiry. It has proposed the concept of inclusive ethics in ethnographic research to make sense of the set of strategies that the researcher uses to relate with the collaborator in a more horizontal way, and which question the researcher's own authority.

Acknowledgements

This study was supported by the research project Trayectorias de aprendizaje de jóvenes universitarios: Concepciones, estrategias, tecnologías y contextos. PID2019-108696RB-I00 funded by the Ministry of Science and Innovation of Spain.

References

Barley, R. (2014). *Identity and social interaction in a multi-ethnic classroom*. London: Tufnell Press.

Bauman, Z. (2007). *Vida líquida [Liquid life]*. Sao Paulo: Editora Schwarcz-Companhia das Letras.

Bengry-Howell, A., & Griffin, C. (2012). Negotiating access in ethnographic research with 'hard to reach' young people: Establishing common ground or a process of methodological grooming? *International Journal of Social Research Methodology*, *15*(5), 403–416.

Bergman, A., & Lindgren, M. (2018). Navigating between an emic and an etic approach in ethnographic research. Crucial aspects and strategies when communicating critical results to participants. *Ethnography and Education*, *13*(4), 477–489.

Blommaert, J., & Jie, D. (2020). *Ethnographic fieldwork. A beginner's guide*. Bristol: Multilingual Matters.

Busher, H., & Fox, A. (2019). Introduction: Overview of the book. In H. Busher & A. Fox (Eds.), *Implementing ethics in educational ethnography: Regulation and practice*. London: Routledge.

Chang, H., Ngunjiri, F. W., & Hernández, K.-A. C. (2013). *Collaborative Autoethnography*. New York, NY: Routledge.

Coole, D., & Frost, S. (2010). Introducing the new materialism. In D. Coole & S. Frost (Eds.), *New materialisms: Ontology, agency, and politics*. Durham, NC: Duke University Press.

Correa Gorospe, J. M., Aberasturi Apraiz, E., & Gutierrez-Cabello, A. (2020). La investigación postcualitativa: Origen, referentes y permanente devenir [Post-qualitative research: Origins, referents and constant change]. In J. Sancho, F. Hernandez, L. Montero, J. De Pablos, J. Rivas, & A. Ocaña (Eds.), *Caminos y derivas para otra investigación educativa y social [Ways and drift to another social and educational research]*. Barcelona: Octaedro.

Correa Gorospe, J. M., Aberasturi, E., & Chaves-Gallastegui, E. (2020). Narrativa y universidad: Aportaciones al debate desde un posicionamiento postcualitativo [Narrative and university: A contribution to debate from a post-qualitative perspective]. *Márgenes*, *1*(3), 133–151.

Facer, K., & Manchester, H. (2012). Mapping learning lives. *BBC*.

Guillemin, M., & Guillam, L. (2004). Ethics, reflexivity, and 'ethically important moments' in research. *Qualitative Inquiry*, *10*(2), 261–280.

Haraway, D. (1988). Situated knowledges: The science question in feminism and the privilege of partial perspective. *Feminist Studies*, *14*(3), 575–599.

Jackson, A., & Mazzei, L. (2012). *Thinking with theory in qualitative research: Viewing data across multiple perspectives*. London: Routledge.

Jornet, A., & Erstad, O. (2018). From learning contexts to learning lives: Studying learning (dis)continuities from the perspective of the learners. *Digital Education Review*, *33*, 1–25.

Koro-Ljungberg, M. (2016). *Reconceptualizing qualitative research: Methodologies without methodology*. Los Angeles, CA: SAGE.

Lather, P. A. (2015). The work of thought and the politics of research. In N. Denzin & M. Giardina (Eds.), *Qualitative inquiry and the politics of research*. Walnut Creek, CA: Left Coast Press.

Lather, P., & St Pierre, E. (2013). Introduction: Post-qualitative research. *International Journal of Qualitative Studies in Education*, *26*(6), 629–633.

Lucas, L. (2012). Ethnographic journeys in higher education. In S. Delamont (Ed.), *Handbook of qualitative research in education*. Cheltenham: Edward Elgar Publishing.

Mills, D., & Morton, M. (2013). *Ethnography in education*. London: Sage.

Nind, M. (2014). Inclusive research and inclusive education: Why connecting them makes sense for teachers' and learners' democratic development of education. *Cambridge Journal of Education*, *44*(4), 525–540.

Nind, M. (2016). Towards a second generation of inclusive research. In T. Buchner, O. Koenig, & S. Schuppener (Eds.), *Inklusive Forschung. Gemeinsam mit Menschen mit Lernschwierigkeiten forschen*. Bad Heilbrunn: Klinkhardt.

Nind, M. (2017). The practical wisdom of inclusive research. *Qualitative Research*, *17*(3), 278–288.

Nind, M., Chapman, R., Seale, J., & Tilley, L. (2016). The conundrum of training and capacity building for people with learning disabilities doing research. *Journal of Applied Research in Intellectual Disabilities*, *29*(6), 542–551.

Nind, M., & Vinha, H. (2014). Doing research inclusively: Bridges to multiple possibilities in inclusive research. *British Journal of Learning Disabilites*, *42*(2), 102–109.

Parrilla-Latas, Á. P. (2010). Ética para una investigación inclusiva. *Revista educación inclusiva*, *3*(1), 165–174.

Pérez-Izaguirre, E. (2021). Can Basque be protected in multi-ethnic environments?: Methodological dilemmas in Basque school ethnography. In L. Sarroub & C. Nicholas (Eds.), *Doing (home) fieldwork: Ethnography of education in familiar contexts*. Lanham: Rowman and Littlefield.

Persson, I. (2017). *Inclusive ethics. Extending beneficence and egalitarian justice*. London: Oxford University Press.

Riera-Retamero, M., Estalayo-Bielsa, P., Hernández-Hernández, F., de Riba-Mayoral, S., & Lozano-Mulet, P. (2021). Los métodos artísticos como desencadenantes de subjetividades en tránsito de la infancia migrante: Un estudio en escuelas públicas de Barcelona [Artistic methods as subjectivity triggers for migrant infants in transit: A study of public scchools in Barcelona]. *Antípoda. Revista de Antropología y Arqueología*, *43*, 167–192. doi:10.7440/antipoda43.2021.08

Romm, N. R. A. (2020). Reflections on a post-qualitative inquiry with children/young people: Exploring and furthering a performative research ethics. *Forum Qualitative Sozialforschung/Forum: Qualitative Social Research*, *21*(1). doi:10.17169/fqs-21.1.3360

Rosiek, J. L., Snyder, J., & Pratt, S. L. (2020). The new materialisms and indigenous theories of non-human agency: Making the case for respectful anti-colonial engagement. *Qualitative Inquiry*, *26*(3–4), 331–346.

Russell, L. (2013). Researching marginalised young people. *Ethnography and Education*, *8*(1), 46–60.

Russell, L., & Barley, R. (2020). Ethnography, ethics and ownership of data. *Ethnography*, *21*(1), 5–25.

Ruth, D. (2015). With the eyes of others: An ethnography of an academic office. *Ethnography and Education*, *11*(3), 359–370.

Seale, J., Nind, M., & Parsons, S. (2014). Inclusive research in education: Contributions to method and debate. *International Journal of Research and Method in Education, 37*(4), 347–356.

Sefton-Green, J. (2017). Representing learning lives: What does it mean to map learning journeys? *International Journal of Educational Research, 84,* 111–118.

Shagrir, L. (2017). *Journey to ethnographic research.* Cham: Springer.

Smette, I. (2019). Ethics and access when consent must come first. Consequences of formalised research ethics for ethnographic research in schools. In H. Busher & A. Fox (Eds.), *Implementing ethics in educational ethnography: Regulation and practice.* London: Routledge.

Smith-Merry, J. (2019). Inclusive disability research. In P. Liamputtong (Ed.), *Handbook of research methods in health social sciences.* Singapore: Springer.

Stith, I., & Roth, W. M. (2006). Who gets to ask the questions: The ethics in/of cogenerative dialogue praxis. *Forum Qualitative Sozialforschung/Forum for Qualitative Social Research, 7*(2). doi:10.17169/fqs-7.2.124

St. Pierre, E. A. (2011). Post-qualitative research: The critique and the coming after. In N. Denzin & Y. Lincoln (Eds.), *The SAGE handbook of qualitative research* (4th ed.). Thousand Oaks, CA: SAGE Publishers.

St. Pierre, E. A. (2013). The posts continue: Becoming. *International Journal of Qualitative Studies in Education, 26*(6), 646–657.

St. Pierre, E. A., Jackson, A. Y., & Mazzei, L. A. (2016). New empiricisms and new materialisms. *Cultural Studies ↔ Critical Methodologies, 16*(2), 99–110. doi:10. 1177/1532708616638694

Veck, W., & Hall, M. (2018). Inclusive research in education: Dialogue, relation and methods. *International Journal of Inclusive Education, 22*(8), 1–16.

Walford, G. (2009). The nature of educational ethnography. In G. Walford (Ed.), *How to do educational ethnography.* London: The Tufnell Press.

Walmsley, J., Strnadová, I., & Johnson, K. (2018). The added value of inclusive research. *Journal of Applied Research in Intellectual Disabilities, 31*(5), 751–759.

Chapter 6

Maintaining Participant Integrity – Ethics and Fieldwork in Online Video Games

Matilda Ståhl and Fredrik Rusk

Abstract

Employing ethnographic methods online offers additional understanding of how online contexts are connected to education (Rusk, 2019; Ståhl & Kaihovirta, 2019; Ståhl & Rusk, 2020). As society evolves, new challenges arise for ethnography to claim its position as a methodology for understanding human sociality. For example, the definition of fieldwork might become blurred when the researcher has constant access to the field from their computer, and accessing a participant's perspective is made more complex when there is no, or limited, face-to-face interaction with participants (Beaulieu, 2004; Shumar & Madison, 2013). This chapter discusses some of the challenges experienced during the process of employing ethnographic methods with students playing the online multiplayer video game Counter Strike: Global Offensive (CS:GO, Valve Corporation & Hidden Path Entertainment, 2012) within an educational context. The challenges included maintaining participant integrity in terms of gaining informed consent from players that became co-observed, defining privacy online during the analysis and in dissemination and portraying participants accurately despite stakeholder interests. These challenges are discussed in relation to maintaining research ethics in situ together with participants and with the research context in mind. The intention is not to portray our approach as best practice, but rather to highlight and discuss the challenges faced.

Keywords: Online; video games; multiplayer games; participant perspective; screen recording; ethnographic case study

Introduction

Conducting research in a society shaped by constantly changing digital technologies offers researchers both new possibilities and challenges. Digitally mediated

Ethics, Ethnography and Education, 87–107
Copyright © 2022 Matilda Ståhl and Fredrik Rusk
Published under exclusive licence by Emerald Publishing Limited
doi:10.1108/S1529-210X20220000019006

practices evolve rapidly, and studying them requires methodological creativity, adaptability and a sustained collaboration with participants (Karpf, 2012; Pink, Horst, Postill, Hjorth, & Tacchi, 2016). Today, 'the digital is transforming what it means to be social and human in the world' (Markham, 2018, p. 653). Social interactions take place both online and offline, and should be reflected accordingly in ethnographic studies (Beneito-Montagut, 2011). To understand the dynamic and shifting online environments, ethnographers need to critically reflect on methodology with a focus on 'which elements of pre-digital research practice should be retained and which have become obsolete' (Quinton & Reynolds, 2018, p. 11). In other words, ethnography, before going online, needs to rethink the process and products of enquiry (Markham, 2018). Evolving ethnographic methods to capture life online creates new demands on the researcher (Beaulieu, 2004; Murphy, 2014; Shumar & Madison, 2013), including ethical challenges regarding online content (Hammersley & Atkinson, 2007; Markham, 2018; Markham & Buchanan, 2012; Sahlström, Tanner, & Olin-Scheller, 2019; Spilioti & Tagg, 2017; Sveningsson, 2003) where the line between public and private is easily blurred. Further, applying pre-digital ethical guidelines might cause complications, such as using non-digital principles of public versus private in an online context (Sugiura, Wiles, & Pope, 2017).

'Online' itself is a problematic term, considering how technology is highly embedded in contemporary society (Markham, 2018). Few contexts are entirely offline, and all contemporary research can be considered online to some extent. The term does, however, have a function when stressing that the fieldwork is conducted online, since this presents a challenge to understand where the line between private and public is drawn in the online context (Beaulieu, 2004; Beneito-Montagut, 2011; Sahlström et al., 2019; Shumar & Madison, 2013; Sveningsson, 2003). Further, according to Quinton and Reynolds (2018), one approaches digital research either as a method (or instrument), or as a phenomenon. Digital research as a method allows access to data in a way that has not been possible using previous technology, in contrast to digital research on a phenomenon that would not exist if not for new technology. However, it is possible to combine them using digital means to get new forms of data on a phenomenon shaped by digital technology. Communicating new forms of data collection and the relevance of a new phenomenon to a research community that is unfamiliar with one or both offers challenges. This chapter discusses the combination of research on digital phenomena with digital data collection through an ethno-case study of an online multiplayer video game.

Several possible and worthwhile questions can be raised about ethics in relation to video games; ranging from the game designers balancing meaningful content with making money (Sicart, 2013) to war-themed games glorifying advanced weaponry (Mantello, 2017), player aggression (Bennerstedt, Ivarsson, & Linderoth, 2012) as well as marginalisation in both the game industry (Johnson, 2018) and online game culture (Taylor, 2016). However, here, we discuss an ethical perspective on researching a digital phenomenon, online multiplayer video games, through digital data collection employing ethnographic methods. As some contemporary research designs are highly experimental (see, e.g. Monge & O'Brien, 2021, where the researchers created a toxic in-game context for unknowing participants), we see a need for a methodological and ethical discussion on online research in general and in-game contexts in particular.

We focus on ethical challenges faced during the process of employing ethnographic methods in an educational ethno-case study on an online game context (Parker-Jenkins, 2018). Case study as a methodology focuses on an immersed understanding of a phenomenon through a specific case (Scwandt & Gates, 2018), here a participant's perspective of an online game in an educational context. Case studies can offer insight into how previous research and empirical data are connected (Cohen, Manion, & Morrison, 2000). The distinction between ethnography and case studies employing ethnographic methods can be blurry on a methodological level, since they are somewhat overlapping. Both focus on a participant's perspective of a phenomenon and use varied forms of data collection. However, in ethnography, more emphasis is put on extended periods of time in the field and gaining insight into this phenomenon from multiple contexts, whereas a case study can be more limited in terms of time and researcher immersion into the field (Parker-Jenkins, 2018). This study is positioned on the borderline between these methodologies, we consider it an ethno-case study and continue to situate our work alongside ethnographic research. This chapter discusses ethical perspectives regarding how online ethnographic fieldwork is conducted in an online game context, how the data can be analysed and how the findings are reported.

Data were collected in 2017–2018 as part of Ståhl's doctoral thesis on identity construction online in collaboration with a vocational school in Finland. The participants (16–18 years old at the time and from two different teams) studied esports as a minor subject but did not play video games together during lessons.[1] As school representatives, they were encouraged to play together as a team in their spare time on a weekly basis. The teammates and the game, in particular, might not be their primary choice otherwise. Activity during the entire programme was required to get course credits. Here, ethnographic methods were employed to gain insight into online games from a participant's perspective and to better understand active players with a serious interest in video games. As present researcher, Ståhl experienced a level of 'otherness' due to her age and gender during the data collection (see Taylor, 2009). However, this decreased as the participants noted that Ståhl identifies as a gamer and that they thereby shared a vocabulary. The participants themselves administered the screen recordings of matches played in competitive mode; however, the matches were not part of organised events. Here, we present the ethical challenges around maintaining participant integrity. These challenges emerged throughout the entire research process; from the data collection to analysis and publication process (Ståhl & Rusk, 2020).

Participant-Centred Research Approaches Online

Next, we present how we utilised ethnographic methods online within an ethno-case study framework whereby participants themselves administered data collection. Additionally, the field of participant-focused research in online games is presented.

One of ethnography's key elements is 'thick description' (Geertz, 1973) that explores a phenomenon or context from a participant's perspective while acknowledging that other perspectives on the studied context exist and communicating this to the reader (Besnier & Philips, 2017). When the studied phenomenon or context is online, it creates new demands on the ethnographer. The definition of fieldwork is blurred when the ethnographer has constant access to the field from their computer, and accessing a participant's perspective is made more complex when there is no, or limited, face-to-face interaction with the participants (Beaulieu, 2004; Murphy, 2014; Shumar & Madison, 2013). Additionally, as interaction mediated via a screen might lower inhibitions, research endeavours need to put emphasis on boundary management in online ethnography.

Accessing an insider's perspective can be done through a research design where the participants themselves administer the data collection, through e.g. screen and/or video recordings. The justifications for relinquishing control of the recordings to the students themselves concern matters of intrusion, access and ethics (Aarsand & Forsberg, 2010; Rusk, Pörn, Sahlström, & Slotte-Lüttge, 2012). Video ethnographic research touches upon private life in a way that is potentially intrusive, and access to the participants' own screens is highly personal data (Paakkari, 2020). A design in which the participants administer the data collection eliminates the physical presence of a researcher, thus minimising the recording's invasiveness (Aarsand & Forsberg, 2010). The data collection can further be seen as a collaboration between researcher and participants, whereby participants feel like research enables their sense of agency (Pink, 2013). Involving the participants in the research has the potential to diminish power imbalances between the researcher(s) and the participants (Russell & Barley, 2020).

When the participants produce the data themselves, the technology they use and their competence in using that technology impacts the form and the content of the data they create (Pink, 2013). Participants ownership of data collection is fairly uncommon with the exceptions for auto-ethnographic endeavours (Bennerstedt, 2013). Previous ethnographic research on online games includes different forms of data collection; interviews during competitions (Rambusch, Jakobsson, & Pargman, 2007), observations and screen shots from Twitch streams (Ruvalcaba, Shulze, Kim, Berzenski, & Otten, 2018) and video ethnography (Taylor, 2016).[2] Ratan, Taylor, Hogan, Kennedy, and Williams (2015) used screen recordings of an online multiplayer game; however, the participants played the game on campus computers with researchers administering the screen recordings. Such a research design offers more researcher control of the data; however, the participants' agency is limited.

Previous ethnographic research on online games has primarily focused on massive multiplayer online role-playing games (MMORPGs) (Taylor, 2009) or massive online battle arenas (MOBAs) (Ratan et al., 2015), despite first person shooters (FPS) being a major genre in esports (Webb, 2019). Nevertheless, research employing ethnographic methods on FPS, such as *Counter Strike: Global Offensive* (CS:GO), has been limited (Kiuorti, 2019; Rambusch et al., 2007; Taylor, 2016), especially in an educational context, with a few exceptions (see, e.g. Rusk & Ståhl, 2020; Ståhl & Rusk, 2020). CS:GO was based on *Counter Strike* (Valve Corporation, 2000); a game originally developed as a modification for the game *Half-Life* (Sierra Entertainment & Valve Corporation, 1998). The organised competitive culture that emerged around the original CS game (2000) transformed an individual pastime activity into something professional with a focus on teamplay (Rambusch et al., 2007). In Finland, the context in focus here, the game series *Counter Strike* remains popular; listed seventh among the most popular digital games in the Finnish Player Barometer (Kinnunen, Lilja, & Mäyrä, 2018).

An Ethno-Case Study in an Educational Esports Context

In the following section, we will discuss the ethnographically informed research design and present the research context.

First-hand experiences of relevant settings, often in combination with interviews, inform researcher immersion and provide the ethnographer with access to a participant's perspective (Hammersley, 2006; Pole & Morrison, 2003), also in online contexts (Parker-Jenkins, 2018). Here, experiences of the relevant setting and researcher immersion were obtained through multiple in-game screen recordings conducted by participants on their own devices. The design was informed by the autonomy principle (Murphy & Dingwall, 2001), as well as insights into ethnographic research design where participants take an active role in the data collection (Rusk, 2019; Sahlström et al., 2019; Ståhl & Kaihovirta, 2019). The research approach was player-centred (e.g. Kiuorti, 2019; Ratan et al., 2015; Taylor, 2009). The focus remained on accessing a participant's perspective on the game in question. As the setting was neither staged for research purposes (Quinton & Reynolds, 2018) nor was the in-game context manipulated by the researchers (unlike the case of Monge & O'Brien, 2021), playing in a setting of the participants' own choice and on their own computers was considered a naturally occurring setting (Hammersley, 2018).

In most games, visuals are relevant to gameplay and how the player perceives the game. The screen recordings are audio-visual data of an embodied experience produced by the participants themselves. Visuality is informed by cultural practices and visual ethnography focuses on images, video material and research online (Pink, 2013). Using visual material in interviews can further facilitate a participant's perspective (Barley & Russell, 2018) by video-stimulated recall (Nguyen, McFadden, Tangen, & Beutel, 2013; Pitkänen, 2015).

There were three levels of communication in the data, and two of these were provided by CS:GO. The game offered a text-based chat (TBC) with two modes: all chat (notifying all players) and team chat (notifying team only) as well as an internal voice chat (IVC) that was audible to team only. The latter could be considered a bit impractical as the players had to press a key each time they wished to speak. Accordingly, most players used an external voice chat (EVC) to speak with their in-game friends. In the data, both teams used a Discord channel to speak freely without the need to press a key.[3] During matches when not all team members were present, they got assigned a temporary co-player, in-game often referred to by the participants as a 'random', and these co-players are as a rule not invited to the Discord channel. The EVC was used for most in-game communication within the team, with a few exceptions where the IVC and the TBC were used. Henceforth, only the players that were officially part of the team are referred to as *team members* and players that join them for one match are referred to as *co-players*.

The focus students volunteered to meet up with the researcher (Ståhl) through a teacher and agreed to participate in the study after being informed on what the study entailed. The data consisted of seven matches and four scheduled interviews per team. Initially there were six focus students, however, as part of team 1 (T1), John became part of the study in the last months of the data collection. The focus students (all male, aged 16–18 at the time) recorded and shared their matches regularly with the researcher through a secure file sharing service. The research design was dependent on the students' engagement due to the physical distance between the researcher and participants as we are based in different parts of Finland. Regular meetings, held at their school, functioned as interviews and were recorded. Stimulated recall (Nguyen et al., 2013; Pitkänen, 2015) on relevant sequences from the screen recordings was employed during all interviews apart from the first. Both teams have submitted wins and losses as well as recordings from various maps.

It is impossible as a researcher, to completely avoid influencing the research context, although the participants conduct the data collection. Through comments made by the participants, it becomes evident that the researcher is present. Therefore, the researchers must instead continuously reflect upon the effects of their presence (Sveningsson, 2003). For example, team 2 (T2) discussed whether or not they were allowed to swear and T1 joked about what certain sounds might sound like when the recording was watched on the researcher's computer. However, this model eliminates the physical researcher presence and, hence, minimises feelings of intrusion and invasiveness (Aarsand & Forsberg, 2010). Furthermore, the participants may be less hesitant or guarded, despite the recording as the participants have agency and control over what, how and when they record (Rusk et al., 2012). The research provided the participants with agency through a collaboration with the researchers (Pink, 2013; Russell & Barley, 2020). While the power differential between researcher and active participants was reduced as the students themselves administered the data collection, the design also put further emphasis on team communication and collaboration as the team themselves had to reach a unanimous decision on which recording to send to the researcher. Apart from access to the material they agreed to share, we have very limited insight into these negotiations as they took place outside of the recordings. However, one such negotiation (focused on sharing wins or losses, match 1, T2) was documented and helped us to clarify that both wins and losses were relevant to us. The participants had access to screen recording software through the esports programme; however, not all participants had used it prior to the study. Apart from joyous in-game exclamations when certain unusual sequences were documented; during an interview, one participant pointed out that he now was able to record his own games and, subsequently, posted certain highlights online.

Ethics within Online Fieldwork: Maintaining Participant Integrity

Next, we discuss the research ethical stance that informs the study, as a whole, to be able to present the practical-ethical challenges regarding participant integrity in Sections 'Conducting Online Fieldwork – Active and Passive Participants, Analysing the Data – Gamertags and Anonymity, and Reporting Findings – Responsibility and Transparency'; gaining informed consent from players that became co-observed and defining privacy online; and portraying participants accurately.

Much has been written about how ethics should be managed with guidelines stipulating various conditions such as avoiding harming participants as well as respecting their decisions and autonomy (Murphy & Dingwall, 2001). However, many, like Pink (2013), argue that no approach to ethical conduct should be viewed as superior to others. Many ethnographers advocate developing a reflexive approach to ethnographic work in relation to ethical guidelines and the context (Pink, 2013; Russell & Barley, 2020). Here, steps were taken to avoid intrusion to the students' privacy (Murphy & Dingwall, 2001). Such steps included, using pseudonyms instead of offline names; informing students, parents and teachers of the study's aim and what participation entailed. Further, screen recordings were sent over an encrypted and secure file sharing service whereby all gamertags (the players' in-game names) were altered or removed (see Fig. 1).

Fig. 1.   Screenshot from Recording of T1 Playing Counter Strike: Global Offensive on the Map Called Mirage. Figure Edited in Order to Secure Player Privacy (Both Active and Passive Participants).

Informed consent was not viewed as a singular act but as a (re)negotiation process (Aarsand & Forsberg, 2010; Pink, 2013; Rusk et al., 2012) involving a continuous collaborative process with the focus participants. For example, due to his research expertise in interaction, Dr Fredrik Rusk joined as a co-author during the data collection. The participants were informed of this, and through ongoing consent (Quinton & Reynolds, 2018), they approved of the additional analytical foci that appeared as consequence. Further, the participants were given control of the data (Murphy & Dingwall, 2001) as they volunteered to be part of the study and handled the screen recording software on their personal computers, and thereby, deciding which matches to send to the researchers. They were instructed to send a total of seven matches, including wins and losses and preferably varying maps, otherwise the decision on which matches to send was theirs. Before showing any in-game data to anyone outside the research project, the specific data were double-checked for participant consent. Only data with the consent from all present active participants are shown. The researchers had prior experience of this approach (Paakkari, 2020; Rusk, 2019; Sahlström et al., 2019; Ståhl & Kaiho-virta, 2019) and the participants have given their permission to use the images and quotes for dissemination. Furthermore, in the recordings, there occurred participant discussions on what content was appropriate to record. Accordingly, as researchers, we had the opportunity to clarify our intentions and discuss details of the research design together with participants.

The excerpts have been translated into English by the researchers, except for statements originally in English. The interview excerpts have been translated with a focus on content and readability, and efforts were made to convey the same points stressed by the participants. In terms of detail and nuance, the translation becomes part of the analysis (Hepburn & Bolden, 2012), and we have therefore employed two-line transcripts (see Excerpt 1) for the in-game data; the

```
1 Martin   ((gets killed by opponent wielding P90))
          åh p nitti skaff ett liv
          oh p ninety get a life

2 John     ((laughs))

3 Joni     men köp en nitti o äg honom
          well buy a ninety yourself and own him

4 Martin  Get a life p90 noob

5         Flashbang out!

6 Martin  plz

7 John    toxic
```

Excerpt 1.   EVC/TBC. T1: Match 7, Mirage.

original statements are presented together with an English translation. Readers with an understanding of Swedish and/or Finnish can find the original statements helpful; however, most readers are limited to the researcher's translation of the language used. We have employed our insight into the research context and language used in online gaming contexts when translating into English. Furthermore, the original statements were the ones being analysed, not the translations.

Conducting Online Fieldwork – Active and Passive Participants

During an initial face-to-face meeting with the students that volunteered to participate, the researcher (Ståhl) presented the project. The students were able to ask questions, the consent form was presented and discussed and the students were informed that they could withdraw their initial consent at any time. Further, additional steps were taken to gain continuous informed consent from the participants and to give them as much control of the data collection as possible. The team members not sharing data with the researchers were informed of the research project and given the researchers' contact information. However, the randomly assigned co-players and the opponents were unaware of the game being recorded for research purposes. When streaming online games, the player often informs the other players, prior to start, of the relevant stream channel. Accordingly, we suggested that the participants would copy-paste a short information text, provided by us as researchers, regarding the focus of the study and our contact information for further questions. However, this suggestion was not well received due to the potential negative effect such an approach would have on the participants themselves. As Jesper pointed out in an interview: 'There could be quite a lot of... I think the other team might be kind of toxic if we lose then'. The members of T2 expressed scepticism towards such a practice and T1, although more neutral, did acknowledge the possibility that this might affect their in-game treatment and potentially cause them harm.

Prior to this question, all suggestions by the researcher regarding the research design had been accepted by the participants or at least negotiated around so that a compromise was reached. Thereby, we noted the participants' reluctance and did not insist on such a practice due to participant autonomy. Correspondingly, although the research design was based on informed consent from the participants, a situation where other individuals were unintentionally documented occurred (Pink, 2013). This resulted in a dataset including both active and passive participants (Quinton & Reynolds, 2018). Passive participation, where the participants are unaware of being documented for research purposes, is fairly uncommon in educational research. Both approaches are practised within online research, and both include possibilities and challenges. On one hand, uninformed, or covert, data collection might be considered an intrusion and breach of user privacy (Beneito-Montagut, 2011), and therefore, transparency and informed consent is advocated within netnography

(Kozinets, 2002). One argument for covert ethnographies, conducted without the consent of the participants, is that it can function as a method to access secretive or stigmatised subcultures.

On the other hand, it is also possible to claim that user awareness of being researched can potentially affect the collection of naturalistic data (Sugiura et al., 2017). Furthermore, it can be argued that ethnographers are 'simply observing daily life as it unfolds' (Besnier & Philips, 2017, p. 130) and, therefore, informed consent might be managed in different ways depending on the situation. While covert research has been heavily criticised due to the concealment, Lugosi (2006) argues that few research endeavours are completely overt and transparent. For example, he refrained from using 'ethnography' and used 'writing' rather than 'researching' to describe his work to avoid alienating potential participants, resulting in limited transparency. Like Lugosi (2006) this study highlights the point that there may not be a clear divide between overt and covert research, and that researcher should thus be reflexive regarding concealment within the researched context.

Further, CS:GO is the fourth most streamed online game on Twitch (Webb, 2019), and matches can be seen as a public domain. They are, in other words, available for research without informed consent, as long as the participants are not identifiable or in any way harmed by the research (Sugiura et al., 2017; Sveningsson, 2003). In a similar situation, Beneito-Montagut (2011) noted that some individuals, through their interaction with the participants, became co-observed and argued that the ethical issues are relatively small, compared to the focus participants who shared more personal interactions through the EVC (see, e.g. 'Reporting Findings – Responsibility and Transparency'). In other words, the activity of the co-observed individuals not being the analytical focus 'but rather some by-product of observing the sample' (Beneito-Montagut, 2011, p. 730); thus different types of participants may require varying ethical procedures within the same research study.

Ultimately, the issue regarding informed consent depends on the research focus. The students participating in the study were our analytic focus, and we decided to respect their wishes and consider random co-players and opponents as passive participants. For example, in Ståhl and Rusk (2020), two active participants were the focus of the analysis and, accordingly, passive participants were only present in the analysis in relevant interactions with the active participants. Since they were not within the research focus, we decided not to gather informed consent from the passive participants. However, such an approach increases the demand on protecting their privacy. To ensure the passive participants' integrity was protected, we needed to increase anonymity and privacy measures for them. Apart from in-game activities, the only information we had about the passive participants were their gamertags and icons (developed or chosen by them). Their gamertags have been either removed or changed and, although they are tiny and have poor resolution, all icons with potentially identifiable features have been edited.

Analysing the Data – Gamertags and Anonymity

When conducting research online, there are two levels of participant anonymity to consider; protecting their offline and online identities (Markham, 2018; Quinton & Reynolds, 2018). Beneito-Montagut (2011) advocates removing all personal information, such as usernames to guarantee participant anonymity. Such an approach can be problematic, for example, in stations like removing a blogger's username and quoting content from their blog with the text being the blogger's intellectual property (Sugiura et al., 2017). Although there might be no, or little, correspondence between the offline and the online identity, there is a risk that the researcher offers enough information so that a connection can be made. While the usernames on Twitter, also known as Twitter handles, can be anonymised, this might not be sufficient to ensure participant integrity due to searchability. Quinton and Reynolds (2018) noted that if the researchers report the Tweet word for word in their research, a reader might find the original post with a simple search and reveal the online identity of the participant. If the research focus allows the researcher to change words so that the central meaning remains and lowers the chance to find the original post by an online search, it would be advisable to do so regarding participant anonymity (Quinton & Reynolds, 2018). However, all data are not possible to summarise or alter without losing its meaning (Sugiura et al., 2017), thereby resulting in a conflict between participant anonymity and researcher transparency and credibility – an issue that this research also tussled with. Focusing on tools for identity (co)construction, we noted the gamertags as one such tool, since they are the players' chosen in-game names. For an esports player, the gamertag can be considered their brand. However, the players did not necessarily consider their gamertags as such. During an interview William stated that they, as esports players, 'are not quite that good yet'. While Jesper in the other team did consider his gamertag his trademark, he further noted that it was only his friends who could identify him by his gamertag (I2, T2, 2017). However, in the analysis, the issue of anonymising the gamertag became evident. The focus students stated that if their gamertags were visible during gameplay, that was fine; however, they would prefer their gamertags not to be associated with discussions on in-game swearing and then preferred it to be anonymised. We decided to anonymise the gamertags, since a mixed approach would have been difficult to maintain.

When discussing alternative pseudonyms, we noticed different interpretations of the original gamertags. Rusk interpreted one gamertag as a noun and suggested a synonym based on that, whereas Ståhl interpreted the gamertag as an adjective and suggested a synonym in line with that. Editing the gamertags would then create an issue when analysing the data. If we analysed the edited version, then edited words would affect the results, since we as researchers might intentionally or unintentionally change the gamertags to align with a certain result. Analysing the original version but reporting the edited version would result in limited transparency. Usernames are chosen by the participants and are an important data source; therefore, changing the username might result in loss of meaning as the changed name does not address the same joke, allusion or association. If the research focuses on self-presentation online, changing the usernames 'would seriously affect the authenticity of data and thereby the quality of research' (Sveningsson, 2003, p. 53). Any anonymous name given to the participants of this study needed to thus reflect the context and nature of the original username's intent in order to maintain data authenticity.

To further complicate the matter, the vocational school in question is the only Swedish-speaking vocational school in Finland offering an esports programme. Although not mentioned explicitly named in here, the collaboration between the researchers and school has had some publicity on a national level. Therefore, it would be fairly low hanging fruit in terms of detective work to establish which school the students attended. A simple online search on the school name and the students' gamertags provides results from different competitions and tournaments. As these reports often contain photos of the participants, their names and personal information, we decided that including the original gamertags was not an option regarding participant integrity.

We then considered discussing the original gamertags without publishing them. However, the additional information needed to explain the allusion or joke (Sveningsson, 2003), without providing the gamertags, might be enough for a reader to identify the original gamertag, especially when combined with transcripts of in-game data or interviews. For example, the beverage associated with Joni's gamertag was not his motivation for choosing it. Instead, it was his interest for a certain animal group that was the motivating factor. Providing any more information than this might be enough to identify his gamertag, but any further analysis based on such a vague description would have limited credibility. Accordingly, any results reported in such a manner would have limited credibility and be too vague to be relevant. We decided to leave this out of the analysis and subsequent dissemination (Ståhl & Rusk, 2020).

Reporting Findings – Responsibility and Transparency

It can be argued that the sole justification, ethically and professionally, for collecting any data is to share the findings by publishing them (Swedish Research Council, 2017). As responsible researchers we should not only share these findings within academia but also share the implications with society (Quinton & Reynolds, 2018). When analysing the data and reporting findings, the researchers should, according to Quinton and Reynolds (2018), bear participant vulnerability in mind and represent them as accurately as possible. The participants, in our study, are not a particularly vulnerable group. However, there are some factors that carry weight in terms of vulnerability. Firstly, most participants were minors (under 18, but over 15 which in Finland is the age limit for giving research consent) at the start of the research project. Secondly, as video games remain a stigmatised hobby (see, e.g. van Rooij et al., 2018), reporting research findings might result in negative attitudes from the general public. Thirdly, and finally, access to the participants' own screens (Paakkari, 2020) and private conversations with their closest teammates is highly personal data and provided the researchers access to discussions otherwise solely meant for themselves and their situationally chosen friends.

In the data, we noted that the participants, as well as randomly assigned co-players and opponents, used offensive language (Ståhl & Rusk, 2020). In fact, offensive language is used frequently enough to be considered standard 'gamer lingo' (Pulos, 2013) or even a 'game within the game' (Vossen, 2018). Here, it is exemplified with the seventh and final match submitted by T1 that they eventually end up losing despite being a close call (see Excerpt 1). Early in the game, the opponents are currently leading the game with five won rounds to T1's four. Martin's distaste for the submachine gun P90 and the players using it was clear as he, when killed by an opponent wielding 'a fucking P90', questioned 'What am I going to do? P90 is so gay ass'. His distaste presumably stems from the fact that P90 is a low risk weapon that fires multiple bullets without affecting recoil that much. Martin referred to these weapons as 'noob weapons' (Excerpt 1), indicating that these require limited in-game skill; echoing the notion that some choices might distort the image of competitive gaming as a level playing field (Harper, 2013).[4] The in-game comments mentioned above were uttered in the EVC and therefore never reached the opponent in question. The majority of the offensive language was used in and through the EVC and, therefore, never reached anyone outside the team. Excerpt 1 covers a situation later in the same match when T1 is currently leading (14 won rounds to the opponents 12) and regarding the same opponent. However, the noob comment is uncharacteristically stated towards the opponent so that they can read it (see Excerpt 1, cursive, lines 4 and 6). Further, when such language was directed at players outside of the team, there were also instances where some team members addressed the toxic language use (see Excerpt 1, line 7).

Offensive language appears to be common in online games and functions as a rapid form of communication and as part of (co)constructing player identity (Kiuorti, 2019). The offensive language was not consistently present, albeit present enough to be relevant to report in the findings. Additionally, the language used in the data is at times misogynistic and homophobic; a language use that is in conflict with societal and educational values, as well as our personal values. We noted that technomasculinity (Johnson, 2018) was the hegemonic masculinity (Connell, 2005) within online gaming, which can explain why players feel justified expressing such language and maintaining a power structure where they are on top (Ståhl & Rusk, 2020). One can question if an academic paper is the correct forum for explicitly presenting this kind of language use. However, ethnography has a long history of employing transcripts of both speech and non-verbal behaviour verbatim (Hammersley & Atkinson, 2007) to provide the reader with insight into the context.

When we have presented our work in progress and shared different versions of the manuscript in diverse academic contexts, we were offered commentary and suggestions by fellow academics who were appalled by the language used in the data. Most of these colleagues were probably surprised by how offensive the 'gamer lingo' actually was, since they have limited insight into (online) games. However, putting emphasis solely on the offensiveness of the language used by the participants and emphasising those specific data sections would distort our findings and could potentially harm the participants. The setting and context would not be portrayed in an ethically responsible manner (Murphy, 2014; Quinton & Reynolds, 2018). In other words, it would only reflect a partial understanding of the data and the participants' perspective but might also provide an inaccurate participant representation.

During one interview and a discussion regarding female players in general, Martin mentioned the generally negative attitude in CS:GO against players clearly stating to be female, for example, by gamertags such as 'grl gamer'. He mentioned that 'they usually get a lot of crap'. He also remembered an instance where a co-player commented that the match was as good as lost, since they had a female player on the team: 'Someone immediately wrote "gg there is a girl in our team"'. He further said that: 'I don't give a damn if you're a girl. If you are good at the game, there should be nothing stopping you. That (female players are not as good as male) is just a stereotype'. It is fair to note that the participants did not express any misogynistic opinions during the multiple interviews. Rather, they stressed that anyone should be able to play if they want to and are good enough. However, there is always the possibility that they believed that this was what the present (female) researcher wanted to hear.

Research on new digital phenomena tends to gain public interest from various stakeholders (Quinton & Reynolds, 2018), which puts further emphasis on representing the studied phenomena and contexts as fairly as possible. Bennerstedt (2013) noted a tendency for normative approaches to game research where the results reflected what the researchers set out to find. In line with Bennerstedt et al. (2012), we have noted a polarised public discussion regarding video games; portraying them as either the road to ruin or the saviour of our classrooms, which is also reflected in academia (see, e.g. the discussion regarding WHO establishing a diagnosis called 'gaming disorder' in van Rooij et al., 2018). In our case, we were provided access to students at the vocational school with an esports programme through one involved teacher. The esports programme is dependent on external funding, and research findings reflecting positive traits of the data would be beneficial for the programme's future funding applications. The data include aspects, such as collaboration, companionship and students employing digital competencies; traits that highlight benefits of an esports programme. Presenting solely the results that reflect the data in a positive manner would provide a skewed picture of the contexts and settings and not align with a non-normative, descriptive, approach. We do not want to shove the offensive language use under the rug, neither do we want to emphasise it. Instead, we strive to portray the culture, setting(s) and context(s) as they are oriented to from a participant's perspective, and report the findings in an ethically, scientifically responsible and transparent manner. We as researchers have a moral challenge, and responsibility, to become better at seeing how our research is interwoven in larger structures of meaning (Silverstone, 2007; referred to by Markham, 2018, p. 664). In the case of offensive language use, the results have been shared with the school and have later been referred to by the teacher coordinating the programme when they needed resources to make the programme more inclusive. Accordingly, we maintain that an esports programme within education is a great forum for addressing the offensive language use within online games and can help to further professionalise esports and, possibly, change the culture from within (Ståhl & Rusk, 2020).

It is also worth mentioning our own, possible, bias as researchers on a gamer context. Neither researcher is actively playing CS:GO. However, both identify as gamers and have previous experience of gamer lingo in online gaming contexts. We are aware that our experiences might make us 'blind' to the severity of the offensive language. However, it can also be argued that our experiences can result in an insider understanding of gamer lingo in a similar practice to that in the data. Ultimately, our integrity as researchers to fairly represent the settings, contexts and phenomena we study (Quinton & Reynolds, 2018), outweighs our own and the stakeholder's interests.

Discussion

The following discussion begins with a short summary of the practical-ethical challenges on maintaining participant integrity presented in this chapter. Then, we discuss these challenges in relation to both the research context and managing research ethics in situ together with the participants. We follow up the discussion with some concluding remarks.

The practical-ethical challenges on maintaining participant integrity presented in this chapter are (1) gaining informed consent from players that became co-observed, (2) defining privacy online and (3) portraying participants accurately. In this study, research ethics was managed *in situ together with the participants* by understanding informed consent not as a singular act but as a (re) negotiation process (Aarsand & Forsberg, 2010; Pink, 2013; Rusk et al., 2012). All of the practical-ethical challenges were (re)negotiated together with the participants, to be able to find the best solution for each of them. Some negotiations were not necessarily specific to the online context, such as double-checking all material with the participants prior to publication. However, such a stance was helpful when online-specific issues occurred. For example, the participants found that informing the co-observed random co-players and opponents of the study might cause them harm, which resulted in a differentiation between active and passive participants (Quinton & Reynolds, 2018). By not applying a 'one size fits all'-approach, but rather a reflective stance regarding ethical considerations (Hammersley & Atkinson, 2007; Pink, 2013), we consider the participants as two different groups that need to be considered separately. When ethics are managed in situ (Russell & Barley, 2020), the ethnographer might find it easier to ensure that the interests and privacy of all participants are considered through this more dynamic research design.

The (re)negotiation process also involves the *research context*, especially as the online context adds an additional layer of personal information for the researcher to handle. Depending on the focus, the practices of handling participant online identities vary, from removing all personal information (Beneito-Montagut, 2011) or slightly editing the content (Quinton & Reynolds, 2018), to publishing usernames due to content being a participant's intellectual property (Sugiura et al., 2017). As the player's chosen in-game name, gamertags are part of the in-game experience, but due to the participants' online visibility, we could not report them as such. However, editing the gamertags might have resulted in loss of meaning and affected the authenticity of data and quality of the research, especially in terms of researcher transparency (Besnier & Philips, 2017). We decided to prioritise participant integrity, since gamertags or usernames have a similar function in CS:GO as in other online games and contexts (Sveningsson, 2003). Further, when analysing offensive language, we noted that tech-nomasculinity (Johnson, 2018) is the hegemonic masculinity (Connell, 2005) within online gaming, which can explain why some players feel justified using certain language and maintaining a power structure where they are 'on top'. As this is true for the online game community as a whole, stressing this behaviour solely among the participants would be unjust, irresponsible and unproductive for the larger discussion of the issue. In vilifying our participants we would not have fairly represented the phenomena we studied (Quinton & Reynolds, 2018). This does not mean that we condone using homophobic, misogynistic and offensive language, but we need to describe the context transparently and responsibly for both the reader and the participants. By discussing our findings in relation to current research on online games, we can illuminate the larger structures at work. By doing so, we can question that offensive language or 'gamer lingo' (Pulos, 2013) is taken for granted in online games and highlight the segregation that technomasculinity enables, while also showing that there are voices in the gaming community that question this language use. Accordingly, we maintain (Ståhl & Rusk, 2020) that an esports programme within education is a great forum for addressing the offensive language use within online games from within. There were competing power differentials and stakeholder interests, especially regarding the offensive language. Despite them, we have tried to convey the complexity of the data as accurately as possible, without taking sides and while also considering the participants' vulnerability.

Concluding Remarks

The research design provided the participants with agency through collaboration with the researchers. While the power differential between researcher and active participants was reduced as the students themselves administered the data collection, the design also put further emphasis on team communication and collaboration as the teams themselves had to reach a unanimous decision on which recording to send to the researcher. Apart from access to the material they agreed to share with us, we have very limited insight into these negotiations as they took place outside of the recordings and were not presented as a problem during the interviews. Future research endeavours with a similar design would benefit from further documentation on these negotiations and discussions regarding how power differential between participants might affect data collection.

While we recognise and welcome further discussion on the topic of ethically sound research, we argue that, for a study like the one presented here, a fixed set of rules for conducting research online might be counterproductive. Instead, informed consent can be understood as an ongoing process that is part of an iterative-inductive approach that emphasises the importance of addressing and resolving ethical aspects in situ, at each stage of the process and together with the participants. A laboriously developed ethically informed stance towards data generation will thus be necessary, as will continuous dialogue between researchers and participants – on the focus and purpose of data collection. In regard to evolving online environments and tools, the potential for organising education is constantly changing. Future research endeavours that aim to better understand the impact of this shift might include online fieldwork, resulting in challenges that are not necessarily covered by current ethical guidelines. Ultimately, we do hope that by adding this chapter to the growing number of texts on conducting research online, we will contribute in forming reflective ethical stances that can adapt to the wide variety of online contexts that are already part of our everyday lives.

Acknowledgements

Initially, we wish to thank the participants that willingly shared highly personal data with us so that we as researchers better could understand what online gaming was to them! We wish to thank the Swedish Cultural Foundation in Finland, Victoriastiftelsen, Stiftelsen för Åbo Akademi and Högskolestiftelsen i Österbotten for research funding and travel expenses on behalf of Ståhl during the process of this chapter. We also wish to thank Inga, Valdemar, Anna-Lisa och Inga-Brita Westbergsfond for covering travel expenses during the data collection phase.

Notes

1. Esports or electronic sports is an organised format of competitive gameplay.
2. An interactive forum for live streaming of primarily playing online games.
3. Free software often used for voice chat in addition to online games as it allows for private channels.
4. A noob (or n00b) is a new player displaying no willingness to change or listen to senior players' advice.

References

Aarsand, P., & Forsberg, L. (2010). Producing children's corporeal privacy: Ethnographic video recording as material-discursive practice. *Qualitative Research, 10*(2), 249–268. doi:10.1177/1468794109356744
Barley, R., & Russell, L. (2018). Participatory visual methods: Exploring young people's identities, hopes and feelings. *Ethnography and Education, 14*(2), 223–241. doi:10.1080/17457823.2018.1441041

Beaulieu, A. (2004). Mediating ethnography: Objectivity and the making of ethnographies of the internet. *Social Epistemology*, *18*(2–3), 139–163. doi:10.1080/0269172042000249264

Beneito-Montagut, R. (2011). Ethnography goes online: Towards a user-centred methodology to research interpersonal communication on the internet. *Qualitative Research*, *11*(6), 716–735. doi:10.1177/1468794111413368

Bennerstedt, U. (2013). *Knowledge at play. Studies of games as members' matters.* Doctoral thesis, University of Gothenburg. Retreived from https://gupea.ub.gu.se/handle/2077/32674

Bennerstedt, U., Ivarsson, J., & Linderoth, J. (2012). How gamers manage aggression: Situating skills in collaborative computer games. *Journal of Computer-Supported Collaborative Learning*, *7*(1), 43–61. doi:10.1007/s11412-011-9136-6

Besnier, N., & Philips, S. U. (2017). Ethnographic methods for language and gender research. In S. Ehrlich, M. Meyerhoff, & J. Holmes (Eds.), *The handbook of language, gender and sexuality* (2nd ed., pp. 123–140). Hoboken, NJ: Wiley Blackwell.

Cohen, L., Manion, K., & Morrison, L. (2000). *Research methods in education* (5th ed.). London and New York: Routledge.

Connell, R. W. (2005). *Masculinities.* Cambridge: Polity.

Geertz, C. (1973). *The interpretation of cultures.* New York, NY: Basic Books.

Hammersley, M. (2006). Ethnography: Problems and prospects. *Ethnography and Education*, *1*(1), 3–14.

Hammersley, M. (2018). What is ethnography? Can it survive? Should it? *Ethnography and Education*, *13*(1), 1–17. doi:10.1080/17457823.2017.1298458

Hammersley, M., & Atkinson, P. (2007). *Ethnography. Principles in practice* (3rd ed.). London and New York, NY: Routledge.

Harper, T. (2013). *The culture of digital fighting games: Performance and practice.* London and New York: Routledge.

Hepburn, A., & Bolden, G. B. (2012). The conversation analytic approach to transcription. In J. Sidnell & T. Stivers (Eds.), *The handbook of conversation analysis* (pp. 57–76). Oxford: Wiley-Blackwell.

Johnson, R. (2018). Technomasculinity and its influence in video game production. In N. Taylor & G. Voorhees (Eds.), *Masculinities at play* (pp. 249–262). Cham: Springer Nature Switzerland.

Karpf, D. (2012). Social science research methods in internet time. *Information, Communication & Society*, *15*(5), 639–661. doi:10.1080/1369118X.2012.665468

Kinnunen, J., Lilja, P., & Mäyrä, K. (2018). Pelaajabarometri 2018. Monimuotoistuva mobiilipelaaminen [Player barometers 2018. Mobile play in many forms]. TRIM research reports, 28.

Kiuorti, E. (2019). 'Shut the fuck up re! 1 plant the bomb fast!' Reconstructing language and identity in first-person shooter games. In A. Ensslin & I. Balteiro (Eds.), *Approaches to videogame discourse: Lexis, interaction, textuality* (pp. 157–177). New York, NY: Bloomsbury Academic.

Kozinets, R. V. (2002). The field behind the screen: Using netnography for marketing research in online communities. *Journal of Marketing Research*, *39*(1), 61–72.

Lugosi, P. (2006). Between overt and covert research: Concealment and disclosure in an ethnographic study of commercial hospitality. *Qualitative Inquiry*, *12*(3), 541–561.

Mantello, P. (2017). Military shooter video games and the ontopolitics of derivative wars and arms culture. *The American Journal of Economics and Sociology, 76*(2), 483–521. doi:10.1111/ajes.12184

Markham, A. N. (2018). Ethnography in the digital internet era. From fields to flows, descriptions to interventions. In N. K. Denzin & Y. S. Lincoln (Eds.), *The SAGE handbook of qualitative research* (5th ed., pp. 650–668). Thousand Oaks, CA: SAGE.

Markham, A., & Buchanan, E. (2012). Ethical decision-making and internet research 2.0: Recommendations from the AOIR ethics working committee. Retrieved from http://aoir.org/reports/ethics2.pdf. Accessed on March 23, 2019.

Monge, C. K., & O'Brien, T. C. (2021). Effects of individual toxic behavior on team performance in league of legends. *Media Psychology*, 1–23. doi:10.1080/15213269.2020.1868322

Murphy, P. N. (2014). Locating media ethnography. In V. Nightingale (Ed.), *The handbook of media audiences* (pp. 380–401). Sussex: Wiley Blackwell.

Murphy, E., & Dingwall, R. (2001). The ethics of ethnography. In P. Atkinson, A. Coffey, S. Delamont, J. Lofland, & L. Lofland (Eds.), *Handbook of ethnography* (pp. 339–351). London: Sage.

Nguyen, N. T., McFadden, A., Tangen, D., & Beutel, D. (2013). Video-stimulated recall interviews in qualitative research. In Proceedings of the Australian association for research in education annual conference, Adelaide, South Australia (pp. 1–10).

Paakkari, A. (2020). *Entangled devices. An ethnographic study of students, mobile phones and capitalism.* Doctoral thesis, University of Helsinki.

Parker-Jenkins, M. (2018). Problematising ethnography and case study: Reflections on using ethnographic techniques and researcher positioning. *Ethnography and Education, 13*(1), 18–33. doi:10.1080/17457823.2016.1253028

Pink, S. (2013). *Doing visual ethnography.* London: Sage.

Pink, S., Horst, H., Postill, J., Hjorth, L., & Tacchi, J. (2016). *Digital ethnography: Principles and practice.* Los Angeles, CA: Sage.

Pitkänen, J. (2015). Studying thoughts: Stimulated recall as a game research method. In P. Lankoski & S. Björk (Eds.), *Game research methods* (pp. 117–132). Pittsburgh, PA: ETC Press.

Pole, C., & Morrison, M. (2003). *Ethnography for education.* Berkshire: McGraw-Hill Education.

Pulos, A. (2013). Confronting heteronormativity in online games: A critical discourse analysis of LGBTQ sexuality in World of Warcraft. *Games and Culture, 8*(2), 77–97. doi:10.1177/1555412013478688

Quinton, S., & Reynolds, N. (2018). *Understanding research in the digital age.* London: Sage.

Rambusch, J., Jakobsson, P., & Pargman, D. (2007). Exploring e-sports: A case study of gameplay in Counter-Strike. In B. Akira (Ed.), *Situated play. Proceedings of the 3rd digital games research association international conference* (pp. 157–164). Tokyo: Digital Games Research Association (DiGRA).

Ratan, R. A., Taylor, N., Hogan, J., Kennedy, T., & Williams, D. (2015). Stand by your man: An examination of gender disparity in league of legends. *Games and Culture, 10*(5), 438–462. doi:10.1177/1555412014567228

Van Rooij, A. J., Ferguson, C. J., Colder Carras, M., Kardefelt-Winther, D., Shi, J., Aarseth, E., ... Przybylski, A. K. (2018). A weak scientific basis for gaming disorder: Let us err on the side of caution. *Journal of Behavioral Addictions, 7*(1), 1–9. doi:10.1556/2006.7.2018.19

Rusk, F. (2019). Digitally mediated interaction as a resource for co-constructing multilingual identities in classrooms. *Learning, Culture and Social Interaction, 21*, 179–193. doi:10.1016/j.lcsi.2019.03.005

Rusk, F., Pörn, M., Sahlström, F., & Slotte-Lüttge, A. (2012). Everything, everywhere, all the time: Advantages and challenges in the use of extensive video recordings of children. In P. Salo (Ed.), *The fourth qualitative research conference* (pp. 67–78). Vaasa: Åbo Akademi University.

Rusk, F., & Ståhl, M. (2020). A CA perspective on kills and deaths in Counter-Strike: Global offensive video game play. *Social Interaction. Video Based Studies of Human Sociality, 3*(2). doi:10.7146/si.v3i2.117066

Russell, L., & Barley, R. (2020). Ethnography, ethics and ownership of data. *Ethnography, 21*(1), 5–25. doi:10.1177/1466138119859386

Ruvalcaba, O., Shulze, J., Kim, A., Berzenski, S. R., & Otten, M. P. (2018). Women's experiences in eSports: Gendered differences in peer and spectator feedback during competitive video game play. *Journal of Sport and Social Issues, 42*(4), 295–311.

Sahlström, F., Tanner, M., & Olin-Scheller, C. (2019). Smartphones in classrooms: Reading, writing and talking in rapidly changing educational spaces. *Learning, Culture and Social Interaction, 22*, 1–5. doi:10.1016/j.lcsi.2019.100319

Scwandt, T., & Gates, E. F. (2018). Case study methodology. In N. K. Denzin & Y. S. Lincoln (Eds.), *The SAGE handbook of qualitative research* (5th ed., pp. 650–668). Thousand Oaks, CA: SAGE.

Shumar, W., & Madison, N. (2013). Ethnography in a virtual world. *Ethnography and Education, 8*(2), 255–272. doi:10.1080/17457823.2013.792513

Sicart, M. (2013). *Beyond choices. The design of ethical gameplay.* Cambridge, MA: The MIT Press.

Sierra Entertainment & Valve Corporation. (1998). *Half-life.* Bellevue, WA: Valve Corporation.

Silverstone, R. (2007). *Media and morality: On the rise of the mediapolis.* Cambridge: Polity.

Spilioti, T., & Tagg, C. (2017). The ethics of online research methods in applied linguistics: Challenges, opportunities, and directions in ethical decision-making. *Applied Linguistics Review, 8*(2–3), 163–167. doi:10.1515/applirev-2016-1033

Ståhl, M., & Kaihovirta, H. (2019). Exploring visual communication and competencies through interaction with images in social media. *Learning, Culture and Social Interaction, 21*, 250–266. doi:10.1016/j.lcsi.2019.03.003

Ståhl, M., & Rusk, F. (2020). Player customisation, competence and team discourse: Exploring player identity (co)construction in Counter-Strike: Global offensive. *Game Studies, 20*(4).

Sugiura, L., Wiles, R., & Pope, C. (2017). Ethical challenges in online research: Public/private perceptions. *Research Ethics, 13*(3–4), 184–199. doi:10.1177/1747016116650720

Sveningsson, M. (2003). Ethics in internet ethnography. *International Journal of Global Information Management, 11*(3), 3484–3498. doi:10.4018/9781599049373.ch233

Swedish Research Council. (2017). Good research practice. Retrieved from https://www.vr.se/download/18.5639980c162791bbfe697882/1555334908942/Good-Research-Practice_VR_2017.pdf. Accessed on March 26, 2020.

Taylor, T. L. (2006/2009). *Play between worlds. Exploring online game culture.* Cambridge, MA: The MIT Press.

Taylor, N. (2016). Play to the camera: Video ethnography, spectatorship, and e-sports. *Convergence: The International Journal of Research into New Media Technologies*, 22(2), 115–130. doi:10.1177/1354856515580282

Valve Corporation & Hidden Path Entertainment. (2012). *Counter-Strike: Global offensive.* Bellevue, WA: Valve Corporation.

Valve Corporation. (2000). *Counter-Strike.* Bellevue, WA: Valve Corporation.

Vossen, E. (2018). The magic circle and consent in gaming practices. In K. L. Gray, G. Voorhees, & E. Vossen (Eds.), *Feminism in play* (pp. 205–220). Cham: Palgrave Macmillan.

Webb, K. (2019). The 10 most popular games on Twitch. *Business Insider.* Retrieved from https://www.businessinsider.com/top-twitch-games-by-hours-watched-fortnite-lol-gta-v-2019-11?r=US&IR=T#5-grand-theft-auto-v-3689-million-hours-watched-6. Accessed on January 21, 2020.

Chapter 7

Adapting Ethnographic Methods in Light of the COVID-19 Pandemic: Scottish Country Dancing

Yang Zhao

Abstract

This chapter discusses the differences between face-to-face and online eth-nographies of Scottish Country Dancing. It draws on fieldwork conducted firstly in Lyon in 2017 and subsequently in Edinburgh in 2017–2018, with further fieldwork in Edinburgh, due to the global pandemic, now taking place online. Online Scottish Country Dancing is challenging, especially given that this social dancing requires a partner and space. Due to the pandemic, how and why individuals do online dancing has shifted because people can now link in and across different locations. As a researcher as well as a dancer, my current project utilises blended ethnography, including textual analysis, fieldnotes, participant observations, interviews and surveys. Conducting online ethnographic practices raises specific ethical consider-ations and challenges, most notably concerning who is being observed and whether the participants are aware of being observed. This chapter addresses how the research aims to adapt ethnography from face-to-face fieldwork to online situations, in response to the impact of COVID-19 and associated ethical challenges.

Keywords: Scottish country dancing; online teaching; blended ethnography; online ethnography; COVID-19; lurking

Introduction

This chapter discusses differences between face-to-face fieldwork and online ethnography, using as examples my previous Choreomundus research (2016–2018) and the dance ethnography for my PhD (ongoing).[1] Both focus on Scottish Country Dancing (SCD), and both are linked to the Royal Scottish

Ethics, Ethnography and Education, 109–127
Copyright © 2022 Yang Zhao
Published under exclusive licence by Emerald Publishing Limited
doi:10.1108/S1529-210X20220000019007

Country Dance Society (RSCDS). Before the pandemic that led to lockdown in the United Kingdom in March 2020, people hardly ever did group social dancing classes online because it presents challenges in relation to space limitation, technology and group participation. Since the pandemic began, some people started doing SCD online. Although some dropped out for various reasons, weekly online SCD classes have continued. Consequently, it is important to explore the ethical considerations for my research that has shifted from face-to-face to online during, and because of, the pandemic. Moreover, although the pandemic has greatly increased the extent to which people conduct their lives online, life in a networked world has already had the effect of blurring boundaries between online and offline (Tummons, 2020). This means that we should not construct false dichotomies between the physical and the virtual, but should rather seek methodologies that can move fluidly between these contexts. However, this can present challenges in terms of ethical considerations and procedures for obtaining ethical approval.

A distinctive feature of SCD is its international reach, with over 12,000 members as reported at the 2019 RSCDS AGM (according to statistics shown at the RSCDS Autumn Gathering on 2nd November 2019 in Perth, Scotland). The RSCDS branches and affiliated groups work locally to organise and offer SCD courses, and some groups/branches offer highland dancing, Cèilidh dancing and one-off workshops. The RSCDS has 161 branches and over 300 affiliated groups throughout the world.

I started doing Scottish dancing in Edinburgh in autumn 2015. In my initial research in 2016, I explored how people participate in SCD in a non-native community in Lyon and a native community in Edinburgh. Fieldwork was conducted in Lyon, with weekly/fortnightly visits to the RSCDS Lyon (January–June 2017) and in Edinburgh, with visits to RSCDS Edinburgh and other SCD groups (Easter 2017; June – July and August – September 2017, and early May 2018). In autumn 2018, I carried out a pilot study for my PhD in the RSCDS Edinburgh with weekly SCD classes. In February 2020, I carried out fieldwork in the RSCDS in Edinburgh. In 2021, I decided to work with a Scottish group (henceforth the B group) that went online after the pandemic started, where dancers are not limited to UK-based participants. Before Covid, this group, like the Edinburgh Branch, only held face-to-face classes but after the pandemic some of the members started doing online SCD classes on a weekly basis. As well as people's engagement in both the dance classes and the society, I also aim to explore their motivation to participate in SCD and the development and values of the RSCDS. The project could perhaps also shed light on the use of ethnography in social dancing educational settings.

As a result of the pandemic, my research will comprise face-to-face and online fieldwork, both of which include SCD classes and chats as well as meetings, where Board members and managers give summaries of activities in the previous year and discuss plans and ongoing projects, and present displays/streams and music/ dance demonstrations and videos. Dancers' chats/online posts will also be observed, if individuals give me consent to observe them. My online fieldwork has not officially started yet because I have only recently changed the research design to online, and it has not at the time of writing (June 2021) been approved by the

Ethics Committee. In order to answer the questions that offline ethnography alone cannot explain, a blended ethnography has been designed. However, online ethnography raises ethical considerations and challenges, such as who is observed and whether the participants are aware of being observed within a virtual setting. To do this, the concept of 'lurking' in an online field will be problematised as well as the need to be flexible and able to adapt to changing circumstances. While as a methodology ethnography is well placed to respond to ethics as they emerge *in situ* the 'one-size-fits-all' approach implemented by university ethics review boards is not as responsive. These tensions will be explored in this chapter.

Face-to-Face Fieldwork in Lyon and Edinburgh in 2017–2018

The RSCDS Lyon branch was established in 1986. It is located in the centre of Lyon, and classes take place in a school activity room, spacious enough for around 20 people who dance there. The group was composed of around 10 women and around five men; most people were French, only one or two British, one American and one Japanese, and I was also a participant in 2017/2018: I attended the Friday night Beginners and Intermediate classes as well as one-off SCD weekends when visiting dancers from other countries would stay with the Lyon Branch members. In Edinburgh, there is more than one Scottish dance society that actively puts on dances, and the same people often attend different meetings. A large number of participants are British, with many more men and university students than other RSCDS branches/groups such as Lyon. Two societies held dance events during the summer holidays, and I conducted fieldwork (interviews and/or observations) during these. I did not film dance classes: this would have meant that the teacher(s) and dancers would not feel relaxed, and the participants would be less likely to approve the fieldwork. However, if others were filming (especially the organisers and attendees), this problem was solved. For example, sometimes at balls in Edinburgh, several people were filming, and so it was not strange that I was also doing so. Fieldnotes were rewritten soon after each dance and later analysed. For reasons that will now be outlined, I drew on a combination of data sources (I also used questionnaires in order to construct basic information about dancers and their dance experiences).

Textual Analysis

The texts in the project were mostly SCD films and related documents created by myself or by others. According to Bernard (2011), artefacts, images, behaviours and events are all texts that may be studied raw or may be coded for textual analysis. Flyers are secondary resources that provide some basic information on dance events. RSCDS Lyon Branch flyers, including simple dance sequences, were printed before dance events. Scottish dance societies in Edinburgh sometimes also print or post flyers online to promote dance events. Some dance programmes can also be found online. I also used photos and videos to analyse dance and people. Pictures taken before or during the dance classes and/or events showed the dance environments. Some videos and pictures were posted on the Branch website, and dance class programmes in soft and hard copies were available on the events registration website, in emails and at the dance venues. I watched the videos many times and identified some interactions on the dance floor that I may not have noticed when I was there. I went through several films looking at their timeline to watch people's interactions and then listed all relevant facial expressions and body movements.

Participant Observation

Some participant observations were conducted with the agreement of the hosts (direct observation was not normally allowed by host dance teachers in Lyon). Unlike online research, the participants were able to meet me face-to-face, which meant that I could establish a personal relationship with them. I informed the dancers that I was working as a dancer and researcher, and every Lyon Branch member who attended weekly classes was notified of my research by the Branch in emails/updates to their members. Moreover, the Branch leaders announced my research and introduced me verbally to everyone who attended weekly classes. In Edinburgh, a similar process was followed, and I emailed the SCD groups beforehand so they knew who I was when I attended the dance events/classes. Sometimes other Edinburgh dancers and teachers promoted my research and asked others if they could help by participating in interviews and/or question-naires. The fieldnotes about dance instructions and people's interactions were written briefly during the break or after dance classes, but people's non-verbal behaviour and social interactions were also recorded in detail in a small notebook. Moreover, in order to record people's interactions and distinguish individuals, I also noted individuals' dress, appearance and behaviour, for example, how many times he or she danced with me during the session. I expanded my jottings to fieldnotes after the dance classes as soon I could, as Hammersley and Atkinson (2019) suggest.

In my experience of SCD it is important to participate, because it is very unusual for someone to observe the dance without participating, and to do so would risk disrupting the dynamic. Indeed, ethnographers should try to reduce their effect on a community and not be obvious, for example, using a notebook that is smaller than 7 inches may not attract much attention or highlight that you are actually making observations (Schensul & LeCompte, 2019). In SCD classes in Edinburgh in 2016 and in Lyon in 2017, I hardly ever saw people sitting without dancing. Therefore, when I realised that the dancers might not feel comfortable, I stopped direct observations and making notes, but joined in the dancing. During breaks or after events, I quickly wrote my notes based on memory. This intuitive response to the dancers' reactions to my presence as a researcher was facilitated by my in-person observation of their non-verbal behaviour and by hearing what they were saying.

Interviews

In Edinburgh and Lyon, participants were mostly interviewed individually. Although some children do learn SCD, only adults were interviewed and observed as participants. According to Thomas (2009, p. 164), semi-structured interviews provide 'the best of both worlds as far as interviewing is concerned, combining the structure of a list of issues to be covered together with the freedom to follow up points as necessary'. However, some participants in Lyon did not speak English very well and it was easier for them to express their ideas during informal chats rather than within more formal interviews. As not all participants had consented to audio recording, notes were taken promptly following the discussions. The themes of interview questions were Scottish dancing experience and personal information such as other types of dance experience and interactions with other participants. Because language (French) was a barrier for me and the dancers were nervous when they spoke English, only one French dancer did an audio-recorded interview in English and the teachers, or callers, and the teaching and transmission of dance were not discussed in depth. I was able to read basic French, but I was not able to speak it very well. On several occasions when I communicated with dancers who had limited English, I wished my knowledge of French was better because fairly basic conversations were not able to provide me with information I needed about the dancers' background and their dance experience. Thus, it was only possible to obtain thick description from interactions with the dancers I stayed with, who were native English speakers and/or proficient in English. Some dancers in Edinburgh agreed their interviews could be audio recorded. Additionally, some people based in Edinburgh were travelling during the summer so one interview was done via Skype (video) and this was audio recorded.

Semi-structured interviews are a commonly used technique in field interviews and normally require audio recording in addition to fieldnotes (Danelo, 2017). However, some interviewees in my research preferred casual chats or informal interviews (Schensul & LeCompte, 2019). I found that casual chats provided informative data since chats regarding Scottish country dance occurred many more times than planned interviews. I was able to ask people a few times about the same questions and I gained some clearer answers. Also, I acquired some unexpected knowledge, which helped to provide a more detailed picture of dance societies and their members. Indeed, Schensul and LeCompte (2019) argue that once the recording starts, people normally speak differently from how they would in daily life. Online research provides fewer opportunities for such casual interactions. Another reason for me to do informal chats was because I was unable to spend time with members in Lyon, since I arrived there on Friday afternoons and went directly to the dance; after the dance classes finished, I went with the hosts to their home, arriving around midnight, and would return to Clermont-Ferrand the following day. Thus, I did not have enough time to get to know the hosts and interview them as the only opportunity was the following morning during or after breakfast. The only opportunity for interviews was one-off dance events such as dance weekends when I spent more time with people.

Fieldnotes

Fieldnotes were transcribed from memory after a casual conversation was held, combining informal chats and semi-structured interviews (Danelo, 2017). Non-verbal and social behaviours of participants, however, were recorded in more detail in a small notebook. I, as an Asian, look different from most other Scottish country dancers. It was almost impossible for people to ignore me when I sat apart and took notes. However, as noted above, following the advice of Schensul and LeCompte (2019), I attempted to reduce the impact of people's focus on me by joining in the dancing.

Research Diary

A diary chronicled how I felt and how I perceived my relations with others around me (Bernard, 2011). Sometimes I brought my laptop with me and typed my observations and feelings after the night dance classes or on the following day before I ate breakfast with the hosts (Lyon Branch members). I also wrote in my diary after dance events in Edinburgh during the summer (mid-June to early July and late August to early September 2017). I stayed with the Lyon Branch members whenever I went to dance with them but I did not stay with any Edinburgh dancers. Staying with the dancers helped me to understand them better, but this was not always possible and was not practical in Edinburgh.

Ethical Considerations during the Choreomundus Research

To communicate clearly the purpose of the research and the expectations of participants, it was essential that the ethical framework should be convincing both for the academic institution and the participants. Prior to fieldwork in 2016 and 2017 I was asked to follow the ASA Ethical Guidelines (ASA, 2016), which state that researchers should clarify the purpose of their research in the appropriate way and should protect original records and fieldnotes. Before I conducted my fieldwork, all participants were informed that I was conforming to these standards. I made great efforts to ensure that ethical considerations were taken seriously. All participants who helped with interviews and also with informal chats, observations and questionnaires had been informed about the study before I conducted my fieldwork. All data collected throughout this project were treated confidentially, and participants were anonymised through the utilisation of pseudonyms. No personal information or contact data of participants were divulged to any organisation, nor could participants be known from any reports or publications arising from the study. Direct quotes from the interviews or observations or from questionnaires were also used in the writings; however, any recognisable data were anonymised, and participants had the possibility to verify data before it was used.

Doctoral Fieldwork: Moving Online

In September 2018, I started a PhD in Education (Dance) at the University of Edinburgh, which was fully funded by the China Scholarship Council. Previously, I had done research in societies such as Edinburgh University New Scotland Country Dance Society (EUNSCDS), a student society (affiliated group of the RSCDS). After a couple of years of discussion with researchers and dancing with Scottish country dancers, it was decided that I would do in-depth research exclusively in the RSCDS Edinburgh Branch (founded in 1924), which has weekly classes and actively engaged SCD members. When I officially joined the Edinburgh Branch of the RSCDS (September 2018), I attended the Beginners class on two occasions in 2018. There I met again one of the SCD teachers whom I had met in May 2018 in Edinburgh. Later, in summer 2019, at his request, I translated an SCD class for some Chinese children during a summer camp in Edinburgh. In 2020 he helped me in many ways, including being interviewed online when I was in China in summer 2020, inviting me to his SCD class for international students who were visiting Edinburgh (not for the RSCDS) before the national lockdown and lending me items from his archives such as SCD books/videos. The main attraction of the RSCDS Edinburgh Branch was that it is based in Edinburgh and is directly linked to the headquarters (HQ) where the Archive (RSCDS, 2022) is located. Furthermore, the RSCDS Edinburgh Branch has its own branch archive, including high-quality facsimiles and books about RSCDS history and SCD practice (excluding music). Moreover, there was a manageable number of participants (less than 20 people in a weekly Beginners class) with whom I could do ethnography, and people came from diverse backgrounds. In ethnography, prolonged fieldwork and in-depth research with a small group are encouraged in order to improve the quality of the research (Schensul & LeCompte, 2019). Before the COVID-19 outbreak, I had planned to do around 12-months fieldwork by attending weekly classes and events to get to know the group well: my concerns included gaining access to the field, holding conversations with dancers and the dance societies' organisers/leaders/board members/ committee members and getting involved in the field. After the ethics application for in-person research was approved in January 2020, I started fieldwork in the RSCDS Edinburgh Branch in February 2020. However, the 'one-size-fits-all' ethical approach implemented by the University Ethical Review Board is contrary to the unpredictable and intimate character of ethnography (Dingwall, 2012). Indeed, Russell and Barley (2020) state that 'ethical guidelines published by the Association of Social Anthropologists of the UK and the Commonwealth (ASA) do not promote this "one size fits all" approach', which is particularly problematic for online ethnography, as I shall explain below.

In March 2020, shortly after ethics approval for in-person fieldwork was granted, the global impact of COVID-19 stopped face-to-face dancing in groups, which could now only take place online. Due to the restrictions on dancing in person that meant I had to meet SCD attendees on Zoom, the aims of the research were changed to explore how the RSCDS has adapted to the Covid pandemic and, in particular, how both students and teachers perceive the shift of SCD tuition to online classes. The objectives of the research are as follows. (1) To provide the first ever in-depth study of the B group as one of the RSCDS groups through an ethnographic perspective. (2) To evaluate online social dancing and dance education, including their successes and failures. (3) To explore in detail online social dance pedagogy and issues of embodiment. (4) To discover how Pierre Bourdieu's theories can be applied to online social dance and particularly to SCD. The Research Questions for the online ethnography have also been amended. (1) In what ways, if any, have the original philosophy and aims of the RSCDS changed during the Covid pandemic and post-pandemic period? (2) How and why do members of the RSCDS engage in SCD and what factors influence their choices in terms of online or in-person engagement? (3) How have the teachers and students of the Bo'ness SCD group adapted to online learning, or changed SCD sequences/movements, during their experience of the Covid pandemic?

Since I needed to move my research online, I had to adapt my methodology accordingly. However, the Edinburgh Branch of the RSCDS took a decision not to organise online classes but to wait till people could dance face-to-face before restarting classes. In April–August 2020, I took an interruption of study and returned to China. Thus, I had to expand the focus of my research on SCD from local dancers and dancing groups to online 'communities' composed of regular attendees who go to the same SCD classes and who come from many different countries. In China, I contacted some SCD teachers/dancers and also participated in some American branches' online SCD classes. Some of the dancers are RSCDS members who attend online classes. The research mainly comprises online SCD classes as field sites and uses pre-COVID in-person physical sessions as background information. In August 2020–April 2021, due to the time zone differences, I changed my online fieldwork with American branches to UK-based groups.

At the time of writing, in summer 2021, the University of Edinburgh Research Guidelines stipulate that due to Covid restrictions, only essential research such as clinical research can be conducted in person. Although some dancers were happy to be observed/interviewed and had signed the consent forms via email prior to the pandemic, because my study is not considered as essential face-to-face research, I can only apply for ethical approval for online research. The research design of my online-only ethnography focusses on archival research on SCD, document/website analysis of the RSCDS and interviews with the management/board of the RSCDS to explore how the RSCDS has adapted to the Covid pandemic. It also uses interviews and observations of online group classes as well as my embodied experience of being a dancer who has been taking part in the classes, and who produces fieldnotes and ethnographic writings, to explore how both students and teachers perceive the shift to online social dance education in SCD.

When Covid restrictions are lifted, I plan to submit an ethics application for a research design based on blended ethnography, where interviews are conducted with the B group attendees and teachers/musicians either in-person or online, but the fieldwork will be conducted in the B group in person. My research design has been amended several times and the PhD is an ongoing project, where the field for what will become a blended ethnography needs to be clarified with a view to minimising ethical risks. The formal parameters of the online fieldwork cannot be finalised until the Ethics Committee has approved the updated research design (pending at the time of writing). I have not officially started collecting online observation data and have only been dancing and building relationships of trust with potential participants online. This is because my supervisors have advised that until the new ethics application is approved, I should not interview anyone and I am not allowed to officially start collecting data, but can participate online.

I have been dancing with the online B group since November 2020, and some of its members have already expressed their interest in participating in the project, for instance, through interviews and observations of their chats/dance moves. The teacher is a fully certified SCD teacher in the original (in-person) B group, certified by the RSCDS as the recognised governing body for SCD. The group contains other fully certified teachers (including American teachers who sometimes teach and some SCD teachers from other countries who participate in the online classes). The B group and the RSCDS agreed to email others about project participation, stating that if they would like to participate in the research, they should email me. Several people have already contacted me to express their interest. I will also ask the B group members if they wish to participate when we chat as part of the classes I am currently attending on Zoom. Only people who respond to my enquiry or email will be included.

Since the research is designed to be conducted in the B group, the research participants are mainly the B group attendees. They will include the RSCDS board/management and the certificated SCD teachers who teach online, as well as individuals who are working towards teaching certification. If the new ethics application is approved, only these participants will be asked to sign the updated forms and to give interviews with new interview questions if they wish to. For practical reasons such as online relationships and online/in-person class times, I can only carry out online and blended ethnographic research with the B group, not with American or any other British groups. Others who participated previously will be excluded, although this material will provide background knowledge. Since this is an ethnographic study, it should focus on participants in a single dance group where in-depth research can be conducted, instead of one-off observations, interviews, or general surveys. To minimise the ethical risks, observations are primarily focused on dance teachers rather than on the online SCD participants. Individual dancers in the B group will be observed only if they give me consent to observe their dancing and/or chats. Some have already given consent, and approximately 5% of dancers will be observed (maximum five participants). Observations will focus almost exclusively on the teachers' online teaching adaptions, as it would be too distracting for me to observe several other dancers at the same time during dance classes. Online participant observations will be conducted in the weekly classes and in total 15 interviews will be conducted online. The 12 interviewees in the B group will include the teachers (around four interviewees), the students and the musicians (around eight student and musician interviewees). Another three interviewees are members of management and/or Board of the RSCDS.

All the teachers and participants to be observed are required to give written permission. I will take notes about teaching strategies and adaptions of SCD during online dance classes and/or chats regarding the SCD classes. Interviews or narrative portraits will focus on participants' dance experience and background, adaption to online SCD, the mode of and reasons for engagement in the online B group/RSCDS and opinions about the RSCDS. The interview/narrative portraits will take place on an online platform such as Skype, MS Teams, Zoom, Blackboard Collaborates, FaceTime etc. The platform that is most convenient to participants will be used as many are older and are less flexible in their choices. Ideally, I would like to audio record and will require consent for this, and all recordings will be destroyed once they have been transcribed manually. Interviews will be recorded by the platform and/or computer screen audio recording. All electronic data will be stored on a password-protected computer file on my computer and backed up in the University of Edinburgh 365 OneDrive.

Blended Online Ethnography

Due to the impact of COVID-19, this research has had to adapt to the online world, and the main focus has therefore switched from face-to-face groups in Edinburgh to online UK- and US-based groups. This approach can increase my understanding of the broader context of the RSCDS/SCD through another perspective that is not limited to Edinburgh or the United Kingdom, but is multi-national because some online attendees are based in different locations and represent different levels of SCD. Later, however, the project will also draw on offline data sources and can therefore be described as blended online ethnography. Once the online ethnography has been approved, a further ethics application for blended ethnography will be required. Beneito-Montagut (2011) has argued that ethnography may be multi-sited, both online and offline, while also comprising flexible multimedia data collection methods. This flexibility facilitates the comprehensive analysis of how social information and communication technologies operate in society on a daily basis (Beneito-Montagut, 2011). As Tummons (2020) argues, the advent of an increasingly networked world necessitates more flexible methodologies, where we construct our observational data from online and offline and the spaces in between them. In order to discuss the topic of ethics in these circumstances, the significance of conducting online ethnographic research first needs to be explicated.

My PhD has shifted from the single location and local situation of traditional ethnography to examining the circulation of cultural meaning, objects and identities in a broader understanding of the temporal and spatial order. Internet platforms are connected through the World Wide Web, which is essential for online research and multi-site structures (Yadlin-Segal et al., 2020). The Internet integrates individuals and mass media, creating a new mode of human communication that enables participants to engage in two-way mass communication. Indeed, Internet users no longer comprise passive audiences of data (Sade-Beck, 2004). Research on such communities' interpersonal communication has primarily investigated virtual support groups, determining that online communication enables users to freely express their emotions and attain a significant degree of self-disclosure (Sade-Beck, 2004). Considering that network platforms are intertwined, connected, shared and embedded through hyperlinks and composed of SCD participants and teachers who use them, multi-sited SCD communities (geographically as well as online) require the ethnographic field to be configured as multi-sited and intertwined. Some SCD participants have been attending different online classes, and there are overlaps of members from different RSCDS branches/groups. Using online ethnography as a research tool and approach can enable exploration of how teachers and dancers adapted to online SCD practices due to the pandemic.

In order to connect the 'online' world to the 'real' world, blended ethnography using complementary methods of online and offline data collection across both types of fields can be undertaken, as opposed to virtual ethnography (VE) which is focused solely on the online rather than the offline (Sade-Beck, 2004). Nevertheless, different researchers offer varying definitions. For instance, the type of VE that studies the impact of communication technologies on everyday life is also named blended ethnography (Antoniadou & Dooly, 2017). A further term, expanded ethnography, involves a choice of offline and online methods by individual researchers. Beneito-Montagut (2011) argues that everyday life occurs online, with no difference between online and offline interpersonal communication (IC). Furthermore, these forms of communication are typically intrinsically linked, with the methodological tools requiring expansion to better capture this social reality. In the context of my project, online dance communication and face-to-face communication have several differences, but the focus is on specific examples of Internet use as opposed to Internet technologies, services, sites or applications.

Ethical Challenges in Blended Ethnography

As noted above, the blended ethnography approach which I adopted as a result of the pandemic raises ethical challenges. For instance, lack of participation in human interaction online, providing lower visibility, is described as 'lurking' (Yadlin-Segal et al., 2020). When researchers in online settings collect data secretly, it is easy for them to 'hide in the dark', especially when the data are obtained as public text such as chats (Wheeler, 2017). Online observers may not be visible, 'either because we are lurking (if the ways in which our virtual field is constructed permit it) or because we have chosen to adopt particular online identities' (Tummons, 2020, p. 185). Although lurking online is relatively easy, it poses ethical challenges. However, these challenges are not insurmountable. Because ethnographers can move frequently and invisibly between different sites and platforms, in order to make their practice transparent, whenever they enter a new field site in the digital environment they should therefore re-introduce themselves and their research (Yadlin-Segal et al., 2020). A researcher entering the virtual community for the purposes of research should explain their aims, and participants should be emailed with the forms in advance. Transparency and confidentiality must be considered carefully.

Thus, whenever I attended the online SCD classes, I emailed the branch/group secretary or teachers in advance to introduce myself and the research, and then I was sent the Zoom links to the classes. Before or during the online classes, I was introduced by the person whom I had contacted so all the other dancers knew who I was. This was done to ensure that participants in the space being studied were aware of the research and my existence as the researcher in the field so that they could choose to protect their information, posts and shared identities. Most attendees at online SCD classes are the organiser's friends, and others including me have been introduced to the organiser by her friends and/or by regular attendees of the online class. Without knowing my identity as a dancer and PhD student, people would not accept me joining the dance classes. Moreover, unlike other research in a virtual space/online community, SCD classes are closely related to embodied experiences in that the attendees, including me as a researcher, are always visually present when online: having the camera on is mandatory during classes, and only regular attendees are included in the Face-book chat group.

In the online research I conducted before submitting the online ethnography ethics application, participants could not choose to opt out unless they turned the camera off. Even if some dancers were happy to be observed, my main focus was on the teacher's teaching, and I was busy with dancing and/or taking notes on the teacher. However, when the dances were repeated and/or moves were practised, I was sometimes able to identify dancers who gave me consent to be observed. In the online B group, all attendees were asked to turn the camera on, whether they were dancing or observing others dance. In my research design for online-only ethnography, I have chosen the speaker view on Zoom, meaning that the dance teacher is the main focus on my screen and the musician who plays music for the class sometimes appears at the top. Personal relationships with online participants are different from those with in-person participants in Lyon and Edinburgh. I can mostly only chat with people online and do not see them in person. However, quite a few attendees, including musicians, are both online and in-person B group dancers, and they are also happy to see me in person. Thus, there is potential to build relationships in person as well as online.

Despite the challenges, there are several advantages to conducting virtual ethnography. For example, I do not need to jot notes during the dance break as when I was in Lyon; rather, I can sit in front of the computer and take notes anytime I want. Wheeler (2017) argues that virtual ethnography enables researchers to bypass physical gender segregation and geographical boundaries and reach under-populated areas. Virtual ethnography can also reduce the financial constraints that limit those who can conduct face-to-face ethnography. Wheeler (2017) observes that researchers don't have to clumsily note their observations at the time, nor do they have to worry about forgetting to turn on the tape recorder to record the interview. Instead, they can take screenshots of instant messaging conversations or download videos for later viewing and experience events 'at this moment' without being disturbed by collection tools, while still ensuring that their data are accurate. However, this presents further ethical challenges because people may not know what has been recorded or saved as a screenshot.

Adaption of Methods for Blended Ethnography

Textual Analysis

As explained earlier, textual analysis involves secondary resources. This method is well suited to answering my first research question, which is about the history, philosophy and aims of the RSCDS. The RSCDS sometimes prints leaflets or posts them online, and now it uses exclusively electronic versions, for instance, the Lyon branch posts the classes/events timetables online. Also, there are programmes of the SCD classes/workshops on the Internet, which include the names of the dances and their musical accompaniments. When the Lyon Branch held international dance weekend events, the dance programmes, which sometimes included descriptions of the dances, were available both in emails and in printed versions in the venues. It is possible to use existing photos and videos to analyse dances and dance teachers/dancers and to explore the background information and discourse of the online SCD classes. Some resources and texts are supplied by the SCD teachers and dancers, including some Facebook groups where dancers/teachers exchange ideas about SCD such as on a Dance Group Facebook page and group chat, and some websites with SCD videos/music and descriptions such as the RSCDS website mentioned earlier. Moreover, some online dance classes are filmed by the organisations, and some reports or e-updates are emailed by the Society to members subscribed to the distribution list or are posted on Facebook.

Changes: Interviews Continued; Questionnaires Discontinued

Given the ethical complexities of observing online, I have chosen to complement online observations with interviews.

In order to discover how teachers and students have adapted to online learning or changed their choices of SCD sequences and/or movements to fit the constraints of dancing in their home space and without a group physically present, I will conduct interviews as well as reflecting on my own embodied experience of being a dancer who has taken part in the classes, using fieldnotes and ethnographic writings. I have considered carefully whether the topic is appropriate for an online interview, or if this poses potential risks. Chats or questions would not normally be included in the notes taken unless people give me consent. One of the ethical challenges of online ethnography is that in order to use Zoom chat as data I need the permission of everybody who types into Zoom. The setting of the interviews should allow privacy for both interviewer and interviewee, and this has been stated in the forms. Interview questions are sent to participants via email after their confirmation of participation in the research. If they do not wish to answer any questions, they can omit them. In line with the Ethics Committee requirements, if personal data are collected, then once it has been downloaded/

transcribed it is important to disaggregate this information from the research data that is saved in a separate file.

Questionnaires have been discontinued but interviews have been continued for several reasons. In interviews, people are encouraged to share their dance stories and experiences including some life experiences as well as their perspectives and perceptions of SCD classes and the RSCDS. Research participants can be asked to clarify the meaning of their responses to questions, and they can be asked for explanations of their teaching. Also, nonverbal data, especially SCD movements, can be observed. These elements cannot be captured in questionnaires. Another reason interviews are used is because the same questions can be asked at several levels to acquire deeper responses from the research participants. Moreover, whereas questionnaires are suitable for large samples and/or a greater amount of data over a broad range of topics, this project only needs a specific number of participants and most of them are in the B group. Also, in my previous experience of conducting MA and PhD research, only very limited numbers of participants were willing to fill in questionnaires and the answers were sometimes fairly short. Thus, without a higher response and retention rate, it is not worth collecting data from questionnaires.

However, this project will not be an entirely online ethnography. I agree with Wheeler (2017) that meeting later with the research subjects in person allows me as the researcher to confirm my explanations of the project and to present myself as a dancer/researcher face-to-face. I contacted key participants online and some people have agreed that in the future we may meet in person when the COVID-19 restrictions are fully lifted. In fact, some dancers who live nearby have already met when the lockdown was lifted in May 2021. I have not yet met the dancers in person. These potential in-person meetings could enable me to establish a stronger relationship with the participants and the information obtained online could be amplified. Moreover, according to information recently obtained from branch leaders based in Scotland, the RSCDS plan to hold in-person classes in Scotland in September. Therefore, to complement my online research, I may attend in-person dance classes in Edinburgh after September 2021, after the pandemic restrictions are lifted.

Fieldnotes

Bernard (2011) points out that research notes may be documented by jotting profiles (for example, on index cards) for each of the people the ethnographer meets. People's behaviour and appearance may be noted on the cards. My notes record the background of the dance classes or events, such as when and where the event took place, how many people took part, the names of the dances and the dance teacher's instructions. I sometimes make notes about people who don't dance but join in and watch online SCD classes, as background information. During breaks, I take fieldnotes or sometimes, when I am not dancing online, I take notes at different times and expand them in detail when I have time to write adequately or type into a computer. I need to observe dancers'/dance teachers' input but Zoom only shows bodies from certain angles and some tiny elements of body language/facial cues cannot be captured. Due to the angle, distance and imaging clarity of the camera and the lack of physical presence, only limited movements can be observed. Because there is no physical contact among dancers on Zoom unless they are in the same room, not many details of interactions between attendees can be perceived and noted. Thus, the missing elements, such as the movements of the dance teacher and her facial expressions, will need to be further explored when I am doing in-person fieldwork.

Fieldnotes are written day by day in an open-ended manner, changing direction rather than being final or fixed (Bernard, 2011). I also use fieldnotes to reflect on my own position in terms of dance experience and knowledge and also in relation to the dancers I danced/talked with. My knowledge of SCD and the online communities has deepened, and so when I look back at the same dance videos/descriptions, my interpretations have consequently evolved. My deeper understanding has resulted in my position moving from that of a novice outsider towards that of an insider. In the online group, all participants have been aware that I am in the class to dance online and to do my research. When I officially start collecting data, participants will have been notified and will have signed and returned the forms. Dancers join from different locations and dance backgrounds. They seem pleased to answer my questions and/or ask questions about me and my understanding of the classes/SCD. Many of them can be considered as novices (who started SCD online during the Covid) and outsiders (most online members were not members of the physical group before Covid). Moreover, I have been dancing with the group online since November 2020: I have got to know people in the group and they have also got to know each other better.

Standpoint and Positionality

In order to decide which research question(s) are needed and to interpret their own data (Kaur-Gill & Dutta, 2017), ethnographers must engage within the context they analyse, participating and interacting with the community. Additionally, Kaur-Gill & Dutta (2017) argue that, from the emic insider's perspective, ethnography becomes a challenge for the practitioner, since he/she needs to establish a direct relationship in the field with participants while maintaining some distance, carrying out structured and unstructured interviews. As I get to know the dancers and the societies better, the dancers are more willing to share with me their knowledge and experience of SCD and their online communities. By understanding the communities and the individual dancers more, my position has become increasingly that of an insider. After several months of attending the dance classes and having been added to their chat group, I am positioning myself as an 'inside-outside' researcher and dancer. The process of becoming an insider involved several stages. From November 2020 I generally attended the group's dance every fortnight online. After a few weeks of continuous weekly attendance at the online SCD classes, on 30th January 2021 I also took part in a film representing the group in response to a call for an online flash mob dance recording.

Along with many others, I was in the Facebook Community group where people posted news and updates, but after I joined this flash mob film, at the end of the weekly dance class on 2nd February, I was also invited to the group's Facebook chat, where people chat frequently, and all the Zoom links for the classes were sent to me. I used to receive the Zoom link/passcode via email and did not know they had an FB chat group where they share updates not only about SCD but also about their wider lives. I look younger than others as the only full-time student in the group, and I am the only Asian dancer. Nevertheless, the group is inclusive, including dancers at different dance levels, nationalities and age groups. After being accepted by the group, I have access to the same information as other members.

The quality of the online relationships seems strong and close, as people who participate in the B group are friendly and open-minded. Compared to in-person relationships, this blended research is proving to be even better for my fieldwork. In Edinburgh in 2018–2020, the secretary and teachers helped me promote my project but only a few people responded to my questionnaires, while in the B group the participants showed me a warm welcome and took a keen interest in my research. Recently, after the B group teacher said in the FB group chat that I needed interviewees, several participants (more than expected) emailed me within two hours to express their interest. Also, since restrictions have been lifted, some of the dancers have met each other in different countries/cities. While some knew each other before the pandemic, others had encountered each other online through the B group and met in person for the first time. Pictures of these meetings were shared in the Facebook B group chat and/or page. When Covid restrictions are lifted completely I will be able to travel to other countries to meet some of the participants or we may meet when they come to Edinburgh. Although this may not happen during my PhD, it does show that people have built relationships online and would like to make friends in person.

Sometimes I attend SCD after having viewed online information or after receiving notifications from the organisers of events/classes. Facebook can be used to find information about SCD meetings and dance classes and is one of my research sources, since there are some online SCD events and classes updates. Dalsgaard (2016) argues that Facebook can be used to access field sites. Moreover, he refers to several studies that report how Facebook is perceived from the outside as a 'network', instead of a 'community', because the users are 'centre-less and dispersed'. However, regular attendees who go to the same SCD classes or classes given by the same teacher(s) are considered as online 'communities'. To avoid ethical issues associated with lurking and ethical risks of 'hiding in the dark', Facebook data will not be imported directly but will only be used as a tool to access the fields and to build relationships with other dancers.

Ongoing Ethical Considerations

A 'one-size-fits-all' approach to ethics clearance is unsuited to ethnographic research, particularly online. In online SCD classes there are always people who have their camera on but are not dancing; rather, some participants may simply watch others dancing or do their own thing, such as knitting. In some other groups during online SCD classes (such as some American and British groups I attended online in 2020), some participants have their camera off. Therefore, when lurking online, the dancers are less self-conscious about the camera. In some online classes, people who would rather not be observed have their cameras off. If most people have their camera on I may decide to leave mine on too. In some group dance classes, all participants are required to turn on their videos whether or not they are dancing. In online settings where all participants are on camera, they become more relaxed than when they are observed face-to-face. When I have the camera on and all or most of the others are dancing, they can see me taking notes on the computer or writing. Unlike in-person classes, where dancers sometimes seemed uncomfortable about me taking notes, I can take notes anytime if I do not dance. Also, some classes are recorded, so if I would like to analyse dancing/teaching, I can also watch the classes afterwards.

Participating in online groups helps to build my knowledge and relationships with the participants, and there are informative and interesting updates in the Facebook pages/groups. I have not obtained consent from all the dancers to use chat box content, so chat boxes and other information obtained by lurking outside the class will only be used as data if individuals have given consent and the ethics application is approved. The chat boxes sometimes contain informative sources such as SCD links and events, especially during the leisure time before and after dancing. Facebook and email data have also been used as background information. However, only the dance classes themselves are considered as my online field sites. SCD dancers can join online dancing wherever they are based; the community is not limited either to the SCD classes or the Facebook group/ page and other online/in-person events. As discussed earlier, online fieldwork boundaries are blurred, but in this ongoing PhD project the SCD classes have been considered as my field to distinguish these online events from other online sites such as Facebook.

Conclusion: Adapting to Online Ethnographic Research

The pandemic has meant that SCD has moved online and therefore my research methods have also had to change. With the help of some key participants and making use of ongoing online events, I have adapted my PhD to continue my research on SCD using blended ethnography, with the main focus currently on online methods. This is advantageous in some respects, as my research now has a wider international reach than previously, and my methods allow me to be multi-sited and to combine offline and online data collection. This flexibility is crucial at a time when the evolution of the pandemic remains uncertain. However, the strict ethical constraints impose limitations on choice of research participants and also restrict the gathering of data on people who don't dance but join in and watch SCD classes online. Being transparent and clear about the research, building trust and keeping the participants updated are key to overcoming the ethical challenges of online research. As lurking in the field presents ethical challenges, interviews have become complementary methods in the blended ethnography design, along with textual analysis, fieldnotes and observation of the participants who have given their informed consent. Nonetheless, further studies are needed to address the implications of the 'one-size-fits-all' ethical approach implemented by university ethical review boards for interpretive fieldwork and in particular for online ethnography.

Note

1. Choreomundus is an international Erasmus Mundus programme. I studied at Norwegian University of Science and Technology, Clermont Auvergne University in France, University of Szeged in Hungary, and University of Roehampton, United Kingdom.

References

Antoniadou, V., & Dooly, M. (2017). Educational ethnography in blended learning environments. In E. Moore & M. Dooly (Eds.), *Qualitative approaches to research on plurilingual education* (pp. 237–263). Dublin: Research-publishing.net.

ASA. (2016, December 4). ASA ethical guidelines. [Adobe Digital Editions version]. Retrieved from https://www.theasa.org/downloads/ASA%20ethics%20guidelines%202011.pdf

Beneito-Montagut, R. (2011). Ethnography goes online: Towards a user-centred methodology to research interpersonal communication on the internet. *Qualitative Research, 11*(6), 716–735.

Bernard, H. (2011). *Research methods in anthropology* (5th ed.). Lanham: AltaMira Press.

Dalsgaard, S. (2016). The ethnographic use of Facebook in everyday life. *Anthropological Forum, 26*(1), 96–114.

Danelo, D. J. (2017). *The field researcher's handbook: A guide to the art and science of professional fieldwork.* Georgetown: Georgetown University Press.

Dingwall, R. (2012). How did we ever get into this mess? The rise of ethical regulation in the social sciences. In K. Love (Ed.), *Ethics in social research (Studies in qualitative methodology)* (Vol. 12, pp. 3–26). Bingley: Emerald Group Publishing Limited.

Hammersley, M., & Atkinson, P. (2019). *Ethnography: Principles in practice* (4th ed.). Abingdon: Routledge.

Kaur-Gill, S., & Dutta, M. J. (2017). Digital ethnography. In J. Matthes, C. Davis, & R. Potter (Eds.), *The international encyclopedia of communication research methods* (pp. 1–10). Hoboken: Wiley Blackwell.

RSCDS. (2022, January 4). RSCDS archive. Retrieved from https://www.rscds.org/about/history/rscds-archive

Russell, L., & Barley, R. (2020). Ethnography, ethics and ownership of data. *Ethnography, 21*(1), 5–25.

Sade-Beck, L. (2004). Internet ethnography: Online and offline. *International Journal of Qualitative Methods, 3*(2), 45–51.

Schensul, J., & LeCompte, M. (2019). *Essential ethnographic methods*. Lanham, MD: AltaMira Press.

Thomas, G. (2009). *How to do your research project*. London: Sage.

Tummons, J. (2020). Online, offline, hybrid, or blended? Doing ethnographies of education in a digitally-mediated world. In M. R. M. Ward & S. Delamont (Eds.), *Handbook of qualitative research in education* (pp. 178–189). Cheltenham: Edward Elgar Publishing.

Wheeler, K. (2017). The ethics of conducting virtual ethnography on visual platforms. *Fieldwork in Religion*, *12*(2), 163–178.

Yadlin-Segal, A., Tsuria, R., & Bellar, W. (2020). The ethics of studying digital contexts: Reflections from three empirical case studies. *Human Behaviour and Emerging Technologies*, *2*(2), 168–178.

Chapter 8

Ethical Dilemmas and Reflections in a Collaborative Study with Children during the Pandemic

Diana Milstein, Regina Coeli Machado e Silva and Angeles Clemente

Abstract

This chapter explores the ethical dilemmas that emerged *in situ* from an ethnographic study in collaboration with Latin American children and youngsters. It was developed in the challenging conditions of isolation and lockdown, during the COVID-19 pandemic. In such times, a group of eight researchers from different geographical locations in the Americas looked into the ways children reorganise, reconstruct and reinterpret their daily lives in social isolation. The methodological approach, which enabled dialogue and conversation, began through a system of correspondence – in oral, written, recorded, drawn, photographed and audiovisual forms – among Latin American children. The expectations about the viability of this field-work modality brought, from the beginning, ethical challenges that required continuous adjustments, agreements, rectifications, adaptations and explicit reflection on such ethical aspects. Here we focus on three challenges that we analyse individually, although in practice they were interconnected. The first one was the dilemma regarding perception and use of time. The second ethical challenge is based on the fact that we recruited the young participants through friendships and kinship networks that each of the eight researchers previously had. The third challenge was connected to the decision to communicate through letters (a markedly confessional, private and intimate epistolary genre) that were both intervened by our 'special' position and also taken as ethnographic documents. In our fieldwork, in the specific spatial and temporal situations we worked, we understand the self as emerging from intersubjectivity and knowledge relations as co-created between researcher and researched. Thus, ethical decisions are made during the research process itself and, for us, *in situ* ethics entails a reciprocal commitment, between

Ethics, Ethnography and Education, 129–150
Copyright © 2022 Diana Milstein, Regina Coeli Machado e Silva and Angeles Clemente
Published under exclusive licence by Emerald Publishing Limited
doi:10.1108/S1529-210X20220000019008

children, youth and adults as co-researchers, to adjust themselves to the developments and boundaries of the ethnographic field. This also allowed the participants to manage the adjustments in this specific and situated context that circumscribed everybody, seeking answers in conversations and paying careful attention to the situation.

Keywords: Child and young participants; ethnographic documents; time and space; pandemic; *in situ* ethics; Latin America

Introduction

This chapter will explore the ethical dilemmas that emerged *in situ* from an ethnographic study in collaboration with Latin American children and young-sters, developed in the challenging conditions of isolation and lockdown, during the COVID-19 pandemic. A group of eight researchers from different geographical regions in the Americas wanted to understand how, in times of a global pandemic, living in different locations in their home countries or abroad, children and youngsters reorganised their daily lives which were previously arranged by the routines of going to school and back home, participating in outdoors activities, playing with friends and using various electronic devices for different purposes.[1] It was precisely from these electronic technologies that we took the first step to develop our methodological strategy: an exchange of elec-tronic letters via Internet. The initial purpose of this research was to understand the ways in which children and young people reconstructed and interpreted social isolation as well as the ways in which these experiences were discussed with their peers.

We believe that *in situ ethics* is part of the constant exercise of reflection on our own ethnographic work, especially taking into account that the unusual fieldwork of this project had no precedent for us. Not only were our theoretical–methodological approaches inseparable but also our decisions, our practices and our mutual responsibilities were constantly present during the investigation.

In situ ethics is about the management of a relational ethics as defined by Wendy J. Austin (2008):

> Relational ethics is a contemporary approach to ethics that situates ethical action explicitly in relationship. If ethics is about how we should live, then it is essentially about how we should live together. Acting ethically involves more than resolving ethical dilemmas through good moral reasoning; it demands attentiveness and responsiveness to our commitments to one another.
>
> (p. 748)

In situ ethics means more than just being aware of the duties and responsi-bilities that should direct our investigation. *In situ* ethics means a reciprocal commitment, between children, youth and adults as co-researchers, to adapt to the developments and boundaries of the ethnographic field and manage ethical considerations in paying careful attention to the specific situation.

We are aware that our fieldwork was original because it was doubly conditioned by Internet technologies and by a context of simultaneous social isolation that affected children, youngsters and adults. These locations included places – urban and rural – in various sites of Argentina, in the capitals of Colombia and Panama, in southern Oaxaca, Mexico, in two southern cities of Brazil, in a northwestern city in the United States and in a central western city in Germany (where one of the participants, originally from Oaxaca, was living).

The expectations about the viability of this fieldwork modality also brought, from the beginning, ethical challenges that required continuous adjustments, agreements, rectifications, adaptations and explicit reflection on ethical aspects mixed with other concerns. For this chapter we will focus on three of these challenges that we want to analyse individually, although in practice they were interconnected, which opened up possibilities (and set up limits) during the fieldwork. The first one is the dilemma regarding perception and use of time. Children and young people showed multiple and simultaneous ways of experiencing time that were opposed to the imposition of a homogeneous and extended time of the pandemic. The second ethical challenge was to have recruited the young participants through friendships and familial relationships that each of the eight researchers previously had. This way of initiating relationships was contrasted with the ways we had recruited research participants before: getting in touch with unknown children and youngsters from a neighbourhood, school, hospital etc., where we usually would develop our fieldwork. The third challenge was to choose to initiate interactions through letters, a markedly confessional, private and intimate epistolary genre, that was intervened by our 'special' position as 'mail carriers', for we were not only in charge of delivering and receiving the letters that they sent to each other, but also, in prior agreement with them, we had access to the content of the messages that, from the beginning, were taken as ethnographic documents. We consider these letters as descriptive documents of everyday life that allow access to topics that not only relativise but also extrapolate what children and young people know, understand, and interpret about dimensions of daily life in times of isolation due to pandemic. Additionally, some children and young people worked with us in online meetings, re-reading letters and asking questions aimed at reconstructing senses/meanings of what was written and drawn. As part of that co-produced knowledge, the letters are not considered primary document data sources but ethnographic data co-constructed in the research process.

To make these dilemmas clearer, we will first present the context and the way we carried out ethnography in times of pandemic, that is, our methodology and the fieldwork. Then we will develop the ethical challenges, relying on reconstructed ethnographic evidence from the fieldwork, before opening a discussion and concluding with some provisional conclusions. We are aware that it is important to highlight the debate about the controversies and limitations of ethics committees and their regulations, which operate in our countries, with more or less rigour. Such controversies, as emphasised by Russell and Barley (2020, p. 7) come from the Cartesian premises of understanding the self (and mind and body) as pre-existing limited consciousness, and knowledge as the exclusive property of those who produce it and as a result of predetermined objective strategies. In our fieldwork, we conceive of the self as emerging from intersubjectivity and knowledge relations as co-created between researcher and researched, in specific spatial and temporal situations. Thus, ethical decisions are made in the research process itself.

Ethnographic Field: The Relational Spaces between Face-to-Face and Virtual Interactions

Our fieldwork consisted of activities carried out virtually due to the exceptional situation of the global pandemic in which we have all been immersed in March 2020. The closure of national borders and social isolation due to the introduction of new hygiene measures had, as one of its effects, the stimulation of virtual interpersonal relationships without face-to-face contacts, with the exception of people who lived in the same household. Far from being spatial, the research context was delineated by an interconnected network initiated by the team of researchers: those of previous interactions and proximity between researchers and children and youngsters, those of other relationships initiated between young participants unknown to each other, those of the more or less heterogeneous participants located in different local/national/international realities, and those of the face-to-face relationships, outside the online universes, who originated, and maintained, these virtual interactions.

One of the strategies to start fieldwork was inspired by the work carried out by Podestá Siri (2004), who had the idea of children and young people communicating with each other through letters. In her study with Nahua communities in Mexico, she was interested in local linguistic traditions, promoting an inter-indigenous epistolary dialogue between children who lived in towns and children who lived in cities. The researcher herself considered that the children were experts in the culture in which they had been socialised:

> Nobody is better than them to talk about the place where they were born. In that sense, from the beginning I tried to make them understand that *I could not do the job with their eyes, ears and feelings*; that, although I could talk about their village, I would not do as if I had been born there, as a native would do it (…).
> (Podestá Siri, 2007, p. 35/36, our emphasis and translation)

Faced with an unexpected and sudden isolation due to the pandemic, we felt that it was important to hear children and young people's voices about their experiences of this unusual situation. We intuited that no one better than them could communicate what 'their eyes, ears and feelings' knew, and that the dialogue between peers would be very fruitful in this regard. They knew a lot about school/schooling because they were students and were experiencing changes to educational practices (whether they liked it or not) in the confinement of domestic life. To our advantage, they were used to using virtual tools since they were little. When we read how Podestá Siri urged children to write to each other, we asked ourselves, how could dialogues between children and youngsters be generated in cyberspace without the possibility of face-to-face encounters? And, more importantly, what would they tell and ask each other?

Of course, these concerns are based on the fact that we are clear that children and young people are social actors who share our present (in opposition to those who place them as *citizens of the future*) and with full agency (understanding that this fullness includes differences of age, generation, social class, gender etc.). This also implies that their participation in the ethnographic process regards them as interlocutors, whose living conditions, knowledge and experiences are essential to understand the social realities that we study.[2] It also reinforces a shared position regarding the dilemma related to researching *with* children and young people, which contrasts with the tendency to research *about* them (James, 2007). This difference of perspective calls into question 'approaches to generic or imprecise objects – the child or the youth – that essentialize, homogenize and neutralize the concrete and tangible presences of children and youths...' (Milstein, 2020, p. 3).[3] The idea is to develop opportunities for young people's agency to unfold in the shared research times and spaces. Agency is here understood as the capacity of social subjects to feel, think and act with relative autonomy in their relationships. So, what they say, do, perceive and/or interpret are unique and necessary contributions to understand new situations and circumstances that, in this context, are the daily lived experiences of isolation in pandemic times. Part of the question to be discussed in this chapter lies on the ethical challenges that this epistemological, methodological and political position presented us when we decided to investigate these circumstances, along with children and youngsters, these new forms of isolation that they/we are still living with.

Their letters – written, drawn, oral, photographed, recorded or filmed – tell of their everyday situations during this period of isolation. For us it was, at the beginning, a way of having records – the letters – that would allow us to get closer to understanding where these children saw their place in the pandemic, what they said about this unprecedented way of experiencing their schooling, domestic life and virtual reality. From the first letters we were surprised by the expressive forms that these young authors used when combining words and colours, drawings, emojis, photos and sketches, among others.

With regards to this multimodality, our inspiration came from the artistic avant-garde movement called mail-art of the 60s and 70s of the last century. The literature made us notice that some of the dilemmas posed by these visual artists could enrich our process of problematising ethical aspects.

> Sending a letter by mail implies the development of a message, and it is an act of communication between two people. Mail intervenes making the message possible through distance (...). Just as the man, when expressing himself, seeks multiple channels, the artist

conveys his creativity through multiple forms. (…) An example of this is offered by the plastic artist who carries out research, who uses the 'conventionally non-artistic' media that alters its function. And proof of the latter is the synthesis that has been reached in this new expressive form, ART-MAIL (…) When a sculpture is sent by mail, the creator limits himself to using a specific means of transport to move a work already made. When making the sculpture, this displacement was not taken into account. In contrast, in the new artistic language that we are analyzing, the fact that the work must travel a certain distance is part of its structure, it is the work itself. The work has been created to be sent by post, and this factor conditions its creation.

(Vigo & Zabala, 1976, p. 1, our translation)

In all cases, the messages meant communication between two young people who did not know each other before the project started. Our intervention consisted in making this distant communication possible. Their enthusiasm to send and receive letters made them search for multiple means that allowed them to channel their creativity to communicate, as was the case with the ART-MAIL artists. In some cases, children and youngsters created coded modes of communication with each other, like trivia games, for example. These coded modes operated as signs of common cultural experiences – memes, emojis, questions, games and challenges. In others, it was also clear that the message 'had been created to be sent', on this form of mail that the team of ethnographers had invented. As mail carriers we were conditioning the form and content of the messages children and youngsters sent to each other. This forced us to raise some practical and ethical questions, as part of the epistemological positioning for reflexivity during the ethnographic fieldwork. By developing unforeseen methodological and epistemological innovations during the unprecedented investigative process, ethical dilemmas are part of the ways in which ethnographers deal with intimate, personal, political and material concerns (Günel, Varma, & Watanabe, 2020; Punch, 1986). Addressing these aspects allowed us to overcome some limitations inherent to technologically mediated encounters between interlocutors and with researchers.

Although there are extensive debates about the differences between ethnography 'online' and 'offline', we consider, like Tummons (2020), that there is no clear difference between them, and that the different scope of each can be complementary. For us, online resources have made it possible to bring together geographically distant participants, and to diversify relationships between strangers. The methodological strategies did not differ significantly. We delimit the ethnographic field by relational spaces (or 'the discursive construction of the research field', Tummons, 2020, p. 180) created by the project's connections. Participant observation, carried out from April to October 2020, allowed us to interact, follow and enquire with each other through dialogues in the exchange of asynchronous messages and some synchronous ones. We also observed offline spaces, the relationships between researchers with children and the adults around them, and the different forms of engagement and participation in the project. This offline participation refers to the observations of researchers around what was happening in their close relationships. They were mainly initiated by family members and researchers. For instance, when a mother sent a letter or when they talked about the children at home, about the project etc. In some cases, researchers were at home with the participating daughter, and in others they found children in the park or in a pueblo in the interior of Argentina, observing and recording. We also used some previous memories that were useful to this project. Participation was intensified through the elaboration of audios, videos and text messages. It was also designed to be accessible, shared and stored. Field records, individual or of small groups, were synchronously made on text sharing platforms so that they were accessible and editable, by the researchers. As a consequence, the very construction of ethnographic data became participatory and was the focus of frequent re-elaborations in the team's online meetings. All data originated from statements by children and young people close to each researcher to create this field in which we emerged through interactions.

Ethnographic Field in Process: Opening Interactions and Building Collaboration

The group of participants and their locations are described in the following (Table 1):

Table 1. Participants and their Locations.

Country	Region	Boys	Girls	Young Women	Young Men	Researchers
Argentina	Metropolitan	2	4			2
	South	1	4	1		1
	Northeast		2	1		1
Brazil	Metropolitan	1				
	South/ Southeast	1				1
Chile	Metropolitan		1			
Colombia	Metropolitan			2	2	
Germany	Central West	1				
Mexico	South		2			1
Panama	Metropolitan		1	3	4	
	North		1			
USA	West			1		2

Most of the authors and recipients of letters are related to the eight researchers by friendship and/or kinship, while those from Panama and Chile were incorporated by proximity between colleagues who maintained professional work links with the researchers. The eight researchers had a previous academic/professional relationship. We are all part of the International Network of Ethnography with Children and Young People (RIENN), and we have shared research projects, publications, and the organisation of symposia, workshops and round tables, among other activities.[4] We have been used to communicating via the Internet for several years, but until March 2020 some of these activities were only carried out face-to-face annually or biannually with the presence of some or all. We all have experience in ethnographic research projects in collaboration with young people and agreements regarding methodological and epistemological criteria from an ethnographic perspective. It was not a novelty that our research included great uncertainty regarding the methodological proposal since this is what distinguishes ethnography. The novelty was not that we were going to carry out fieldwork totally online with children and youngsters, but that we were doing that with what we could call distant participant observation and collaboration. That is, participant observation is distant in spatial but not in temporal terms. It was distant because each participant was in different location, but all of us were observing and participating in the relational spaces that the children and young people were creating, collaboratively with the researchers.

Thus, we began the research that productively oriented a good part of the uncertainty generated by the new form of daily life that had been imposed on everybody. The restrictions were not the same among the countries where the researchers and participants resided; moreover, there were differences between regions with some countries. In some places, governments had imposed social isolation or compulsory social distancing controlled by the security forces. In others, restrictions were imposed but the obligation was relativised, and in two locations, the USA and Brazil the restrictions were rejected by government officials. This gave us the opportunity to get in touch with original, unique and situated knowledge, constructed by both, children, youngsters and ourselves. This also presented us with ethical problems *in situ*, which had already been experienced in other fieldwork situations, but which had not prompted us, used to face-to-face interaction, to analyse sensitively and reflectively.

We provisionally defined the space for fieldwork as an interconnected network (Burrell, 2009), which was set up by the invitation that each researcher made to the children and/or youngsters who might have been interested. From the beginning, doubts and discomforts arose because it was not easy for all the researchers to find participants that they could invite. For those of us that were easier, it was strange to organise fieldwork that seemed limited to people from our closest circles: grandchildren, nephews, our own children, and children of friends and colleagues. On the other hand, we assumed that children and youngsters wanted relationships with their peers and that was why we imagined that the proposal to send a letter to establish a friendship could be very attractive.

Each invitation was made individually, based on the relationship we had with a specific child, girl or young, or with his/her parents. What we commonly agreed was to tell them what the project was about, and how the exchange of letters was going to be developed. We were very welcomed by the participants. Within the first 10 days we had a list of 25 participants. We assigned each participant to another participant on the list to send a first letter. At the same time everyone received a first letter. Therefore, everyone became an author and possible destination at the same time. Everyone had the opportunity to send and receive. To organise them, we wanted pairs of similar ages, but different birthplaces and/or contexts. With the three children between 6 and 7 years old, we organised a triad, thinking that being in a group would be more appealing for the youngest of the study. To begin with, each researcher asked each participant – by chat, email or phone call – to write a letter (handwritten, on the computer, or using WhatsApp) to introduce themselves as they wanted and tell their partners how they were living under lockdown, what they did at home and how they did things related to school. We started receiving and delivering letters right away. Some letters were written on paper, photographed and sent by WhatsApp or other digital formats. Others were written as Word documents, or similar, and sent as attachments via email or WhatsApp. They also wrote messages directly via WhatsApp and some sent videos with oral messages, which we called video letters because of the type of message they contained. Some exchanges between dyads lasted several weeks – from 6 to 12 – others were interrupted earlier, and few had no response from the recipient. Some of these interruptions and lack of response generated discomfort in the researchers. We did not know whether to intervene or not, or what was the right amount of involvement. We are aware that in all fieldwork the right amount is always a learning experience that highly depends on face-to-face social negotiations. In this online fieldwork, with this modality of participatory observation, and explicitly open to collaboration, our doubts and dilemmas increased.

With the participants who held the exchange more regularly and who were interested in collaborating more with our project, we also held virtual meetings. We selected some dyads and proposed meetings to get to know each other and their mail carriers and to talk about what was written in their letters. This gave us the possibility to shorten the distance, so to speak, and to interact with them, share their perspectives, motivations and interests regarding what they had written and about what the meeting in itself would generate. These sessions lasted more than an hour and they were exceptional opportunities to let ourselves be carried away by the children and youngsters involved. They were firm and serious in this virtual mode of encounter but, at the same time, they displayed a playful and amusing way of interaction.

We also got involved with relatives of the children and young people. At the starting point we had conversations with family members of each participant. During the fieldwork, almost all the children received support from their relatives to send messages on the technological supports of the Internet. Some mothers and an aunt communicated with the ethnographers and/or actively participated in the online encounters.

For reading and analysing the letters and other materials and texts, for discussing the interruptions and other issues that arose in the process of sending and receiving letters, and for reflecting on our involvement with the authors/recipients and with their adults – mothers, parents, aunts etc. – the eight researchers met periodically (every week for the first three months and subsequently every other week) using digital platforms. During these meetings we experienced a process of joint construction of knowledge, with ever-increasing levels of collaborative work. This process produced a type of relational logic, implemented in the digital world from face-to-face relationships, which also enabled a collaborative construction of knowledge that raised significant ethical dilemmas.

Ethical Dilemmas *In Situ*

Making distant communication possible in the ethnographic study in collaboration with Latin American children and youngsters living in different locations (in their home countries and abroad) brought ethical dilemmas. Such dilemmas became visible and were equated at the very moment when interactions were engaged. We describe three implicit ethical dilemmas arising from the proposal and the agreements made to develop ethnographic work. The first is about the ubiquity of the time lived in isolation from the pandemic in the encounter with the young people. The second is about the authority contained in interactions with children and youth interlocutors through friendships and family relationships previously established, and the third is about letters and messages as a means of communication between participants.

Experiences of Time during the Pandemic

The imposition of a homogeneous and extended time of the pandemic, taken as 'our time' as researchers, in contrast to the use and perception of time of the young people became clear, for the first time, in the exchange of messages between Becky, Alfonso and Julian, the youngest children in the project.[5] Alfonso currently lives in Germany. He is from Oaxaca, Mexico, like Becky, who was born and lives there. Julian is Argentinian and lives in Buenos Aires. By their messages, we quickly realised that their rhythms were different from each other and that those rhythms were not ours. This unexpected situation made us reflect, *in situ*, on the mismatch between Alfonso, for whom there was no 'cuarentena', Julian, who was, to a greater extent, aware of the 'cuarentena', and Becky, for whom the 'cuarentena' was the experience of an omnipresent time, but 'drained' by the counterpoint of the absence of the powerful school rhythm, as revealed in her videos.[6] In the investigation process, we continue to face multiple times experienced by children and young people in their different locations. They challenged the presumption of the existence of a unique and extended time for everyone by the suppression of the school and domestic rhythm, brought about by the physical and universal time of health management. Additionally, discovering with children the concreteness of a time lived and inseparable from subjectivity, cognitively and symbolically differentiated, placed us in the ethical dilemma involved in this pre-established conception of a homogeneous time for all.

During a virtual meeting that two researchers had with Keysha, a girl from Panama, Sofía, Lucía and Julián, three children from Buenos Aires, plus the participation of two mothers and an aunt, we used a shared virtual whiteboard, so that the children could write, draw and paste photos and stickers while we talked, and they would express how they were experiencing their everyday life. At one point they began to talk about their experience of 'missing', sparking yet another discussion about time. We asked them to write these ideas on the board (Fig. 1):[7]

Fig. 1.   Time in the Pandemic, According to Keysha and Sofía.

The researchers were surprised by the depth of what was expressed and because, in the dialogue we had, the idea of unified time did not take on relevance. Rather, it was about putting feelings and emotions into words. That moved us. When we discussed this with the team of researchers, it was clear that the differences for the children not only consisted in the fact that 'quarantine' did not mean the same thing for everyone, but that they presented us with ways and strategies to mean time in different contexts and lived individually. What it took us time to realise was that for us adults, was the same, that is to say, there was not a single and homogeneous time imposed by health management and global media coverage. It was obvious that the question was not to contrast children and adults' experiences.

Johannes Fabian (1981) warned that it was imperative for ethnographers to realise that the natives with whom he had produced his ethnographies were contemporaries and that his failure to acknowledge this had ethical – as well as political and epistemological – implications. That present time that organises the writing of ethnographies, places the real social actors in a fixed past, that of the time experienced in ethnography. In our ethnography, the ethical dilemma emerged when we looked at the notion of time, not as an object of knowledge, but as a dimension of subjectivity. Our subjectivity as adults living in confinement coincided with an idea of relative uniformity in the way we perceive time in a pandemic. The subjectivity of these four children who also lived in confinement brought other specific ways of perceiving time.

The context of our virtual meeting, where what we were doing and saying was making sense for all of us, hinted at the dilemma that dislocated the researchers. The assumption of the same present for all denies that 'each present provokes the appearance of a new time' (Sánchez, 1994, p. 288) and hinders the possibility of 'differentiating the "absolute present" from the "temporary present"' (Sánchez, 1994, p. 292). Ultimately, this ethical dilemma is also linked to the naturalisation of North Atlantic perceptions about what time is, as Gell (1996) argued in his critique of anthropological approaches to temporalities.

Recruiting via Kinship and Friendship Networks

From the beginning of the project ethical dilemmas emerged in relation to our recruitment strategies and practices and the researcher's positionality as mail carrier. These dilemmas were directly linked to the fragile nature of the young people message exchanges and the use of family and personal networks to recruit participants.[8] Reflecting on these dilemmas, Veronica, one of the researchers, recalls:

> But I don't remember if it [our previous relationship with the children] was exactly an issue of this type of collaboration. What I remember is …[]… happened to me when one of the girl's letters had not been replied. I felt that I wanted to write the reply! I wanted to intervene to get a reply, or mediate with the mother, tell her that her daughter was about to receive an answer. I recalled that you made me realize that I had to let that anxiety go. I had to accept that we were not the teachers, neither the mothers, and to relocate myself in my role as mail carrier.

In the tangle of the interconnected network that was the 'field', Veronica explains the concerns about the collaboration we had requested from the participants and the hesitations caused by the intermediation of previous kinship, academic and social relationships of each researcher. Taken as an initial strategy, this intermediation was maintained. Written messages, drawings, videos and audios were sent by parents and teachers via WhatsApp and email. As mail carriers, we formed small groups and used the same means to receive, deliver and exchange messages between children and with adults. For example: Maria, in Oregon USA, invited her nephew who lives in Rio de Janeiro, Brazil, and Regina, in Brazil, invited her nephew of the same age, who lives in Belo Horizonte, also in Brazil. This link was designed considering the similar age of the two boys and the use of the same language, Portuguese. Each one sent their messages to their respective aunts who, in their role of mail carriers, received them and sent them to their respective nephews. In the field record of one of our meetings Alba mentioned that we were not only the ones that generate the interaction but we were also the means of interaction. She, for example, explained: 'I am a friend of Andres' and Martina's mother, and as friends, we talk about the project, and as intermediaries we also read the letters. That sets unusual conditions'. Silvina also raised 'the importance all of us registering everything, and reconstructing everything'. Frequent concerns, such as these, always accompanied our strategic intermediation to trigger the collaboration and participation of children as co-researchers. The concerns made us reflect on our ethical limits in the interaction between the children and youngsters and with them, on the messages themselves, on our 'external' interference in the exchanges, and on whether or not to seek mediation with mothers or friends to re-establish communication when there was a delay in the answer, or a lack of it. The question of who we were brought with it the fear of exercising, as adult researchers, authority over children, assuming the role of teachers, mothers, aunts, grandparents or friends, and inducing the collaboration of our nephews, grandchildren, students and children of friends. The dilemmas of this self-reflection fluctuated between our role as researchers/friends/family and the levels of the children and young people's participation in our project. It also dealt with the fact that, whether this participation was voluntary or induced, we needed to consider the asymmetry between children and grown-up friends of their parents, grandmother and grandchildren, aunts and nephews, teachers and students. It was crucial to ask ourselves about the space of this sociability and if there were interactions with some degree of equivalence between children, youth and adults as participants and collaborators, since, on the one hand, any kinship relationship implies relationships with rights and obligations, but, on the other, friend relationships are spontaneous and are associated with affective attitudes and conventional behaviours.

If in kinship relationships there is social recognition that is expressed in legal and ritual procedures, in relationships between teachers and students there are conventional relationships of authority and hierarchy, as can occur in the ways of acting between adults and children. However, in addition to these conventional and asymmetric relationships, the reflexivity about our practices and our mutual responsibility led to the invitation to collaborate, which sounded like 'a promise to *something* we could not respond to', as Flor, another researcher, described her uncomfortable feeling in relation to the girl she invited, who had not received a reply. In this 'something' that we could not define is the ethical dilemma in the tensions between these relationships that inevitably permeated the collaboration. These tensions, however, did not stop the collaboration. Under epistemological vigilance, the originality of their possibilities turned to be more evident: the intertwining of these previous relationships between researchers and young participants who did not know each other made possible by the Internet and other technologically mediated modes of interaction (Hine, 2000). Those who accepted the invitation and remained in the project were driven by reciprocal curiosities. From the interaction and conventional relations between adults, they started to exchange messages sent by virtual means that, little by little, were also adapted by the children and youngsters themselves. The messages started in the form of social rites of self-presentation, in codes present in written messages, and in exchanged audios and videos. We are borrowing a term from Goffman (1989), 'interaction rituals' marked by the collaboration that was beginning. Often, after self-identification, 'My name is Ana, I am 12 and I am from Buenos Aires', for example, they begin talking about where they were: 'My native country is Panama, but I live in a province called Chiriquí. I don't know if you have heard about it but it is on the other side of Costa Rica. I lived my first 5 years in Chiriquí, then I moved to Panama till I was 10 and now I am back in Chiriquí'.[9] In addition to self-identification and self-presentation, they wanted to know about each other: 'Do you have any pets?', 'What do you like to do?', '... do you know something about handicrafts?'

As can be seen, in the first messages, children start their messages inserted in the appropriate context to the invitation, and they are focused on their interlocutors. They make it clear, when identifying themselves, that they are talking about themselves and politely seeking to know who their interlocutors are, for they have no previous knowledge of them. They know that the motivation for the messages comes from the invitation to asymmetries. And it is the effects of this invitation that matter, as participation is gradually transformed in the process, and asymmetries are no longer invoked. This did not mean that interactions between children and young people, mediated by previous relationships, whether of kinship, friendship or of professional nature, were no longer permeated by ethical dilemmas. On the contrary, they were part of the experimental and self-critical ethos that accompanies ethnographic research in general: it not only apprehended the context in which it is inserted, but this context also determined how anthropology would apprehend it. That is, it is an inseparable part of the strategies, practices and reflexivity of any ethnographic field, included and performed by forms of online interaction, as Tummons (2020) argued.

Letters/Messages as a Means of Communication and Ethnographic Documents

The methodological strategy of using letters brought ethical tensions that were disclosed from the very beginning by the uneasiness of one of the youngest participant's, Alfonso. Personal letters are markedly confessional, private and intimate. For the purposes of the project, we had access to them. This unusualness, we thought, could be alleviated by the previous agreement made in the invitation to participate, and by the expectation that these terms conditioned not only the content of the messages, but also the interactions provided by the interchange between children and youngsters. This happened for most exchanges, but others did not take this ethical position. This was the situation of the three youngest children: Alfonso, Julián and Becky.

When we began to try to connect children, Angeles contacted a good friend of hers, Alfonso's mother. Alfonso accepted the invitation. They have been living in Germany for the last two years. To find a match for Alfonso, Diana thought about Julian, her grandchild. Also, a good coincidence, Julian had lived in Germany with his family for six months. When Diana spoke with Julian, he commented with incredulity: '¿Por qué se quedaron en Alemania?' [Why did he stay in Germany], alluding to the fact that many people returned to their country due to the pandemic. That dyad, which did not start immediately, was joined by Becky, a girl from Oaxaca. Becky's idea was a video that she sent to Julian and Alfonso. The strategy of including Becky worked, but not in the way that the researchers expected. Watching the video, Julian was moved by this form of communication and also made a video addressing Alfonso. Alfonso was also motivated to initiate communication, but surprisingly, he chose the written letter, which he completed with three pictures. His mother explained to him that she and Angeles would be the mail carriers to deliver the letter by email. However, he insisted that he 'needed' to send the letter by physical mail. Alfonso's letter is full of imaginative and playful games. He begins it by trying to guess the name of the 'friend' that, of course, he knows:

> Hello Max
>
> No, your name is not Max … Ah, now I remember!
>
> Your name is Tulian
>
> No, no…
>
> Your name is Julian.
>
> My name is Alfonso[10]

Alfonso puts together two social rituals in this imaginative game: that of the basic elements to initiate encounters and that of the rules of the epistolary genre. First, the game begins with a 'friend' that he knows exists, but that he has not met yet. With the written letter, he sends some paint art, like a colourful reproduction of his left hand or the three flags of the countries involved in the exchange (Germany, Mexico and Argentina). His illustrations are completed with some riddles, games and questions for Julian to guess. In his video, Julian introduces himself and says that the 'cuarentena' is more or less for him. He presents his daily routine, with activities organised at home throughout the day. The first thing in the morning is to do homework, which is organised by the days of the week: Monday, math; Tuesday, language; Wednesday, knowledge of the world; Thursday, again language; and Friday, again math.

In Becky's first video, she appears in front of a board where six pictures are showing the activities that she has been doing during the 'cuarentena'. With a ruler in hand, Becky describes, in a teaching style, the different things that she has been carrying out at home. She ends the video by saying that she hopes the children will tell her what they do during the 'cuarentena'. Both Julian and Becky re-enact rhythms at home demarcated by school practices: Julian engaging in homework and experiments in formal education and Becky acting as a teacher. For Alfonso, on the contrary, school activities do not occupy his time, which he conceptualises as a vacation or a long weekend. Through the letter, Alfonso justifies, for himself and for Julian, that the letter is the means to make him his friend.

Alfonso, the Mexican boy, asked for Julian's direction in Buenos Aires, Argentina. He 'needed' to send the letter physically and did not want his messages 'to be read by everybody'. He wanted to participate in the project but he did not want his messages to be public. Public to what extent? Could we, the researchers, read the messages, analyse them and include them in publications? He thought that only Julian, his recipient, should read his letter. His message, a three-page written letter, was sent to a 'friend' of whom he feels close enough to write about personal facts, including word games and riddles. His understanding is that letters consist of an exchange of messages between friends. Knowing that we, the mail carriers, would read them, he asked his mother 'Who's going to read it?', and immediately replied that he did not want us to. Alfonso urges us to reflect. With great perplexity, his refusal made us think of our choice of the letter, a personal communication, as our methodological instrument. For us, the exchanges of letters were taken for granted. They were made possible by a network of people with previous relationships, mobilised and deepened by the virtual possibilities that, we supposed, could generate, and facilitate, distant dialogues without face-to-face encounters, as Podestá Siri (2007) inspired us. We did foresee a hiatus between the reflective intention at the beginning of our project and its concrete possibilities, due to deviations arising from our role as mail carriers. However, the ethical issue of confidentiality and privacy emerged in the reciprocal nature of the relationship (unknown children connected to each other through previous known bonds) and in these conditions of interaction (through virtual means during the epidemic) that assigned different meanings to the encounters (Guber, 2011, p. 57). If the issue of authorship and anonymity spells out ethical questioning, it does not follow that we have to renounce participation and collaboration nor that we are able to resolve it, as is often the case in fieldwork. But, reflecting on this forced us to rethink that the meaning we attributed to our previous bonds (friends, relatives and colleagues) was not the same for all the participants, to whom we were not connected directly and who were unknown to each other. Thus, without necessarily stressing the notion of 'preserving privacy' as a 'well-founded fiction' of the individualist ideology, we pursued to deepen our mutual responsibility and, at the same time, be aware of the different ethical positions that could intersect.

Our ethical commitment was to maintain our position only as mail carriers, that is, as facilitators for the children to receive their letters. In other words, in the face of unexpected situations and in order to be faithful to our claims and decisions of no intervention (neither to request follow-up communication nor to insist on specific content). Our mutual responsibility (between children and youngsters, their parents and the researchers) made us change our objective about what we had asked and, at the same time, precisely because of the imbalances, our limits became visible.

The ethical tensions underlying the interactions with and between children and youngsters, and mediated by the researchers/mail carriers and other adults, are inseparable from the methodological strategy of enabling forms of collaboration through the exchange of letters using Internet resources. None of the conditions of the project (the agreement made to read the content of the messages exchanged, the intermediation of other adults – parents, aunts, teachers, grandparents and friends – connecting the researchers and the young participants, and their support to access Internet platforms, and to receive and send messages from their cell phones) dismissed our ethical doubts. As Geertz (1968) stated, recognising the moral tension and ethical ambiguities implicit in the encounter, and being able to dispel them through their own attitudes, is what the encounter requires from all participants to actually take place. Ethical issues emerged in various ways in this ethnographic project. One was raised by the direct and explicit strangeness brought by the children ('will you read the letters?'). Another one juxtaposed the homogeneous time of the pandemic with the singular times in their diverse experiences. Our assistance for sending letters was not neutral and the possibilities and limits of the letters exceeded the conventional world of distances with that of virtual communication, emblematic of physical isolation and online communication blurred the boundaries between an intimate document and one accessible to all.

Concluding Thoughts

The reconfiguration of time, space and sociability was a triple disengagement triggered by the COVID-19 pandemic that, still ongoing, has affected, everyone's experience worldwide. Our ethnographic context and corresponding fieldwork were the result of this triple disengagement: the imposition of a homogeneous and generalised time corresponding to the pandemic, dislocated by specific and multiple perceptions described by children and youngsters, the compression of the distance between places, the messages sent simultaneously, and the resulting virtual meetings and interactions. None of these was previously imaginable to us. This unique setting was due to the context of the situation, which guided our purpose of knowing what the children said about isolation and how they were experiencing it. It also made us develop strategies to create and participate in relationships between children and youngsters that were linked to our previous interactions. It also prompted the use of technological communication enabled by the Internet and allowed us to share different meanings communicated by these technologies. And, finally, it raised some ethical dilemmas. We are aware that the use of these technologies does not exclude the ethnographic focus on immersion and participant observation. In other words, technology-mediated ethnography does not differ substantially from conventional fieldwork (Miller, 2020; Tummons, 2020) with child participants. As Hine (2004, pp. 16–17) has discussed, quoting Grint and Wolgar (1997), 'the impact of technology is not due to its intrinsic qualities. On the contrary, it is the result of a contingent series of social processes. The so-called inherent qualities of technology are built, and acquired their form, from processes such as negotiation of the users' nature'.

Internet technologies neither changed the core of our epistemological, theoretical and methodological perspectives nor the ethical implications common to ethnographic work in collaboration with young people. Two key principles guided our project, first, participatory ethnographic strategies with children and, second, the conceptualisation of what children say as co-participants in the construction of meaning. In the first case, we start from the basic assumption that there are no recipes or models to be followed and that children's participation in itself creates a particular relational configuration inseparable from the researcher's active reflexivity in the field. As co-builders of the interaction process, children and youngsters are actors and producers of meanings, they know about themselves, where they are, what is part of the dynamics of their lives and what are the groups to which they belong. Rather than being regarded as performing autonomous actions, children are seen as agents that perform actions triggered by social relationships that bring their corresponding constraints. Nevertheless, they also reinvent themselves permanently and compose themselves in relationships with others. Children's self-understanding is not a mere reproduction of practices and knowledge observed by adults. It is built by the inescapable insertion of their relationships in context (Silva, Dantas-Whitney, Borges, & Oliveira, 2018).

In the second case, in the context of this project, understanding what children say as co-participants in the construction of meaning implies the need to consider the letters, in the various forms, as ethnographic documents. What they said about the reorganisation of their daily lives – previously organised by the routines of going to school, being at home and spending time with friends – is not taken here only as the apprehension of meanings contingent on the pandemic. To take them as documents is to follow the ways in which young participants, in this context, learn, relativising, but also extrapolating, the acquisition of knowledge from schooling processes (Silva, 2016). First, because the participation of children and young people in different spaces of their shared lives is inseparable from the cognitive capacities of experiencing these social lives (Lave, 1988, 1996, 2011). Secondly, because they emphasise the paradox entailed in the fact that we focused our interests on children and youngsters as a strategy to make explicit important social and political phenomena, meanings and themes. When children and youngsters are related to the actions triggered by adults, not only do they participate but they also create/develop knowledge processes. Thus, taking the content of the letters as ethnographic documents entails a process of understanding how knowledge is constructed and communicated, collectively and inter-subjectively. It is about placing the analysis of relationships between people at the centre of our understanding, given that inter-subjectivity always unfolds in specific relationships between particular people (Toren, 2009).

This way of understanding inter-subjectivity is especially enlightening to understand the content of the exchanged messages. Triggered by our previous interactions in ethnographic fields, we paid attention to the ethical dilemmas that, *in situ*, arose with our commitments, professional and personal, to each other. They emerged, as we have tried to show here, from our surprise about the privacy issue in the different times lived in the pandemic.

Underlying *in situ* ethics which considers the context in situation in its relational bases is, therefore, a meta-ethics that comes from our theoretical assumptions and methodological strategies adopted in this unique ethnographic field.

Notes

1. Bogotá, Colombia; Buenos Aires, Corrientes and Bariloche, Argentina; Foz de Iguaçu, Brazil, Oaxaca, Mexico, Corvallis, Oregon, USA.
2. We use the term collaboration to indicate that 'professional researchers seek to establish research teams with girls and boys in a relationship of temporal equality in which the researchers seek to perceive themselves as contemporaries of

children – participants in the same context and at the same time – and seek not lose sight of what they think and know through their emotions and their bodies just like girls and boys do, and that is how they generate conditions in which it is possible to achieve the intersubjective flow that enables the collaborative production of knowledge' (Milstein & Guerrero, 2021, p. 6, our translation).

3. See also Christensen and James (2000), Christensen and Prout (2002) and James and Prout (1990).

4. Di Caudo and Milstein (2019), Guerrero, Clemente, Milstein, Dantas-Whitney, and Silva (2017), Guerrero and Milstein (2020), Meo et al. (2018), Milstein, Clemente, Dantas-Whitney, Guerrero, and Higgins (2011) and Milstein, Clemente, and Guerrero (2019).

5. We benefit from the contributions of Fabian (1983) and his problematisation of time in the ethnographic encounter and Benedict Anderson (1991) on the emergence of imagined communities (without face-to-face interaction and with the same interests).

6. 'Cuarentena' is the term commonly used in Latin America to refer to the lockdown.

7. ['Thinking about something that happened in April now seems like a lot of time to me. It seems that this time has passed in another epoch'.] ['I think that the quarantine is a time to realise that perhaps you never imagined that you were going to miss something as much as now'.] ['Time can be a feeling, an emotion, it can also be mixed with a feeling, and there can be a happiness that turns into sadness because you miss something. Also not everyone misses, one may not miss, and that is not uncommon, we all have a different personality'.] [Time] ['Some say that time is a feeling, for me they are right, although it also seems true to me that it is not A feeling, but that is different from a feeling. It depends on the person, since the time, apart from being a feeling, could also be an emotion'.] ['Missing and thinking about what we miss is seen as two feelings, but now that we are locked up it seems that it is the same feeling. We never thought we were going to be so far from something for so long'.].

8. Including 'family familiarity' (Bourdieu), in addition to the researcher's inseparable subjectivity, was also a strategy of Bourdieu (2005) and Leach (1989). Likewise, it is common to problematise delicate relationships that are established in fieldwork in similar situations, including closeness with relatives, friends and other personal and professional networks.

9. 'Mi nombre es Ana, tengo 12 años y vivo en Buenos Aires', 'Nací en Panama, pero vivo en una provincia que se llama Chiriquí. No sé si alguna vez escuchaste pero está del otro lado de Costa Rica. Hasta los 5 años viví en Chiriquí, después me mudé a Panamá hasta los 10 y ahora volvía Chiriquí' 'Tenés alguna mascota?', 'Qué te gusta hacer?', '...sabes algo sobre artesanías?'

10. HOLA MAX
NO NO NO TE LLAMAS MAX...
A YA LO TENGO TE LLAMAS TULIAN
NO NO NO TE LLAMAS... JULIAN
HOLA JULIAN ME LLAMO ALFONSO
TE MANDE ESTA CARTA PORQUE NO TENGO AMIGOS
ASI QUE TU ERES EL UNICO QUE ENCUENTRO
POR FABOR ¡MI AMIGO!
RESCATAME ¡POR FABOR! ¡POR FABOR! ¡¡¡POR FABO!!!

References

Anderson, B. (1991). *Imagined communities: Reflections on the origin and spread of nationalism* (2.a ed). London: Verso.

Austin, W. (2008). Relational ethics. In L. M. Given (Ed.), *The Sage encyclopedia of qualitative research methods* (Vol. 2, pp. 748–749). Thousand Oaks, CA: SAGE Publications. doi:10.4135/9781412963909

Bourdieu, P. (2005). *Esboço de auto-análise*. São Paulo: Companhia das Letras.

Burrell, J. (2009). The field site as a network: A strategy for locating ethnographic research. *Field Methods*, 21(2), 181–199.

Christensen, P., & James, A. (Eds.). (2000). *Research with children: Perspectives and practices*. New York, NY: Routledge Falmer Press.

Christensen, P., & Prout, A. (2002). Working with symmetry in social research with children. *Childhood*, 9(4), 477–497.

Di Caudo, M. V., & Milstein, D. (2019). Presentación de dossier: Etnografías colaborativas con niños, niñas y jóvenes en América Latina. Temas, problemas y hallazgos. *Revista del Cisen Tramas/Maepova*, 7(2), 23–43. Retrieved from https://ppct.caicyt.gov.ar/index.php/cisen/issue/view/864/showToc

Fabian, J. (1981). Six theses regarding the anthropology of African religious movements. *Religion*, 11, 109–126.

Fabian, J. (1983). *Time and the other: How anthropology makes its object*. New York, NY: Columbia University Press.

Geertz, C. (1968). *Nova luz sobre a antropologia*. Rio de Janeiro: Jorge Zahar.

Gell, A. (1996). *The anthropology of time. Cultural construction of temporal maps and images*. Oxford: Berg.

Goffman, E. (1989/1956). *La presentación de la persona en la vida cotidiana*. Buenos Aires: Ediciones Amorrortu.

Grint, K., & Wolgar, S. (1997). *The machine at work*. Cambridge: Polity.

Guerrero, A. L., Clemente, A., Milstein, D., & Dantas-Whitney, M. (2017). *Bordes, límites y Fronteras. Encuentros etnográficos con niños, niñas y adolescentes*. Bogotá: Editorial Pontificia Universidad Javeriana.

Guerrero, A. L., & Milstein, D. (2020). Introducción al dossier Etnografía y educación: estudios colaborativos con niños, niñas y jóvenes. *Magis, Revista Internacional De Investigación En Educación*, 13, 1–12. doi:10.11144/Javeriana.m13.idee

Günel, G., Varma, S., & Watanabe, C. (2020, June 9). A manifesto for patchwork ethnography. In *Society for cultural anthropology*. Retrieved from https://culanth.org/fieldsights/a-manifesto-for-patchwork-ethnography?fbclid=IwAR0QBUjXRr_hF-tBc28jTOly6JIf3umRHx-ea0BNai9mhvC1FlBTers5ZBk

Hine, C. (2000). *Virtual ethnography*. London: Sage.

Hine, C. (2004). *Etnografía virtual*. Retrieved from https://seminariosocio antropologia.files.wordpress.com/2014/03/hine-christine-etnografia-virtual-uoc.pdf/. Accessed on April 3, 2021.

James, A. (2007). Giving voice to children's voices: Practices and problems, pitfalls and potentials. *American Anthropologist*, 109(2), 261–272.

James, A., & Prout, A. (Eds.). (1990). *Constructing and reconstructing childhood: Contemporary issues in the sociological study of childhood*. London: Falmer.

Lave, J. (1988). *Cognition in practice: Mind, mathematics and culture in everyday life*. Cambridge: Cambridge University Press.

Lave, J. (1996). Teaching, as learning, in practice. *Mind, Culture and Activity*, 3, 149–164.

Lave, J. (2011). Hacia una ontología social del aprendizaje. *Revista de Estudios Sociales*, 40, 12–22.

Leach, E. (1989). Masquerade: The presentations of the self in holiday. *Cambridge Anthropology*, 13(3), 47–69. Retrieved from http://www.jstor.org/stable/23817412. Accessed on March 29, 2021.

Meo, A. I., Fernández, S., Jaramillo, J. M., Milstein, D., Carrera, C., Tammarazio, A., … Solórzano, M. F. (2018). *Panorama sobre etnografía con niños, niñas, adolescentes y jóvenes en Argentina, Brasil, Colombia y Ecuador: 1995-2016*. Ciudad Autónoma de Buenos Aires: Silvina del Carmen Fernández. 2018. ebook, PDF. Retrieved from http://encuentrosetnograficos.weebly.com/uploads/7/4/6/5/7465057/panorama_sobre_etnografi%CC%81a_con_nin%CC%83os_nin%CC%83as_adolescentes_y_jovenes.pdf

Miller, D. (2020). Cómo conduzir uma etnografia durante o isolamento. Retrieved from https://www.youtube.com/watch?v=WC24b3nzp98&feature=youtu.be

Milstein, D. (2020). Children, youths and ethnography: Education and de-centering. *Diálogos sobre Educación*, 11(20). doi:10.32870/dse.v0i20.690

Milstein, D., Clemente, A., & Guerrero, A. (2019). Collaboration in educational ethnography in education. In G. W. Noblit (Ed.), *Oxford research encyclopedia, education (oxfordre.com/education)*. New York, NY: Oxford University Press.

Milstein, D., Clemente, A., Dantas-Whitney, M., Guerrero, A. L., & Higgins, M. (Eds.). (2011). *Encuentros etnográficos con nin@s y adolescentes: Entre tiempos y espacios compartidos*. Buenos Aires: Miño y Dávila.

Milstein, D., & Guerrero, A. L. (2021). Lecturas de etnografías colaborativas con niñas, niños y jóvenes en contextos educativos latinoamericanos. *Magis, Revista Internacional de Investigación en Educación*, 14, 1–33. doi:10.11144/Javeriana.m14.lecn

Podestá Siri, R. (2004). Otras formas de conocernos en un mundo intercultural. Experiencias infantiles innovadoras. *Revista Mexicana de Investigación Educativa*, 9(20), 129–150.

Podestá Siri, R. (2007) Encuentro de miradas: El territorio visto por diversos autores. México, Secretaría de Educación Pública. Retrieved from http://dgei.basica.sep.gob.mx/files/fondo-editorial/educacion-intercultural/cgeib_00041.pdf

Punch, M. (1986). The politics and ethics of fieldwork. In *Qualitative research methods* (Vol. 3). London: Sage.

Russell, L., & Barley, R. (2020). Ethnography, ethics and ownership of data. *Ethnography*, 21(1), 5–25. doi:10.1177/1466138119859386

Sánchez, A. (1994). Un acercamiento al tiempo desde la perspectiva de Merleu-Ponty En Endoxa. Series Filosóficas No 3. UNED. doi:10.5944/endoxa.3.1994.4810

Silva, R. C. M. (2016). Do Ipê Roxo na cidade Nova: Experiência etnográfica e aprendizagem situada. *Etnográfica*, 20(1), 119–142. Retrieved from http://etnografica.revues.org/4225

Silva, R. C. M., Dantas-Whitney, M., Borges, A., & Oliveira, R. (2018). Do inesperado em etnografia com participação de crianças e jovens. Revista del Cisen. *Tramas/Maepova*, 7(2), 23–43. Retrieved from https://ppct.caicyt.gov.ar/index.php/cisen/issue/view/864/showToc

Toren, C. (2009, Summer). Intersubjectivity as epistemology. *Social Analysis, 53*(2), 130–146. doi:10.3167/sa.2009.530208

Tummons, J. (2020). Online, offline, hybrid, or blended? Doing ethnographies of education in a digitally-mediated world. In *Handbook of qualitative research in education*. Cheltenham: Edward Elgar Publishing.

Vigo, A., & Zabala, H. (1976). Arte-correo – Uma nueva forma de expresión. Retrieved from https://post.at.moma.org/sources/23/publications/240

Chapter 9

Ethics and Ethnographies of Education: Current Themes and New Directions

Jonathan Tummons

Abstract

In this final chapter, I offer some conclusions relating to the issues discussed across the volume as a whole. Drawing together common as well as contrasting themes from the different empirical accounts that have been presented by the different authors, I argue for a reflexive and necessarily unpredictable mode of research ethics in the context of ethnographies of education.

Keywords: Agency; ethics; ethnography; methods; methodologies; research

Introduction

In my main contribution to this book (Chapter 2 of this volume) I put forward a series of conceptual think pieces, drawing on the philosophical anthropology of Bruno Latour, for informing an approach to research ethics that foregrounds the agency that ethics, as a social actor, might possess and exercise. Engendering a non-human social actor with agency is not unique to a Latourian standpoint, however, and while 'traditional' anthropological ethnographies arguably maintain a human-centric perspective, other iterations such as multi-sited ethnography and virtual ethnography have increasingly come to occupy a similar perspective (Falzon, 2009; Fitzsimons, 2013; Hine, 2007; Pierides, 2010): the notion that we might focus, as ethnographers, on entities such as documents, meetings or buildings is a well-established one. From this point of view and reflecting on the different chapters in this volume that have provided so much empirical as well as conceptual food for thought, it becomes germane to open up a new line of enquiry in relation to ethics: what is it that they actually do?

Ethics, Ethnography and Education, 151–159
Copyright © 2022 Jonathan Tummons
Published under exclusive licence by Emerald Publishing Limited
doi:10.1108/S1529-210X20220000019009

Ethnographies of Education across Place and Space

The different chapters that make up this volume perfectly encapsulate the heterogeneity of ethnographies of education, taking the reader from the North of England (where the editors of this volume are based) to Scotland, and then to South America, India and Basque Country. The different contexts that these ethnographic studies rest on are not only geographically, but institutionally diverse as well, from young children in primary schools to university students. Some of the ethnographies that have been revisited for this volume took several years to complete whereas others were more rapid; and some exemplify the tradition of single-site anthropological ethnography, whereas others are framed in terms of more recent approaches to online and blended ethnographies – the latter sometimes framed as a response to the COVID-19 pandemic and concomitant requirements to change the design of planned research activities, but sometimes equally designed as online or blended from the start. In some of these accounts, the ethnographers are very much on the inside; in others, they occupy a more liminal status. Some are still ongoing; others have been returned to intermittently; and others are now the focus of retrospection and reflection. Notwithstanding this variety in terms of geographical and cultural locale, the length of time spent in the field, the structures of the educational contexts being explored and the people and practices being observed and written about, a number of common themes emerge that pertain specifically to the ethics of educational ethnography, in such a way as to continue the processes of problematisation of the ethics of ethnography that have emerged over several decades.

These problematisations are at one level remarkable for their persistence: issues such as the need for ethnographers to respond to ethical dilemmas *in situ*, in ways that cannot be straightforwardly predicted or even anticipated by a review panel, appear very clearly in the account given by Elizabeth Pérez-Izaguirre, Jose Miguel Correa Gorospe and Eider Chaves Gallastegui (Chapter 5 of this volume) of their post-qualitative ethnography amongst Basque Country university students – a methodological standpoint that necessarily involves ethical decision-making. In contrast to this, more recent ethical problematics emerge through considering ethnographic research that relies on information and communication technologies in order to be operationalised: particular problems relating to representation, as well as participation make up important elements of the blended ethnographic research being undertaken by Yang Zhao (Chapter 7 of this volume), who has opened up to scrutiny the adjustments that are sometimes needed by ethnographers in responding to the exigencies of fieldwork (although a global pandemic is of course more than 'mere' exigency), highlighting the roles played by not only methodological but also ethical improvisations in ethnographies of education.

For Pérez-Izaguirre et al., the post-qualitative turn acts as a kind of exercise in 'mass problematisation', an empirical but also ontological commitment to unpacking the assumptions of positivism and modernity and to foregrounding the involvement, not to say activism, of critical ethnographic practice within a discursive space that embraces the liquidity or even messiness of the post-modern condition. From this standpoint, it is a logical epistemological–ontological step for Pérez-Izaguirre et al., to draw not only on critical ethnography from an anthropological tradition but also on the more explicitly political emergent perspectives offered to the researcher by collaborative autoethnographies as a lens through which the agency of research participants is repositioned in terms of collaboration. While they do not draw on Lapadat (2017) in their chapter, the latter provides a definition of collaborative autoethnography that is useful to contextualise the present discussion: 'an autoethnographic qualitative research method that combines the autobiographic study of self with ethnographic analysis of the sociocultural milieu within which the researchers are situated, and in which the collaborating researchers interact dialogically to analyse and interpret the collection of autobiographic data' (Lapadat, 2017, p. 599).

Zhao likewise provokes us, as readers and as ethnographers, to consider the entanglements of ethics and methods/methodologies. Once again, we see a shift away from the 'traditional' single-sited anthropological ethnography of education, towards a blended ethnography that encompasses research sites that are both physically and digitally constituted. As Zhao responds to the pressures of the COVID pandemic in terms of not only her research design but also her physical as well as epistemological standpoint, her geographical position becomes immaterial to the research being conducted, the times as well as places that she can choose to occupy become more varied, and her participation-as-researcher can extend to informal as well as formal spaces – in this instance, to the Facebook community group established amongst her research participants. In this way, Zhao provides a further worked example of the ways in which Facebook has begun to emerge as an important site for ethnographers: 'methodologically, Facebook presents the ethnographic/literacies researcher with a new research context and a valuable source of data that offers unique pathways into participants' [...] thoughts and attitudes towards their [...] practices' (Baker, 2013, p. 137).

The Expansion of the Digital: Ethics and Multimodality in Online Ethnographies

Mindful of the online pivot that has characterised much work, as well as research work, during the pandemic, it is noteworthy that several of the contributors have written – either in this volume and/or in earlier publications – about online/blended ethnographic research and, specifically, the ethical and methodological questions that arise when doing research in an online space. Thus, the online ethnographic research discussed by Diana Milstein, Regina Coeli Machado e Silva and Angeles Clemente (Chapter 8 of this volume) stands out as an example of how the pandemic has acted as an impetus for not only the kinds of questions that the ethnographers sought to find answers for (their team consisted of eight researchers in total, distributed across South and North America) but also the ways that the research would be conducted. A very different kind of ethnography is discussed by Matilda Ståhl and Fredrik Rusk in their exploration of identity construction amongst young people playing video games (Chapter 6 of this volume). For Ståhl and Rusk, their sites of interest can be seen as part of a small but increasingly well-established area for study amongst social researchers more broadly as well as ethnographers more specifically (Taylor, 2016).

Diana Milstein, Regina Coeli Machado e Silva and Angeles Clemente arguably stretch contemporary definitions of educational ethnography, operating at an intersection of collaborative ethnography, multi-sited ethnography and online ethnography: iterations of ethnographic research that encapsulate the concerns raised by Hammersley in seeking to establish coherent methodological definitions of ethnographic research that are able to reconcile the post-modernist impulse for pluralism with a need to maintain coherence: 'what is at issue in different definitions of "ethnography" is frequently not limited to methods of research design, data collection, and analysis, but extends to methodological, ontological, epistemological, *ethical*, and political ideas' (Hammersley, 2018, p. 6, emphasis added). In their chapter, Milstein and her colleagues note the affordances of digital technologies in particular for generating spaces for new forms of meaningful collaboration between researchers and respondents as a vehicle for generating self-knowledge and agency: a political as well as ethical outcome from their work.

A qualitatively different digital modality underpins the online ethnography discussed by Matilda Ståhl and Fredrik Rusk, in which the digital not only creates the discursive spaces in which the research can be conducted but also the practices that are of interest to the ethnographer. Here once again ideas about the nature of the collaborative between researcher and researched are provoked: in allowing the gamers – who are the focus of the enquiry – to moderate the digital data by choosing amongst themselves which screen recordings were to be viewed for the research, Ståhl (who conducted the fieldwork) shifts the locus of control away from the researcher in favour of the researched, entailing risk but also affording differing levels of participation (described by Ståhl and Rusk as 'active' and 'passive') with particular differentiated requirements for integrity and confidentiality.

In Praise of 'Traditional' Anthropological Ethnography

Whilst the four contributions to this volume that I have referred to so far encapsulate the pandemic and/or digital *zeitgeists* to varying degrees, the recognition, not to say appreciation, of more 'traditional' anthropological ethnographies of education are nonetheless germane to the discussion. It is all too easy to be seduced by the digital and the online and to overlook the critical ethnographic contributions that can only be afforded by extended periods of fieldwork, of participant observation, of getting to know the cultures and practices of the spaces and locations within which the ethnographer moves and works. Mindful of the arguments for extending definitions of ethnography put forward by Hammersley (2018), the paradigmatic definitions offered latterly by Mills and Morton (2013) and earlier by Troman, Gordon, Jeffrey, and Walford (2006) continue to hold fast, which can be neatly summarised as 'a commitment to immersive and invariably long-term research, resting primarily on participant observation and engagement with the material artefacts of the field whilst also drawing on other methods such as interviews or document analysis, foregrounding the positionality of the researcher, and with an explicit commitment to iterative theory building' (Tummons, 2020, p. 179). From this standpoint, the research accounts of Lisa Russell and Ruth Barley (Chapter 3 of this volume) and Poonam Sharma (Chapter 4 of this volume) provide exemplary points of entry.

Lisa Russell and Ruth Barley provide retrospective accounts of a number of ethical dilemmas that emerged during their respective research: in the case of Russell, the account pertains to a three-year ethnography of young people (augmented by a series of subsequent follow-up meetings) in the North of England who were not in education, employment or training – NEET; Barley's research occupies an even longer time span – seven years – carried out in four distinct, though overlapping, phases. For Russell, the periods of fieldwork led to the disclosure of sensitive and potentially incriminating materials and issues within which she found herself entangled, having to come to terms with events that were unpredictable at best, leading her to worry about her own safety as well as that of one of her respondents. Russell's research work was accompanied by a considerable effort in terms of emotional labour, an issue deserving of wider methodological and theoretical scrutiny (Carroll, 2013). Barley's ethnography at a primary school in a different city in the North of England could not provide a greater contrast in terms of context, but the impulse to intervene provides a common thread. For Barley, it was the inability to stand by when racist attitudes were voiced that led to her intervention.

Poonam Sharma likewise highlights moments of ethical difficulty, if not distress, for the ethnographer, and in reflecting on a specific event that she witnessed during her fieldwork – a pupil being beaten by the principal of the school even though a national ban on corporal punishment had been instigated – she critically interrogates her own action – and lack of action – in how she responded to the incident at the time, as well as how she made sense of the incident in hindsight. In unpacking an episode that was self-avowedly difficult to return to upon rereading her field notes, Sharma questions her actions, even going so far as to posit notions of a hierarchy of incidents for the critical ethnographer: in deciding when to intervene and when not to, is there a taxonomy of events, or an identifiable cut-off point at which the ethnographer can decide which things she can let pass and which she has to try to do something about? For Sharma, there are no easy solutions, only the ongoing commitment to the culturally sensitive conduct of the ethnographer through which ethics of fieldwork can emerge.

Drawing on the empirical warrant established through the chapters that make up this book, I propose that we can discern four distinct – though at the same time overlapping – areas of work for ethics. These also have implications for methodology and method, and I shall touch on these matters also, but it is the ethics work that is the main focus. The four areas of ethics work to discuss are: doing research with, not about, people and practice; the emergent and unpredictable nature of ethics of ethnography; reflexivity and sensitivity as to when to intervene and when to stay silent and the ethics of being a witness to, or hearing a report of, illegal action in the field. I am not suggesting that these are in themselves novel, however; rather, I am suggesting that it is through empirical accounts such as those presented here that they can be positioned without demur as being fundamental elements of an ethnographic sensibility and commitment during our post-structural/post-modern/post-qualitative times.

Ethics Work (i): Research with, Not about, People and Practice

The politics of research and representation are writ large within ethnographies of education, where the people whose practices are at the heart of our research are welcomed, encouraged even, to speak up, moving the researcher–researched relationship beyond well-established – and also, arguably, well-worn – notions such as respondent validation or member checking towards a more meaningful dialogue between the ethnographer and the people who inhabit her field(s) of enquiry and interest. However, we should be chary of proposing democratic, 'partnerships amongst equals' within our ethnographies. The writing of the work remains the responsibility of, most commonly, the individual academic, although collaborative and team ethnographies are – as in this present volume – increasingly common (Horiguchi & Imoto, 2015). It is right that participatory approaches (of various kinds) should be encouraged – indeed, it may be necessary to present such an approach as a condition of access to the field – but not at the cost of abrogating responsibility for the ways in which the research will be written up and talked about in conferences, workshops, journal articles and monographs. Irrespective of whether or not we occupy a critical position as looking to enact change or reform, or whether we argue that our role as ethnographers is to generate knowledge and theory but not to participate in reform processes, we have, I suggest, moved far beyond 'us and them' approaches to research that concentrated meaning-making and analysis entirely in the hands of the ethnographer. It is often the case that we are not 'the experts'.

Ethics Work (ii): The Emergent and Unpredictable

It is not possible to anticipate many of the ways in which ethical dilemmas might impact on our progress when in the field. Nor should we try to do so: the unpredictability of everyday life is an inevitable corollary of a research paradigm that by definition is conducted in the everyday (as distinct from research conducted in controlled conditions or in evaluating an intervention that otherwise would not constitute part of the everyday repertoire of the people being observed). It is hard for ethics committees to reconcile themselves to the fact that we often cannot specify the research questions that we are looking to answer through conducting empirical work. Nor can we specify the kinds of ethical problems, other than those that might be neatly captured on an application form, that we might encounter. Consequently, we are sometimes required to describe our research plans in ways that are permissive or vague, in order to render them sensible to a committee and a process – a practice that is, arguably, unethical in and of itself. The extent to which an ethnographer should or should not dissemble or otherwise choose to omit elements of the purposes of their research when presenting themselves within the field is contestable: some will argue for full disclosure all of the time whilst others will argue that it surely must be necessary sometimes to hold back certain details, ideas or themes (Sin, 2005).

Ethics Work (iii): When to Intervene and When to Stay Silent

Participant observation remains the *sine qua non* of ethnography (Gold, 1958), but participation in the field and intervention in the field are, self-evidently, qualitatively different, and any decision to intervene – to speak or to act – in response to events that are challenging, upsetting or even distasteful is complex at best (Dennis, 2009). In choosing to adopt a different standpoint to that of the researcher – that of the critical friend or advocate, for example – the ethnographer draws on an empathy that is, arguably, not only developed through but also demanded of ethnography (Mills & Morton, 2013). The decision whether to say or do something that takes the ethnographer outside their role as a researcher generates equivocal responses from the standpoint of an enacted ethics. For example: for Barbour (2010), the costs of speaking up – the risk of the research being impacted, the need to not betray the trust of gatekeepers, the sense of being disloyal to colleagues – outweighed an interventionist approach. By contrast, Puttick (2017) positioned his decision to intervene explicitly as a consequence of the time spent in the field, of the rapport and collegiality that had been engendered, in order to speak out against specific aspects of the practices that he had observed. There is no automaticity in such decisions, and the reflexive commentaries present within this volume speak to this same ambiguity. Once again, ethics are found *in situ*, in a manner incapable of being anticipated, let alone captured, by an auditable process. Observing something that is philosophically, intellectually or even ethically disagreeable to the ethnographer is not necessarily a cause for intervention.

Ethics Work (iv): Observing the Illegal

The legality, or otherwise, of events or practices that ethnographers observe or participate in has for several years been a focus for investigation although one that, happily, is rarely of direct concern. Nonetheless, as Chapter 4 in this volume has clearly shown, witnessing an illegal action does not automatically require direct intervention. But it can – and, arguably, should – lead to a rigorous process of reflection involving the ethnographer in scrutinising her own positionality within the field in relation to the cultural milieu in which she is situated, the practices that she witnessed, and her own interrogations of her responses both in the moment and in hindsight. But for the most part, the responsibility for action rests with the ethnographer herself, not with a committee or other institutional process that might be deferred to (if such a process were indeed able to accommodate the unearthing or observing of such practices). There are in fact only a very few instances of criminal activity that an ethnographer (or other social researcher such as an oral historian) would be legally required to report, but any professional and moral impetus to do so is arguably equally compelling, not least when considering that in the United Kingdom (where I am located) 'researchers […] are currently under no legal obligation to report child abuse or neglect where they suspect it, nonetheless it is universally agreed that researchers have a duty to do so. Upholding this convention also fulfils our collective obligations to the public and our profession' (Elliott & Fleetwood, 2017, p. 9).

Some Tentative Conclusions: Continuing the Enquiry

In Chapter 2 of this volume, I argued that for the ethics of educational ethnography to be properly made sense of, they ought to be considered not as matters of fact but as matters of concern. The neoliberal discourses of audit that dominate the contemporary field of higher education practice (ethnographers of education are not solely to be found within universities, but my sense is that this is where the vast majority of them are institutionally based) render research ethics in a concretised, unproblematic form – a checklist dominated by clinical/medical and positivist understandings of research. Mindful of the *in situ* ethical issues that have been discussed within this volume, it is perhaps hardly surprising that ethics committees work in the ways that they do, and that ethnographers grow frustrated if not weary with their strictures and requirements (Wynn, 2018). Once research ethics become matters of concern, the inadequacies of the audit system become all too transparent. What should ethnographers of education do?

There are two ways to proceed that I wish to mention here. The first is pragmatic and administrative: ethnographers need to volunteer to join ethics committees and to argue for changes to institutional processes as they pertain to their institutional contexts. And there may be other steps that we can take as well. The second is empirical, conceptual and reflexive, and is encapsulated in this – as well as other – volumes: ethnographers need to continue to advocate for the scrupulous unpacking of ethical practices and discussions not as academic solipsism but as a necessary enquiry into how and why we do our research in the ways that we do. So, let us look through our anthropological lenses at ethics, at how they are discussed, written about, argued over and enacted. If some members of our academic community are able to not only unpack the ethics of ethnographies of education – whether single-sited, multi-sited or virtual – but also to make those same ethics the focus of the enquiry, then we can start to do the painstaking work of establishing what, exactly, it is that ethics actually does – as a discourse, as a body of practices, as a moral perspective, as a researcher's standpoint and as a commitment to doing no harm.

References

Baker, S. (2013). Conceptualising the use of Facebook in ethnographic research: As tool, as data and as context. *Ethnography and Education, 8*(2), 131–145.

Barbour, A. (2010). Exploring some ethical dilemmas and obligations of the ethnographer. *Ethnography and Education, 5*(2), 159–173.

Carroll, K. (2013). Infertile? The emotional labour of sensitive and feminist research methodologies. *Qualitative Research, 13*(5), 546–561.

Dennis, B. (2009). What does it mean when an ethnographer intervenes? *Ethnography and Education, 4*(2), 131–146.

Elliott, T., & Fleetwood, J. (2017). Law for ethnographers. *Methodological Innovations, 10*(1), 1–13.

Falzon, M.-A. (Ed.). (2009). *Multi-sited ethnography: Theory, praxis and locality in contemporary research.* Farnham: Ashgate.

Fitzsimons, S. (2013). The road less travelled: The journey of immersion into the virtual field. *Ethnography and Education, 8*(2), 162–176.

Gold, R. L. (1958). Roles in sociological field observations. *Social Forces, 36,* 217–223.

Hammersley, M. (2018). What is ethnography? Can it survive? Should it? *Ethnography and Education, 13*(1), 1–17.

Hine, C. (2007). Multi-sited ethnography as a middle range methodology for contemporary STS. *Science, Technology & Human Values, 32*(6), 652–671.

Horiguchi, S., & Imoto, Y. (2015). Fostering learning through unlearning institutional boundaries: A 'team ethnography' of a liminal intercultural space at a Japanese university. *Ethnography and Education, 10*(1), 92–106.

Lapadat, JC. (2017). Ethics in autoethnography and collaborative autoethnography. *Qualitative Inquiry, 23*(8), 589–603.

Mills, M., & Morton, M. (2013). *Ethnography in education.* London: Sage.

Pierides, D. (2010). Multi-sited ethnography and the field of educational research. *Critical Studies in Education, 51*(2), 179–195.

Puttick, S. (2017). Performativity, guilty knowledge, and ethnographic intervention. *Ethnography and Education, 12*(1), 49–63.

Sin, CH. (2005). Seeking informed consent: Reflections on research practice. *Sociology, 39*(2), 277–294.

Taylor, N. (2016). Play to the camera: Video ethnography, spectatorship, and e-sports. *Convergence, 22*(2), 115–130.

Troman, G., Gordon, T., Jeffrey, B., & Walford, G. (2006). Editorial. *Ethnography and Education, 1*(1), 1–2.

Tummons, J. (2020). Online, offline, hybrid, or blended? Doing ethnographies of education in a digitally-mediated world. In M. Ward & S. Delamont (Eds.), *Handbook of qualitative research in education* (pp. 178–189). Cheltenham: Edward Elgar Publishing.

Wynn, L. (2018). When ethics review boards get ethnographic research wrong. In R. Iphofen & M. Tolich (Eds.), *The Sage handbook of qualitative research ethics* (pp. 248–262). London: Sage.

Index